Communicating in
GLOBAL BUSINESS
NEGOTIATIONS

*Our thanks and gratitude to family and
friends, especially
Tim, Johnna, and Zachary
and Jim*

Communicating in GLOBAL BUSINESS NEGOTIATIONS

A Geocentric Approach

Jill E. Rudd
Cleveland State University

Diana R. Lawson
St. Cloud State University

SAGE Publications
Los Angeles • London • New Delhi • Singapore

For information:

Sage Publications, Inc.
2455 Teller Road
Thousand Oaks,
  California 91320
E-mail: order@sagepub.com

Sage Publications India Pvt. Ltd.
B 1/I 1 Mohan Cooperative
Industrial Area
Mathura Road, New Delhi 110 044
India

Sage Publications Ltd.
1 Oliver's Yard
55 City Road
London EC1Y 1SP
United Kingdom

Sage Publications Asia-Pacific Pvt. Ltd.
33 Pekin Street #02-01
Far East Square
Singapore 048763

Printed in the United States of America

Library of Congress Cataloging-in-Publication Data

Rudd, Jill E.
Communicating in global business negotiations: A geocentric approach/
Jill E. Rudd, Diana R. Lawson.
    p. cm.
Includes bibliographical references and index.
ISBN-13: 978-1-4129-1658-5 (pbk. : alk. paper)
    1. Negotiation in business. 2. Business communication.
    3. Intercultural communication. I. Lawson, Diana R. II. Title.
HD58.6.R83 2007
658.4'052—dc22

2006031958

Printed on acid-free paper.

07 08 09 10 11   10 9 8 7 6 5 4 3 2 1

Acquiring Editor:	Todd R. Armstrong
Editorial Assistant:	Katie Grim
Production Editor:	Sarah K. Quesenberry
Marketing Associate:	Amberlyn M. Erzinger
Copy Editor:	Brenda Weight
Proofreader:	Dorothy Hoffman
Typesetter:	C&M Digitals (P) Ltd.
Indexer:	Nara Wood
Cover Designer:	Michelle Kenny

Table of Contents

Preface ix

Chapter 1. Introduction and Overview 1
  The Dynamic Nature of the Global Environment   3
  The Need for an Integrated Geocentric Approach   5
  Centricity and the Geocentric Approach   6
  An Interdisciplinary Examination   15
  An Integrative Framework   16
  Structure of the Book   18
  Discussion Questions   20
  References   21

Chapter 2. A Geocentric Perspective 23
  Country Classification   26
  Impact on International Negotiation   28
  Foreign Direct Investment   30
  Growth of Developing Economies   32
  Small- and Medium-Size Firms   40
  Technology   44
  The Big Picture   45
  Discussion Questions   46
  Notes   47
  References   47

Chapter 3. A Geocentric Negotiation Process 49
  A Geocentric Approach to Negotiation   50
  Prenegotiation → Negotiation Process →
    Agreement → Renegotiation   51

Prenegotiation Stage   51
Negotiation Process Stage   67
Agreement   76
Conclusion and Development of a New Dynamic   77
Guidelines for Global Negotiation Success   78
Discussion Questions   79
References   79

Chapter 4. Influence of Cultural Goals and Values   **83**
Importance of Culture   84
Culture and Business   85
Are Generalizations Enough?   107
Intercultural Challenges and Issues   108
Guidelines for Global Negotiation Success   114
Discussion Questions   114
References   115

Chapter 5. Communication Profile: Characteristics,
Behaviors, and Skills   **119**
Our Perspective   119
An Integrative Communication Approach
   for International Business Negotiations   120
Argumentativeness   121
Verbal Aggressiveness   127
Intercultural Communication Apprehension   132
Self-Monitoring   138
Conclusion   140
Guidelines for Global Negotiation Success   140
Discussion Questions   141
References   147

Chapter 6. The Role of Intercultural Communication
Competency in Global Business Negotiations   **153**
Overview of Intercultural Communication
   Competency   154
Conclusion   172
Guidelines for Global Negotiation Success   173
Discussion Questions   174
References   174

Chapter 7. The International Business Context   **179**
Economic Integration   181
European Union   184

The Americas   187
Impact of Economic Integration on Business   190
Important Issues for Negotiators   202
Conclusion   202
Guidelines for Global Negotiation Success   203
Discussion Questions   204
Notes   205
References   205

Chapter 8. Alternative Dispute Resolution   **207**
Renegotiating   212
Alternative Dispute Resolution Option   212
Mediation in International Commerce Disputes   220
Conclusion   222
Guidelines for Global Negotiation Success   223
Discussion Questions   223
References   224

Chapter 9. A Practitioner Perspective   **225**
The Interview Framework   226
Success Factors: Summary of the Practitioners'
    Perspectives   242
Conclusion   243
Guidelines for Global Negotiation Success   244
Discussion Questions   245

Chapter 10. Conclusion   **247**

Index   **251**

About the Authors   **275**

Preface

The idea for this book resulted from numerous conversations between the authors over many years. Integrating the areas of international negotiation from the communication discipline and international business from the business discipline seemed to make sense. Most work done in academics occurs vertically, within a discipline. We saw a benefit of a cross-disciplinary approach to the topic of international negotiation. The book was the result of this vision.

The cross-disciplinary approach used in this book should benefit both communication students as well as business students. Business students who may have some understanding of the international business environment will be able to strengthen that understanding and integrate negotiation into it. Likewise, communication students with some understanding of negotiation will be able to expand that understanding to include the international context. For all students, this book provides a macroperspective of the international business negotiation environment along with a microapproach to what is required to be an effective international business negotiator. Our aim is to offer the knowledge and skill base needed to develop a geocentric approach to international business. The convergence of cultures and economies makes it difficult to remain ethnocentric or polycentric in our interaction with businesses and people from other countries. Cross-cultural understanding requires a cross-disciplinary approach.

The book is organized in a manner that allows the reader to build a base of knowledge and apply what is learned earlier in the book to what is presented later in the book. Each chapter has a set of chapter-specific guidelines for effective international negotiation. Discussion questions are also included to help students integrate and apply material presented in the chapters.

Chapter 1 presents a model for effective geocentric negotiation and discusses the need for an interdisciplinary approach to the study of international business negotiation. Chapter 2 presents a geocentric perspective of the world. It provides the "big picture" of the international business environment. Chapter 3 presents the negotiation process in the international business context, and Chapter 4 follows with a more in-depth discussion of the role of culture in international business. Chapter 5 discusses the role of the individual negotiator's communication characteristics, traits, and behaviors as influencing factors in global business transactions. Chapter 6 looks at the importance of intercultural communication competency in successful negotiation in the international business context. Chapter 7 then presents and discusses the growth of economic integration and its effects on international business activities, followed by a discussion of some of the more common types of business transactions taking place internationally. The differences in political and legal systems between countries increase the importance of using alternative dispute resolution practices to resolve conflict. Chapter 8 addresses this critical component. For Chapter 9, we went to the practitioners to ask them about their experiences in the international business environment and to ask for advice for students interested in the field of international business negotiations. The responses from those interviewed confirmed the need for a broad-based understanding of the international business environment along with a geocentric attitude when negotiating in that environment. Chapter 10 summarizes the main focus of the book. We hope you enjoy it. Because the contribution to this book was shared equally by the authors, authorship order was determined by a flip of the coin.

Acknowledgments

We would like to acknowledge the contribution of many individuals in the development and revision of this book. The reviewers helped us to improve the clarity and focus of this book. We especially thank Melissa S. Cardon, Pace University, Lubin School of Business; Dan DeStephen, Wright State University; Larry A. Erbert, University of Texas at El Paso; Garold Lantz, King's College; Sandra Loeb, Europa Universität Viadrina; and Wallace V. Schmidt, Rollins College. Their suggestions were greatly appreciated. We also thank Dr. Patty Burant for her insights. Research and office assistance from Donna Helmreich and Julie Esmer and assistance with the references from Sharon Snyder-Suhy helped keep us on track and organized. Thank you.

The interviews with practitioners provided valuable insight into the reality of negotiating in an international business environment. We thank Donna Bard, Gary Giallanardo, Cynthia Lee, Noel Penrose, Odail Thorns, David Turner, and Al Zaremba.

We also would like to thank D. Timothy Hughes for his editorial review of the final revision of the book. An outside pair of eyes helped us to improve the flow and consistency of the chapters. We are especially appreciative of his willingness to work according to our time schedule.

Finally, we would like to thank Todd Armstrong, Deya Saoud, Sarah Quesenberry, and Brenda Weight of Sage Publications for their guidance and support throughout the process. We appreciate their patience and flexibility in the development of this project.

1

Introduction
and Overview

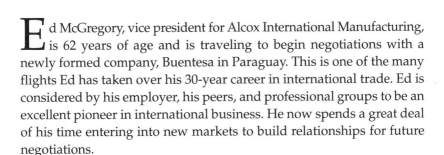

Ed McGregory, vice president for Alcox International Manufacturing, is 62 years of age and is traveling to begin negotiations with a newly formed company, Buentesa in Paraguay. This is one of the many flights Ed has taken over his 30-year career in international trade. Ed is considered by his employer, his peers, and professional groups to be an excellent pioneer in international business. He now spends a great deal of his time entering into new markets to build relationships for future negotiations.

Ed is typically accompanied by other employees, some of whom are newcomers to international trade. This trip, Ed is traveling with a new hire, Tanya Lee, team product manager for one line of products in the International Division of Alcox. Tanya is 27, has an MBA in international marketing, and speaks fluent Spanish. If all goes well, Tanya will be the person in charge of the new account. Tanya seizes the opportunity presented by the long flight to learn everything she can from Ed's experience.

The conversation goes something like this:

Tanya: Ed, what should I know about international business negotiations? Have they changed much from when you started?

Ed: There is a lot happening in the international market today. I think someone with your training in language, history, and communication is a great asset for our company in international negotiation. I wish I had learned as much as possible about other cultures when I was younger. I had to pick up enough of foreign languages on my own to really conduct successful negotiations. I always enjoyed learning about other cultures and experiencing life from different ways.

Tanya: Me, too. I love to travel and spent a couple years in France after graduation. So is international business negotiation all that different from when you started?

Ed: When I first got into international business, I was the only representative from the company. There were very few markets that we were interested in, so most of the time I was in Europe. Then the Asian market opened and I spent my time traveling to Europe and predominantly Japan and South Korea. However, as you know, today we have a whole department dedicated to the international market. Technology has changed so much of how we negotiate. Foreign companies are communicating globally with each other, and there is a constant flow of information. We are able to learn about each other. I used to be able to simply read up a little about the country and the company I was about to meet with. We expected to get our way in international negotiations, and most of the time we did. Later, it became imperative to learn in depth about the company and the country's culture and sometimes adapt my behavior to fit the cultural norms. But now, because of the increased world trade and the vast numbers of people involved, international negotiations have evolved more. Cultural issues will always be a factor. But recently, there seems to be a new, worldwide culture composed of veteran international negotiators like me. We seem to have our own language and customs, regardless of the country from which we come. The old ways of communicating in international trade are outdated.

Tanya: Then what approach will work in today's market, and tomorrow's?

Ed: The geocentric approach.

Tanya: What exactly do you mean?

Ed: Read this book and I think you will be ready for what lies ahead.

❖ THE DYNAMIC NATURE OF
    THE GLOBAL ENVIRONMENT

Today, more than at any time in history, nations, organizations, and companies must be prepared to negotiate in the global market not only to thrive, but to survive. With the 21st century's economic and technology advancements, the global marketplace is no longer reserved for the large, well-established transnational corporation, but is now a place where all types and sizes of organizations have an opportunity to compete. With advances in areas such as communication technologies and transportation services, small- and medium-size firms are able to more easily and cost effectively expand into the international marketplace. There are around 61,000 transnational corporations with over 900,000 foreign affiliates (UNCTAD, 2004).

The rapid advancement of technological innovation has played a major role in the internationalization of firms from both developed and developing countries. As a result, developing countries have been able to advance economically at a faster rate than in the past. The economic advances of developing countries have occurred primarily because of foreign direct investment into these countries, usually from developed countries. This expansion has increased the scope and breadth of cultural understanding needed for success in the international business negotiation environment. In other words, there are more countries and more cultures involved in international business today.

Historically, foreign direct investment (FDI) focused solely in the developed world, with developing-country FDI targeted at access to raw materials. While developed countries are still the major recipients and providers of FDI, a larger proportion of FDI is targeted toward the developing world in today's international environment. The growth potential in developing countries has made them very attractive to many firms. Developing countries offer great opportunities for business as they grow economically. At the same time, knowledge and expertise about operating in these countries is more dissimilar and less familiar than in most developed countries, especially in terms of cultural values and behaviors, political and legal processes, and business practices. Thus, business negotiators face greater challenges conducting international business trades in these countries.

In the 1980s, developing country transnational corporations accounted for less than 6 percent of FDI flows globally. By 2004, they accounted for approximately 10 percent (UNCTAD, 2004). In 2003, China became the largest recipient of FDI worldwide. As FDI grows in developing countries, the economic strength of these countries will also increase, thus increasing the demand for many products and services from developed countries. The end result is that developing countries, which far outweigh developed countries in terms of number and population, will play a larger and larger role in the global economy and in conducting international trade negotiation.

In addition to the contribution of technology and FDI to international growth, the economic integration of countries has changed the face of competition worldwide. Countries no longer compete independently in many parts of the world. Multilateral agreements, known as economic integration, between countries have formed strong competitive groups within regions of the world. Leading the movement of economic integration is the European Union, with a population of over 450 million and a GDP (gross domestic product) comparable to the United States. The most recent ten members, joining in May 2004, are Eastern European countries, adding a great deal of cultural diversity to the mix. These countries are developing countries with a very diverse set of cultures and languages. Although there may be some general similarities across the European Union cultures, each country maintains its own unique character. It is these unique elements that factor into the success (or failure) of a negotiation.

The North American Free Trade Agreement (NAFTA) involving Canada, the United States, and Mexico is another well-known example of the economic integration of countries that influence trade negotiation interaction. For over 10 years, these countries have been working together to reduce trade barriers in order to increase intercountry trade. Farther south in the Americas, multilateral agreements have been in place for more than two decades. Mercosur and the Andean Pact involve a number of Latin American countries. Over time, the member countries have worked to increase the level of economic cooperation in order to enhance economic growth and activity. In 2005, the newest free trade agreement in this region, CAFTA-DR, was formed and includes the United States, Central America, and the Dominican Republic. As with Mexico, through NAFTA, we should see an increased rate of economic growth, especially between member countries.

Finally, in Asia and Africa, countries have been moving toward more economic cooperation with their neighbors. The Association of Southeast Asian Nations (ASEAN) was formed in 1967 in order to encourage trade between member countries through cooperative industrial policies. For several decades, African countries have struggled with attempts to cooperate economically due to political instability and poor economic conditions. However, they continue to work toward economic integration with nine trading blocks (cooperative agreements) among African countries in existence today (Hill, 2004), including the Economic Community of West African States (ECOWAS), the East African Community (EAC), and the Southern African Customs Union.

The economic cooperation between countries has modified the competitive borders between countries. Almost 20 years ago, Kenichi Ohmae (1987) argued that the world was becoming regionalized and firms must develop strategies for competing within and across regions in order to be successful. This has certainly occurred. It is no longer sufficient to develop strategies on a country-by-country basis because countries are no longer competitively independent. Firms must develop strategies for individual countries, and for multicountry regions, as well as globally. Therefore, understanding the negotiation style of a single country may not suffice.

The cumulative effect of technological innovation, increased FDI, growth of developing countries, and economic integration has been a convergence of cultural behaviors. As products, services, and people continue to cross borders and interact, it becomes increasingly risky to assume that cultural behaviors remain unchanged. It is no longer sufficient to learn about a country's culture and expect interaction with people from that culture to follow the "rules" of that culture. As we interact with people from other cultures, we change, they change, and behaviors and attitudes change. It is a dynamic process. Change occurs continually. For negotiators, it is critical to develop a strong understanding of the elements that form the framework for negotiating in an international setting, and to attain the attitude and skills needed to adapt to the changing environment.

❖ THE NEED FOR AN INTEGRATED GEOCENTRIC APPROACH

Much of the study of international negotiation has taken a Western, or developed country, approach. The contribution of this approach has been substantial, and research has aided the development of negotiation expertise of businesses. However, a Western perspective is just that—a Western perspective. The majority of the world's population is non-Western. The majority of countries with the greatest growth potential are non-Western. The majority of work in the area of international negotiation remains Western. A non-Western perspective is needed in order to better understand the world.

This is not to say that we cannot use the theories and research that currently exist. In fact, current theories provide an excellent base from which to expand our understanding of the negotiation processes and practices followed by other cultures. For example, in the field of communication, scholars such as Gudykunst (2005) have provided an excellent overview of communication theories that explain intercultural communication. These theories, especially face-negotiation theory (Ting-Toomey, 1988) and anxiety/uncertainty management theory (Gudykunst, 2005), help us understand the communication interaction between people of different cultures. However, the specific nature of the international business negotiation context requires looking beyond the general intercultural theories and necessitates an integrative approach. Not only do we need to understand how communication behavior may vary by culture, we must also consider the uniqueness of the negotiator's communication style (Gundykunst, 2005) and how the exchange process is a mutually influencing process that often results in a "third culture." Today's global market requires negotiators to know more than general culture guidelines to become successful, competent business managers. The individual's characteristics that facilitate understanding the dynamic nature of the international business negotiation environment are important factors in success or breakdown of a negotiation. Thus, there is clearly a need to incorporate intercultural and individual communication knowledge to better understand the international business experience. This integrative approach must continue by incorporating important negotiation principles, communication factors significant to the international business negotiation context. In addition, viewing business from a worldview is necessary and, with this, is the need for renegotiation and alternative dispute resolution. Therefore, successful negotiation in international settings requires us to examine negotiation from a geocentric approach.

❖ CENTRICITY AND THE GEOCENTRIC APPROACH

Negotiating in an international business context is about building relationships. The depth and strength of these relationships will vary by definition and by culture. But they must exist in order for the business transaction to occur. The view for the international manager/negotiator and the firm is long term, and this requires substantial investment in terms of time and money. Negotiating approaches of problem solving and conflict resolution help maintain the relationship by focusing on positive outcomes for both sides.

Long-term success as an international negotiator requires an individual to step out of his or her own shoes and into the shoes of others in order to understand the "other" perspective. Negotiators with a geocentric approach have the ability to do this, which increases the potential for long-term success in the international environment. As discussed later in the book, the ability to do this well requires that an individual possess certain characteristics as part of his or her communication style. Further, we identify the characteristics needed to gain competence in intercultural communication. In the global environment, the breadth and depth of cultural communication differences are vast. Understanding and adapting to these differences is a necessary part of effective international negotiation.

Along with the capabilities of the negotiator, the attitude, or mindset, of the firm also plays a role in determining the long-term success of the firm. Research has shown that firms with a geocentric mindset perform better in the international environment than firms with other orientations (Calof & Beamish, 1994). The following section explores the framework for determining the international attitude or orientation of a firm doing business in the international business negotiation environment.

A Few Definitions

When discussing managerial and personnel issues in the context of international business, there are specific terms used to explain the relationship of the individual to the headquarters and subsidiary of the company. The country in which the headquarters of a company is located is referred to as the *home country*. When a citizen of the home country works for the company in another country (at a foreign subsidiary of the company), he or she is referred to as an *expatriate*.

The foreign country where a subsidiary is located is called the *host country*. Employees in the subsidiary who are citizens of the host country are referred to as *host-country nationals*. Finally, employees in the subsidiary who are neither citizens of the home country nor citizens of the host country are referred to as *third-country nationals*.

International business negotiation is a communication process involving two or more parties from different cultures who come together, each with their goals of reaching an agreement that will result in a successful outcome.

Organizational Culture

Several factors influence the negotiation interaction and outcomes, such as personality, communication style, or characteristics of the individual negotiator, as well as the national cultures of the negotiation team members, and the perceptions of the partners' behaviors, which is related to cultural background. In addition to these elements affecting an international negotiation, the culture of the organization plays a substantial role in influencing the attitudes and behaviors of negotiators. Just as an individual's culture and background affects his or her negotiation behaviors, the values and attitudes of the firm for which the individual works will also affect his or her negotiation strategies and behaviors.

This book presents the elements of culture that help to form an individual's cultural values and norms. Institutions make up one of these elements. The most important institution in most cultures is the family, and, in many cultures, religion. In a business context, the business organization, or firm, plays a major role in the development of its employees' values and attitudes regarding business.

Within the business context, the culture of a business organization affects the strategic development and operation of the business itself. Organizational culture is defined as "the pattern of shared values and beliefs that help individuals understand organizational functioning and thus provide them with the norms for behaviors in the organization" (Deshpande & Webster, 1989, p. 4). Each organization has its own unique culture as a result of its history (Detert, Schroeder, & Mauriel, 2000) and its members (Trice & Beyer, 1993).

Organizational culture can be divided into two components. The first is the mental activity (Detert, Schroeder, & Mauriel, 2000) that holds the general beliefs and values of the organization's members. Collectively, these members make up the organization. The mental activity, or cognitive component, of organizational culture is the substance of culture (Trice & Beyer, 1993) and provides the answer to "why" regarding organizational behaviors (Schneider & Rentsch, 1988, as cited in Deshpande, Farley, & Webster, 1993, p. 24).

The second component consists of attitudes and behaviors that exhibit the general beliefs and values (mental activity) of the organization's culture (Detert, Schroeder, & Mauriel, 2000). While the mental activity is the substance of organizational culture, this component is the "form" of culture (Trice & Beyer, 1993).

Understanding organizational culture can be as difficult as understanding other cultural groupings. As outsiders to a firm, we can only see the behaviors and attitudes of a firm (i.e., its members). Without knowing the reasons behind the behaviors, it is difficult to determine the best way to respond to those behaviors. As with country cultures, this does not necessarily help us understand the "why" of those behaviors. In order to understand the thought processes behind those behaviors, we must understand the perspective of the organization's members (Trice & Beyer, 1993). Calof and Beamish (1994) found that the *firm orientation* (the organizational culture) was held by the executives of the firm and therefore would be expected to trickle down through the organization. Thus, alignment of the attitude of the firm and the attitude of the negotiator is needed for long-term effectiveness in the international environment.

Centricity

The concept of centricity originated in the late 1960s, when researchers began to analyze the differences in strategic approaches taken by firms doing business in the international environment. Because the strategy of a corporation is created by the individuals within an organization, this implies that the attitudes and values of the individuals would influence strategy development. Thus, the attitude or orientation of the firm would emulate the attitude or orientation of the individuals of the firm and vice versa.

When we think of personality, it is usually in terms of an individual, but in the business environment, it is important to also understand the personality of the organization. Organizations are made up of people and processes. The personalities, especially in terms of attitude of the people of the organization, create or influence the personality of the organization. As would be expected, the executive level of the organization has the greatest influence on forming or modifying the organizational culture. In a study assessing the centric orientation of Canadian firms and its relationship to international success, Calof and Beamish (1994) found that the centricity of senior executives matched the centricity of the organization. And, the stability of the attitude of an organization is maintained through the hiring of like-minded personnel. Personnel within an organization are socialized to the firm's operating philosophy and organizational values. Thus, understanding the firm's perspective aids in understanding the mindset of the individuals within the organization.

From a global perspective, multinational firms take different approaches to dealing with foreign markets. The type of approach taken affects the firm's strategic decision making, management of foreign subsidiaries, how it interacts with foreign firms, and the managers it hires.

The type of approach a firm takes in foreign markets is known as the firm's centricity. Centricity relates to the attitude toward foreign markets and cultures that is held by executives with decision-making power regarding strategic activities and operations in foreign markets (Calof & Beamish, 1994). The seminal research in developing centric profiles (Perlmutter, 1969) continues to be used in assessing the international mindset of a multinational corporation.

In his original work, Perlmutter (1969) identified three centric profiles held by multinational corporations: ethnocentrism, polycentrism, and geocentrism. In later research (Heenan & Perlmutter, 1979), a fourth profile, regiocentrism, was identified. The type of centric orientation held by a firm influences its decisions at an operational level (hiring practices) as well as at the strategic level (types of entry modes to use as well as level of presence in the foreign market). Centric orientation affects decisions in all areas of a business, including research and development, human resources, production and operations, marketing, and finance. As negotiation is present at some level in all of these areas, the centric orientation of a firm and its individuals will affect negotiation strategy and behavior. Further, centric orientation will also affect the relationship development component of international negotiation, which is so important in many regions of the world.

Ethnocentricity

An individual with an ethnocentric attitude believes that his or her values, beliefs, and ways of doing things are superior to those of other cultures. Thus, business decisions will reflect this type of perspective. Firms that use an ethnocentric strategy tend to view the world from a home-country perspective. Foreign operations are typically viewed as secondary to home-country activities and usually are managed so as to support and strengthen the goals of the home country. Managers in an ethnocentric firm come from the home country. Business practices and processes in the home country are exported to foreign operations. There is a strong reliance on "what works best in our country will work best in another country." Adaptation to foreign cultures and business practices is minimal.

When making decisions, international managers are sometimes faced with the challenge of balancing the goals and needs of the home country with those of the host-country subsidiary for which the manager is responsible. Managers from an ethnocentric firm will usually put the needs and goals of the home office before the needs of the host-country operation. Communication between the home- and host-country offices will usually be close, and headquarters will have a great deal of influence over the decisions made in foreign subsidiaries.

The headquarters staffing of an ethnocentric firm seldom places many foreigners in executive positions, which further strengthens the ethnocentric perspective. Little effort is made to integrate other cultures and business perspectives into the firm's strategic direction or operational activities.

As previously discussed, the personnel within a firm help structure the personality, or mindset, of the firm. Further, the firm's mindset, or strategic perspective, influences the type of people hired as well as the type of person attracted to that firm. In other words, an ethnocentric firm would attract potential employees who also have an ethnocentric attitude. This cycle reinforces the organizational behavior of the firm, making it more difficult to effect change in strategic orientation (Calof & Beamish, 1994).

Negotiation behavior of ethnocentric managers would be expected to follow the same tendencies as their strategic and operational behavior. With headquarters' goals being most important, looking at the needs of the foreign company with whom they negotiate would tend to be limited. Negotiation behavior would be expected to follow that of home country. Thus, ethnocentric firms would be least likely to adopt a worldview in which the integration of home and host needs prevails.

Polycentricity

For many firms, a polycentric approach to international expansion was beneficial in developing a global learning and knowledge advantage. A polycentric mindset looks at each country/culture as a unique entity and adapts strategies and behaviors to fit the unique characteristics and needs of the foreign entity. Decisions are made on a country-by-country basis, and the needs of the host-country subsidiary supersede the needs of the home-country headquarters.

International managers from a polycentric firm are typically the most knowledgeable people in the firm regarding the host countries and their respective cultures. Managers readily adapt business processes and behaviors (as well as products and services) to fit the needs in the host countries.

In a negotiation situation, a polycentric manager can be expected to learn about and adapt to the negotiation behaviors and practices of the foreign culture. Goals of the negotiation would be host country oriented first, followed by the needs of the company as a whole. The polycentric approach has benefited companies in their global expansion activities. Local adaptation on a country-by-country basis helps a company to establish a solid local presence in each foreign market and gain valuable knowledge and know-how for doing business in that country. As global competition increases, however, the redundancy of activities from one country to another hinders competitiveness due to increased costs, variability in brand identity, and lack of coordination and integration between country markets. Thus a firm's worldwide activities may seem somewhat fragmented.

For the international negotiator, adaptation is key to success. Understanding cultural differences and modifying negotiation behavior to meet some of the differences are necessary. Organizations with a polycentric orientation depend on their international managers to acquire the knowledge and skills needed to operate effectively in the foreign environment and to develop the ability to determine what behaviors need to be modified in various situations.

Regiocentricity

As firms increase their presence in other countries and competition worldwide grows, firms begin to look for ways to integrate activities and exploit global learning advantages. Typically, firms that begin with a polycentric orientation can strengthen competitive position by moving to a more regiocentric orientation. Regiocentric firms (and managers) view the world with a regional perspective. Countries within specific geographic regions typically share some cultural values and norms. Tastes and preferences are more similar (than with other countries), political and legal systems have similarities, and business practices tend to have more commonalities. Business decisions within a region tend to be affected by the firm's overall strategic direction (for that region). Thus negotiations with one host country will be influenced by the needs and goals of firm activities in other countries within the region.

Managers with a regiocentric perspective identify common threads throughout the cultures within a region and try to adapt to them in a manner that will maximize the strategic goals of the firm for that region. Unlike polycentric firms, which typically have a manager for each country market, a regiocentric firm will select a single manager to oversee and coordinate operations and activities in all countries within a geographic region. Thus regiocentric managers will have negotiation responsibilities in many countries, and negotiation strategies will encompass the regional needs of the firm. In this case, managers would need to have the ability to adapt negotiation behavior to fit a specific regional situation. In other words, a manager would need to understand the cultural values and behaviors of each country in which he or she operates and have the ability to determine which behaviors to integrate into negotiations involving more than one country from the region. In many cases, behaviors may vary from person to person within the negotiating team if it is a regional team.

Geocentricity

Firms with a geocentric orientation view the world as a whole and build practices and processes that maximize the benefits of its presence in each country or region around the world. A geocentric orientation typically evolves from the global learning and knowledge accrued by a firm as a result of its international activities over time.

In a geocentric firm, there is strong integration of operations and activities across countries globally. Host-country subsidiaries do not operate independently of others. Instead, there is cooperation, interdependence, and communication among subsidiaries. Each country subsidiary is assessed for its strongest competitive advantage, which becomes the strategic focus for decisions in that country. In the aggregate, country advantages create a strong global position of the firm.

Decisions made by geocentric managers must take into account the global strategy of the firm. The home country is perceived as being on an equal basis with all other countries in which the firm operates.

A geocentric manager accumulates knowledge and experience about culture, political and legal systems, business practices, organizational behaviors, and many other aspects of doing business in other countries. He or she then applies this know-how to his or her intercultural interactions and business strategies in order to build lasting relationships and reach solutions that benefit all involved in the business interaction.

As a negotiator, the geocentric manager is able to interact with others from a variety of cultures and meet the goals and needs of the home country while allowing others to also benefit from the relationship. This win-win solution to international negotiation occurs because the geocentric manager is able to see things not only from his or her own perspective, but also from the perspective of others, and can assimilate this knowledge to help create mutually beneficial outcomes.

An Argument (Rationale) for a Geocentric Approach

Company strategies must reflect the international marketplace. Strategies, or the mindset, used to operate in the international marketplace have been categorized as being ethnocentric, polycentric, regiocentric, or geocentric strategies. Although ethnocentrism is strong in many countries, an ethnocentric approach to negotiation may not be effective in international negotiation situations in today's global environment. Negotiators cannot afford to judge others by their own cultural values and rules. This self-centered approach is likely to result in negotiation suicide. It is difficult to take a country-by-country approach when developing negotiation strategies today. In other words, one of the underlying goals for many firms involved in international negotiation is the development of a long-term relationship with the partner firm. An ethnocentric approach tends to convey a message of superiority on the part of the ethnocentric negotiator or firm and reduces the ability to build trust between the two parties.

A polycentric approach, using a country-specific negotiating strategy, is no longer as effective as in the past, especially in light of the increase in economic integration worldwide. As a result of integration and a more regional or global approach taken by firms, a negotiating team may consist of members from a variety of countries who all work for the same company. Their negotiation styles may differ as well as their goals for the global firm. Thus, the convergence of cultures and regionalization of firms worldwide make a polycentric approach risky.

While a regiocentric approach is useful, especially in economically integrated areas, it may limit the global opportunities available to a firm. Firms use regional strategies within the context of their broader, more global, planning. However, the broader global approach is critical to maintaining competitiveness and efficiencies throughout the firm's global activities. For firms to maintain competitiveness, managers negotiating within a region of the world must take into account the strategic goals of the firm for other parts of the world as well as their own region. What happens in one region of the world may very well affect another region.

A geocentric approach offers the greatest possibility for success in the international negotiation setting. Understanding similarities and differences among and between countries and their cultures is important. As international managers gain more experience in the international environment, their attitudes and behaviors are affected by these interactions. Further, the manner in which geocentric managers behave in an international setting is influenced by the breadth and depth of their international experiences. The accumulation of knowledge and experience from countries and cultures around the world improves the geocentric manager's communication competencies across cultures and enables him or her to adapt to the variety of settings faced when negotiating in various countries. The geocentric negotiator develops an identity that is no longer representative of a single culture but rather a true integration of the negotiator's history, experiences, and worldview.

❖ AN INTERDISCIPLINARY EXAMINATION

The need for combining the study of business, negotiation, culture, and communication to understand global business negotiation is upon us. Now, more than any other time in history, individual disciplines must come together to address the changing world in which we live. We are specifically interested in a combined effort of disciplinary approaches for the examination of negotiation in an international business context.

For several decades, researchers operated within their own area to study the issues, problems, and theories of intercultural interactions. All, however, in one form or another, are helping to formulate an understanding of who we are and why we behave in certain ways. And most would agree, regardless of their area of study, on the following premises:

1. The culture in which an individual is reared influences the manner in which the world is viewed.

2. The expectations of how people should conduct themselves in social interactions and how to interpret those interactions are created in part by the culture.

3. Culture facilitates or prevents clarity in communication during international negotiations.

4. Cultural behaviors change as intercultural interaction occurs.

5. Company values are represented in the organizational culture that influences negotiators' strategies and practices, as well as expectation of others conducting a business negotiation. The workplace culture may be very similar to our understanding of human nature or it may require us to learn and take on new behaviors.

6. The individual is a critical component for explaining the dynamics of the communication process in intercultural business negotiations.

It is the individual who communicates and finds ways for reaching an agreement—not nations, companies, or cultures. The importance of examining how these precepts are intertwined requires a collaborative, interdisciplinary approach. Thus, using an integrative approach, we propose a framework for achieving a successful geocentric negotiation.

❖ AN INTEGRATIVE FRAMEWORK

Olaniran and Roach in 1994 argued, "Before cultures can bridge gaps in intercultural interactions, more understanding is needed of the specific communication patterns of other cultures" (p. 380). We must consider both the general culture and how this interrelates with the individual characteristics of a negotiator for a more meaningful understanding of global negotiation. Given the globalization effect that is currently underway, we can no longer cling to a singular discipline or focus in order to understand or successfully manage the negotiation process in business transactions. Specifically, we are compelled to reexamine the boundaries that constrain a much richer and much needed perspective—an integrative framework. The integrative approach is one in which we can turn to find an understanding of global negotiation. Focusing on negotiation as a communication process in the context of the international business environment will help us better understand the integration of communication, culture, and negotiation.

The significance of negotiation as a communication process–centered procedure has been acknowledged by negotiation scholars for several decades (Fisher, Ury, & Patton, 1991; Gelfand & Brett, 2004; Lewicki, Saunders, Minton, & Barry, 2003). But little research has focused on the international business negotiation experience. In addition, the intercultural communication research (although plentiful) lacks clarity on how or what intercultural communication means in terms of impact on the negotiation process, especially in the business transaction. The intercultural communication research is predominantly focused on the development of cultural generalities that are helpful to learn about homogenous cultures. However, with the technological and intercultural communication advances, pure forms of cultural representation are greatly diminishing. To fully understand the international business negotiation process, we must examine the international business negotiation from more than one viewpoint. The geocentric perspective allows one to examine the international business transaction by examining the impact of individual factors, cultural factors, the business environment, and the dynamics of the intercultural business communication. The framework of individual characteristics integrated with cultural influences and contextual factors (e.g., negotiation relationship) will lead us to a much richer understanding of the business negotiation for the next century.

The dynamic nature of the international business environment makes it difficult to generalize practices and processes for interacting with companies and individuals from other countries, especially in a negotiating setting. However, understanding the foundational elements of the people involved in international business negotiations as well as the environment in which international business negotiations take place provides a framework that can be applied to the numerous transactional settings that occur in the international environment.

The purpose of this book is to provide a framework that explores the elements necessary for effective negotiation in the international business environment. The two foundational categories needed for effective international negotiation are the *individual negotiator* and the *environment* (See Figure 1.1).

The Individual Negotiator

The individual involved in the international business negotiation matters. At the macro level, the goals and values of the negotiator's culture will influence his or her negotiation behaviors and practices. *Cultural goals and values* vary from country to country and can complicate a negotiation if differences are not clearly understood.

At the micro, or individual, level, *communication styles* vary from person to person and influence an individual's potential for effective negotiation strategy selection and collaborative relationship building. Some individuals, based on their communication characteristics, may find it easier to be effective as international business negotiators than others. In addition, negotiators have different skills and motivations to negotiate successfully in the global market. Obtaining a high level of intercultural *communication competency* is essential for maximizing success in international business negotiations. The negotiator's achieved intercultural communication competency used in the international business negotiation is an important ingredient in international business trade. Competency is more likely to be achieved when the negotiator is: adaptable, empathic, sensitive, knowledgeable, provides face honoring, and is mindful and effective in achieving his or her goal. The negotiator's style of communication coupled with his or her intercultural communication competency level will clearly influence the end result: the success or failure of international business negotiations.

Negotiators as Managers

International business negotiators are managers. Negotiation is only part of their roles and responsibilities. It is difficult to understand their role as a negotiator without some understanding of the management issues and other responsibilities facing the international manager. As we discuss the various aspects of the individual, such as communication characteristics, behaviors, and competency, and the international business context, there will also be some reference to the individual as a manager. What makes an individual successful as an international negotiator also makes that person successful as an international manager and vice versa. The broader scope of the international manager adds perspective to understanding the position and role of negotiation and the negotiator within the international business context.

Environment

The environment in which international business takes place is the second foundational category important for effective international negotiations. These elements tend to be more fluid. At the macro level, the *international business environment* changes as countries and relationships between countries change. Factors such as economic development, political changes, and technological development will affect relationships between countries. At the micro level, organizational situations as well as *business relationships* between firms will influence the negotiation process between firms and countries. As relationships change, negotiation processes and strategies also change. The challenge becomes the ability to identify and fluidly adapt to these changes.

As we will develop throughout the book, a geocentric approach to the *negotiation process*, including strategy and practices, is required for long-term success in the international business environment. The international negotiator must take into account not only the immediate need of a current negotiation, but also the long-term global strategy of the firm. Relationships with foreign companies take a prominent position in the development of global strategy, thus developing and maintaining those relationships become paramount to negotiating success. A geocentric negotiator is able to adapt to the ever-changing international business setting.

❖ STRUCTURE OF THE BOOK

In this introductory chapter, we presented the framework for a geocentric strategy for a firm and its managers and briefly outlined the

Figure 1.1   A Geocentric Approach to Successful Negotiation

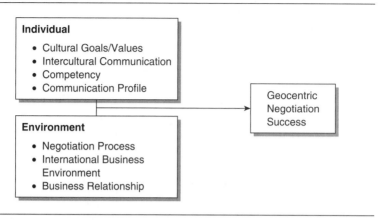

importance of a geocentric approach for successful negotiation in an international business context. This chapter provides the foundation for understanding and developing a geocentric mindset to international negotiation.

The world overview developed in Chapter 2 provides a base for developing a global perspective necessary for understanding the dynamics involved in successful international communication and negotiation. This sets the stage for the remaining chapters by giving the reader a frame of reference for applying the elements of the geocentric approach to international negotiation.

Chapter 3 reviews the negotiation process. This chapter presents a general framework of the negotiation process, an analysis of negotiation from an international perspective, and suggested guidelines to consider in a geocentric business negotiation. Chapters 4 and 5 address two of the elements of the framework presented. From a macro perspective, Chapter 4 discusses the commonly accepted models for differentiating cultural goals, values, and behaviors between countries in a business context. The communication profile (Chapter 5) focuses on the individual and the communication characteristics and behaviors important in effective international negotiation.

Chapter 6 focuses on intercultural communication competency. Skill, motivation, knowledge, and communication behaviors influence the communication competency level of international business negotiators. This chapter is a discussion concerning the role of intercultural communication competency in global business negotiation. A brief review of the communication competency research is presented, followed by a discussion of eight factors for enhancing negotiator intercultural communication competency. This chapter concludes by suggesting key communication guidelines for negotiating in the international marketplace.

Chapter 7 returns to the international business environment and examines more closely the organizational context of international business negotiations. Differentiating between types of business strategies used in the international environment should help the international negotiator in developing the appropriate negotiation strategies.

Chapter 8 discusses the role of alternative dispute resolution, or ADR, in international business negotiations. ADR is especially important in the international environment, where differing political and legal systems from country to country may result in misunderstandings of negotiation expectations, and diminish activities due to uncertainties and lack of knowledge. Third-party participation in negotiations is widely accepted in some cultures and highly avoided in other cultures. The role of the third party and the timing of intervention, as well as critical issues and benefits of using third-party intervention, are discussed. In addition, the available ADR options are reviewed. This chapter concludes by presenting guidelines for assessing when to use ADR.

Chapter 9 offers a practitioner perspective on international negotiation. A number of businesspeople whose careers involve international business negotiations were interviewed in order to provide a real-life perspective on what it is like to negotiate across cultures. Each person interviewed offered advice for students and businesspeople interested in pursuing a business career involving international negotiation.

The paradigm shift has begun in our world. It is our obligation to reexamine, reconfigure, and, if necessary, disregard what we know from yesterday to gain knowledge for tomorrow.

❖ DISCUSSION QUESTIONS

1. How is technology influencing globalization?

2. What role does FDI play in the globalization of developing countries? How does FDI relate to international negotiation?

3. Why is the globalization of developing countries important?

4. Discuss the pros and cons of each category of centricity. As an international negotiator, how would each affect your negotiating environment?

5. Why are issues such as technology, FDI, economic integration, and centricity important to international business negotiation?

❖ REFERENCES

Calof, J., & Beamish, P. (1994). The right attitude for international success. *Business Quarterly, 59*, 105–110.

Deshpande, R., Farley, J., & Webster, F. E., Jr. (1993). Corporate culture, customer orientation, and innovativeness: Japanese firms: A quadrad analysis. *Journal of Marketing, 57*(1), 23–37.

Deshpande, R., & Webster, F. E., Jr. (1989). Organizational culture and marketing: Defining the research. *Journal of Marketing, 53*(1), 3–15.

Detert, J. R., Schroeder, R. G., & Mauriel, J. J. (2000). A framework for linking culture and improvement initiatives in organizations. *Academy of Management Review, 25*(4), 850–863.

Fisher, R., Ury, W., & Patton, B. (Eds.). (1991). *Getting to yes, negotiating agreement without giving in* (2nd ed.). New York: Penguin.

Gelfand, M., & Brett, J. (2004). *The handbook of negotiation and culture.* Stanford: Stanford Business Books.

Gudykunst, W. B. (2005). *Theorizing about intercultural communication.* Thousand Oaks, CA: Sage.

Heenan, D., & Perlmutter, H. (1979). *Multinational organizational development: A social architecture perspective.* Reading, MA: Addison-Wesley.

Hill, C. (2004). *International business: Competing in the global marketplace* (4th ed). Boston: McGraw-Hill/Irwin.

Lewicki, R., Saunders, D., Minton, J., & Barry, B. (2003). *Negotiation.* Boston: McGraw-Hill/Irwin.

Ohmae, K. (1987). The triad world. *Journal of Business Strategy, 7*(4), 8–18.

Olaniran, B., & Roach, D. (1994). Communication apprehension and classroom apprehension in Nigerian classrooms. *Communication Quarterly, 42*(4), 379–389.

Ondrack, D. A. (1985). International human-resources management in European and North-American firms. *International Studies of Management and Organization, 15*(1), 6–32.

Perlmutter, H. (1969). The tortuous evolution of the multinational corporation. *Columbia Journal of World Business, 4*, 9–18.

Ting-Toomey, S. (1988). Intercultural conflicts: A face-negotiation theory. In Y. Y. Kim & W. B. Gudykunst (Eds.), *Theories in intercultural communication* (pp. 213–238). Newbury Park, CA: Sage.

Trice, H. M., & Beyer, J. M. (1993). *The cultures of work organizations.* Englewood Cliffs, NJ: Prentice-Hall.

UNCTAD. (2004). *World investment report: 2004: The shift toward services.* Geneva: United Nations.

2

A Geocentric Perspective

One of the greatest competitive advantages for global managers is knowledge. As managers gain experience in foreign business activities, the knowledge they gain increases at a faster rate due to synergy. The more a manager learns about various countries, the better he or she will be able to understand and interpret their systems for operating. The aggregate knowledge and information begins to create a manager with a worldview, or global perspective. In one of his well-known works, *The Competitive Advantage of Nations*, Michael Porter (1990) identifies human capital as the most important factor of production for successful nations and firms. Increasing the value of human capital through improved skill levels is a strong factor in the success of firms. For firms doing business in other countries, one of the most important skills for a manager is the ability to learn. From a competitive perspective, worldwide learning and the ability to integrate and apply that knowledge is a key capability for sustainable competitiveness in the global business environment (Bartlett, Ghoshal, & Birkinshaw, 2004).

The difficulty remains that "despite the fact that people are innately curious and naturally motivated to learn from each other, most modern corporations are constructed in a way that constrains and sometimes kills this natural human instinct" (p. 456). Thus, a global manager must be internally motivated to learn from experiences in other countries. This chapter provides a general global overview focusing on the level of development of countries and the role of foreign direct investment in the world economy. Additionally, the role of small- and medium-size firms in the global economy is discussed. These elements contribute to the international negotiator's understanding of some of the issues he or she may face when negotiating internationally. Although the topics discussed in this chapter do not directly relate to a negotiation, they are important because they help the negotiator understand the context from which his or her counterpart operates.

A first step in global learning is to understand the general economic framework in which international business transactions take place. This is an important component in developing successful strategies for international negotiations as it helps you to begin to gain knowledge of the countries around the world in which cross-border business takes place in terms of the size and scope of the international business environment and its participants. Several of the elements discussed also impact the environment or setting in which international negotiation takes place. As you will see, the ethnocentric (my way is best) or polycentric (treat each country independently) approaches for international negotiation are no longer ideal in most cases. The interconnectedness of countries demands the more complex geocentric view of international business interactions and transactions.

In order to fully understand the need for a geocentric approach to business transactions and negotiations, it is important to understand how the world looks today. For a large part of the 20th century, the world was powered by the United States and the now former Soviet Union. Generally, countries were aligned with one of these two superpowers. With the fall of the Soviet Union in the late 1980s, the orderly framework in which countries operated began to shift. The disassembling of the Soviet Union left only one superpower, the United States. More important though, it created opportunities for countries to review past strategies and determine how best to compete in a new world market that was no longer dominated by two major economies.

At the same time the Soviet Union was being disbanded, the European Union was growing and deepening its level of integration (or cooperation) between member countries. As discussed in Chapter 7, the European Union has become a major economic power in the world today.

A third factor has influenced the framework in which we operate in the international environment today, and that is China. The need for developed countries, such as the United States, the European Union countries, and Japan, to find good sources of low-cost labor provided great opportunities for economic growth in China and other Asian countries. Of course, for China, this opportunity was helped along by the Chinese government's decision to move toward a more market-oriented economy in order to prevent a similar situation as that experienced by the former Soviet Union. The result has been the rapid ascent of China becoming a major player in the world economy today. In terms of GDP in 2004, China was the second largest economy in the world (estimated GDP of 7.26 trillion dollars), following the United States (Central Intelligence Agency, n.d.). However, given the size of its population, it is still considered a relatively poor country. China's GDP per capita in 2004 was about $5,600 (as a comparison, the U.S. GDP per capita was about $40,000).

Other areas of the world are also important to examine. India, the second most populous country in the world, has not had the speed of growth that China has experienced, but it is undergoing economic and policy changes that will increase its potential for growth. Latin America and Central America are also in transition. They are especially important to North American countries because of their geographic proximity to the United States and Canada, as the greatest amount of trade between countries usually occurs between neighboring or geographically close countries. As the economies of Latin America grow, the United States and Canada should benefit. Likewise, Latin American countries should also benefit from their northern neighbors.

As you read through this chapter, you may question the importance of this type of information to international negotiation. It is important. The world is changing. Business dealings are not always two-directional; more than two countries may be involved. Additionally, a deal you negotiate in one country may affect a deal in another country or a deal in another division of your company. As countries change economically, their business practices evolve, many times to more Western-oriented behaviors. The presence of foreign firms in a country influences its business and economic development.

When developing negotiating strategies, a relationship or need with one country may influence a relationship with another country. This is especially true when political issues come into play. As the integration of economies increases, there is a greater degree of cross-national or multinational interaction, usually regionally delineated. Thus negotiation tends to become a little more complicated. It is important that the international business manager/negotiator understands the global context in which he or she operates.

To get a clear picture of the world in which we live, it is also important to look at the economic position of countries relative to their populations, as well as the amount of foreign activity in the form of foreign direct investment (from an economic position) in which the country is involved. While there are numerous other measures that could be used to help define the economic status of a country, these should sufficiently provide a view of the world today.

❖ COUNTRY CLASSIFICATION

The World Bank classifies all countries that are members of the World Bank as well as all other countries with populations greater than 30,000 (a total of 208 countries). This classification aids in policy development as well as in providing a general picture of the world's population. Detailed information regarding country classifications by the World Bank can be found at http://www.worldbank.org/data/countryclass. Here we will create a general picture.

The World Bank classifies countries into four categories based on gross national income per capita (World Bank Group, 2005): low income ($765/capita or lower), lower-middle income ($766–$3,035), upper-middle income ($3,036–$9,385), and high income ($9,386/capita or higher). There are 61 low-income economies, 56 lower-middle-income economies, 37 upper-middle-income economies, and 54 higher-income economies. These classifications are usually consolidated into two groups: developing countries, which include the low-, lower-middle-, and upper-middle-income economies; and the developed countries, which include the remaining 54 high-income economies. Already, the economic imbalance of the world should be apparent. Of the countries included in the World Bank classification, 154 are considered developing countries, whereas only 54 countries are classified as high income. Low-income countries have the fastest population growth: almost three times that of the high income, or developed economies (World Bank Group, 2005). The majority of business transactions take place in the developed economies. However, there is an increasing level of economic activity in developing countries as their governments develop plans to attract FDI.

Table 2.1 provides the world population distribution across the classification categories. As you can see, the largest proportion of population is from the developing countries. In fact, more than 80 percent of the world's population is in developing countries.

Table 2.1   Population Distribution by Country Classification for 1999 and 2003

	Low Income		Middle Income [a]		High Income	
	1999	2003	1999	2003	1999	2003
Population	2.1 B[b]	2.3 B	2.9 B	3.0 B	892.6 m[b]	913.6 m
Population Growth	2.0%	1.8%	1.1%	0.9%	0.6%	0.5%
GNI[c]/capita	$390	$450	$1,700	$1,920	$26,500	$29,310

SOURCE: World Bank Country Classifications
[a]Middle-income countries = lower-middle-income countries and upper-middle-income countries
[b]B = billion, m = million
[c]GNI = Gross National Income

The distribution of population between developed and developing countries is important for several reasons. First, one of the goals of most country governments worldwide is to improve the standard of living of its citizens. The way to do this in today's competitive environment is through economic growth. For developing countries, usually internal (within the country) wealth is concentrated in the hands of only a few and is not large enough to facilitate sufficient economic growth for an improved standard of living for a large portion of the society. The former Soviet Union is a good example of this. The former Soviet Union was a closed economy in that the majority of economic growth and development was with internal assets (little support from outside the Soviet bloc countries). While development was beneficial to many sectors and groups of people within the Soviet bloc, the standard of living for the majority of people within the bloc continually declined.[1]

As economic growth through internal mechanisms is not sufficient, developing countries have realized the need for external sources of support for economic growth. The primary mechanism for this is referred to as foreign direct investment (FDI), which will be discussed in more detail later in this chapter. Basically, FDI involves the investment of capital by firms into another country. There are several advantages of FDI to the developing country. FDI provides needed capital for economic growth, as well as more advanced technology relative to the technology existing within the developing country. Further, it provides management know-how and business systems that help improve the competitiveness of the developing economy in the international marketplace.

A second reason for the importance of understanding the population distribution of the world is to understand and appreciate the demand for aid being placed on developed countries. Developed countries hold the responsibility to financially support developing countries for humanitarian and security purposes. The dilemma then becomes how to balance the needs of other countries with the needs of one's own country. One way to reduce the support needs of developing countries is to help them grow economically so they can become more self-sufficient.

Finally, a third reason to understand the structure of the world's population is to understand the direct impact on the developed countries through immigration. As the population in developing countries increases, more and more people migrate to the urban areas of those countries in order to find more economic opportunities to support their families. Unfortunately, in many cases, the urban population grows faster than the support services of the city, thus putting severe pressure on the infrastructure in areas such as safety, sanitation, and education. The standard of living decreases.

Because of these difficult conditions and lack of opportunities (especially with little FDI), people begin to migrate to the developed countries in search of better economic (and sometimes political or social) conditions. Large migration flows occur from Latin America and Asia to North America and from Eastern Europe, the former Soviet bloc, and North Africa to Northern and Western Europe (Population Reference Bureau, 2004). Although watched closely and managed through immigration policies, immigration has become a major issue in many developed economies today. Developed countries must address not only what levels of immigration to allow, but also the issue of illegal immigration.

❖ IMPACT ON INTERNATIONAL NEGOTIATION

The growth of the role of developing economies in the international business environment adds to the complexity of international negotiation strategy. On one hand, as developing countries do not have the same level of international interaction as countries long involved in international business, cultural norms and values may be more stable, thus easier to learn about. On the other hand, since the level of interaction is relatively low for the country, it may be more difficult to attain information regarding the culture from secondary sources, making it a "learn as you go" process. For most countries, basic cultural information is available, but it is the application of this information over time that provides the insightful experiential knowledge that is useful in negotiating situations.

Keep in mind that the number of developing countries far outweighs the number of developed countries. Thus the cultural and business practices knowledge that needs to be understood could be quite challenging. In addition to cultural behaviors and business processes, each country differs in terms of its legal and political structures. These areas are particularly important to the negotiation in terms of contract and ownership issues. In many developing countries, the government maintains strong controls over commercial activities through regulation as well as ownership. Further, the policies and regulations for foreign firms may differ from the same policies for domestic firms, often putting the foreign firm at a disadvantage.

When we think of international negotiation, we typically refer to negotiations with a party from another country. This is a valid perspective. However, a secondary application of some of the strategies and tactics used in international negotiation could be applied to domestic situations. With the increasing level of immigration of people from developing countries to developed countries, the face of negotiation within one's own country may change. As a large number of legal immigrants into developed countries are highly educated and highly skilled, it is likely that the number of foreign-born negotiators on domestic negotiating teams will increase. Even with acculturation of the organizational culture, individuals maintain many of their home-country cultural characteristics. Thus domestically focused negotiation strategies and tactics may require modification.

Finally, a third area of impact of negotiation involving developing countries is that of balance. The goal of most firms is to maximize profit and advantage in all transactions; we want to get the most out of a negotiation. As discussed earlier, however, a responsibility of developed countries to developing countries is to aid in the development efforts of the country (typically referred to as social responsibility). This applies to economic growth and carries over into the activities of firms. For developed-country firms negotiating with firms or organizations from developing countries, the challenge becomes determining the appropriate balance between maximizing company goals and contributing to the economic well-being and growth of the developing country. This is important not only from a humanitarian perspective, but also from a stockholder perspective. More and more stockholders in companies, as well as potential stock investors, are expecting companies to be more socially responsible in their business activities, especially when developing countries are involved.

❖ FOREIGN DIRECT INVESTMENT

As mentioned in the "Country Classification" section of this chapter, FDI is critical to the economic development of developing countries as well as developed countries. By definition, FDI is "an investment made to acquire lasting interest in enterprises operating outside of the economy [country] of the investor. Further, in cases of FDI, the investor's purpose is to gain an effective voice in the management of the enterprise" (UNCTAD, 2004). Typically, an investor would have ownership of 10 percent or more of the entity in order to have an effective voice in management (OECD, 2005). In most instances of FDI, the "investor" is a firm (ownership of that firm varies by country and can be privately held, publicly held, nationally held, or a combination).

FDI is typically viewed from two positions: the *inward* flow of FDI and the *outward* flow of FDI. FDI is measured on a country, regional, and worldwide basis. Inward FDI refers to the value of FDI capital (money) that flows into a country from all other countries. Outward FDI refers to the value of the FDI capital that flows out of a country to all other countries. Understanding the magnitude of FDI (both directions) is important in understanding the "playing field" of the international environment as well as helping to determine the direction of future international business activity. FDI is important to the international negotiator because it requires the interaction of people and firms from different countries and cultures in order to plan and implement the FDI activity. A basic understanding of FDI activity is needed to understand a very important component of negotiation in the context of international business. This section will present a brief overview of FDI activity worldwide and in specific regions and countries. Chapter 7, "The International Business Context," will discuss some of the types of business activities that require FDI.

Foreign Direct Investment Trends

Historically, the majority of FDI has taken place between developed countries, with the United States being the largest receiver of FDI (FDI inflow) as well as the largest investor in other countries (FDI outflow) cumulatively. Developed countries also make substantial investments in developing countries; in 2002, China was the second largest recipient of FDI (UNCTAD, 2004). Although a large majority of FDI activity remains within developed countries, the amount of FDI activity involving developing countries is increasing. Initially, FDI involving developing countries consisted of developed countries investing in the developing countries, such as the United States investing in China to set up manufacturing plants in order to benefit from the lower labor costs available in China. In 2003, developing countries accounted for 31 percent of FDI inflow, with ten countries accounting for almost 75 percent of total investment (UNCTAD, 2004). While FDI inflows to developing countries continues, there has been an increase in FDI coming out of (FDI outflows) developing countries as well, reaching 6 percent of total flows in 2003 (UNCTAD, 2004), with the fastest growing activity being between developing countries. Asia and Latin America were the two largest outward investors in the developing countries (developing-country-to-developing-country FDI).

Another trend in FDI activity is the move from FDI in manufacturing to FDI in services. Table 2.2 summarizes the proportion of FDI in services for developed and developing countries. As can be seen, services now (2001–2002) comprise a much larger proportion of FDI than those of about a decade earlier (1989–1991). Outward flows of FDI in services had a larger proportional change over the time period reported. In the time period 1989 to 1991, 55 percent of FDI outflows were related to service activities (e.g., banking, insurance, etc.). By 2001 to 2002, 77 percent of FDI in the world was service related. It is the nature of service businesses that makes this change noteworthy.

As we know, there are substantial differences between the operations of firms that manufacture products and those that offer services. Whereas human interaction is required in both cases, the level and frequency of human interaction in service firms tends to be more involved. The manufacture of products offers tangible results that can easily be assessed prior to the purchase of the product. Services, on the other hand, are intangible and typically not received until after the purchase agreement has been made. Thus, other factors such as the relationship between the parties involved in the transaction(s) become more important.

FDI drives much of the global economy. Developing countries depend on it for development opportunities. Not only do they need the capital investment associated with FDI, but they also need the technology advancements and the managerial know-how that accompanies the capital investments into the country. FDI in turn improves the economic landscape of the country and increases employment. This in turn increases the economic strength of the people of the country, which results in an increase in demand for goods and services. The increase in economic strength increases investment, and the cycle continues. At some point, firms from FDI-receiving countries become

Table 2.2 Proportion of FDI in Services Coming From Developed and Developing Countries

	FDI in Services			
	Inward Flows of FDI in Services		Outward Flows of FDI in Services	
	1989–1991	2001–2002	1989–1991	2001–2002
World	54%	67%	55%	71%
Developed Countries	58	73	55	71
Developing Countries	35	50	39	77

SOURCE: UNCTAD, 2004.

strong enough (economically) that they begin to look at investment opportunities in other countries. If we look at China, we can see this cycle. Throughout the 1980s and 1990s, China was a net receiver of FDI. Billions of dollars were invested in China by foreign companies. While China is still a major receiver of FDI, they are also beginning to look at investment opportunities in other countries. In 2004, FDI by Chinese companies increased by 27 percent ("Spending Spree," 2005).

Developed-country firms use FDI as a major vehicle for international expansion. It provides access to other developed markets and it allows firms to enter developing countries that have market potential for future economic growth. At the same time, it helps the developing countries to strengthen their competitiveness in the international environment.

❖ GROWTH OF DEVELOPING ECONOMIES

The growth of developing economies presents real competition to firms in developed countries. This is illustrated by the country of origin of firms that make the *Financial Times* Global 500. The *Financial Times* Global 500 lists the 500 largest firms in the world as measured by a number of economic factors ("Global 500," 2005). Table 2.3 shows the number of firms from each country between the years of 2002 and 2005. Of particular note is the decrease in the number of firms from the leading world economies. Between 2002 and 2005, the largest decrease in the number of firms (35.7 percent) was in the Netherlands, followed by the United Kingdom (19.5 percent) and Japan (14 percent). While these

Table 2.3   *Financial Times* Global 500, 2002–2005

	2002	*2003*	*2004*	*2005*
Australia	9	7	7[a]	8
Austria	0	0	1	1
Belgium	5	5	7	6
Brazil	2	2	4	5
Canada	18	22	22	22
Denmark	2	4	3	3
Finland	2	2	3	2
France	9	25	26	28
Germany	21	21	18	19
Hong King	8	9	8	8
India	1	2	5	5
Ireland	2	3	3	3
Israel	0	0	1	1
Italy	11	12	11	12
Japan	50	47	50	43
Malaysia	0	1	0	0
Mexico	6	3	4	4
Netherlands	14	8	10[b]	9
Norway	2	2	4	4
Portugal	1	1	1	1
Russia	4	5	4	4
Saudi Arabia	2	5	6	8
Singapore	5	3	3	3
South Africa	0	0	0	2
South Korea	6	5	5	6
Spain	7	8	10	9
Sweden	5	7	8	7
Switzerland	12	9	11	12
Taiwan	2	3	5	5
Thailand	0	0	0	1
UAE	1	1	1	1
UK	41	34	33	33
US	238	241	225[c]	219

SOURCE: "Global 500," 2005.
[a]Two companies are Australia/UK owned.
[b]Three companies are Netherlands/UK owned.
[c]One company is US/UK owned.

decreases may appear substantial, it should not be interpreted that the leading world economies are losing leadership positions; they still hold a large majority of the largest global firms and are the world leaders in international business. To illustrate, Table 2.4 shows the G8 countries and the number of Global 500 firms from these countries for 2005.

As you can see, 76 percent of the largest firms globally in 2005 still come from the world economic leaders. If the other developed countries are included (Australia, Sweden, the Netherlands, etc.) this percentage becomes even greater.

Table 2.4   Number of 2005 Global 500 Firms From G8 Countries

Country	# of Global 500 Firms
Canada	22
France	28
Germany	19
Italy	12
Japan	43
Russia	4
United Kingdom	33
United States	219
Total	380

SOURCE: "Global 500," 2005.

If the developed economies have such a stronghold on the global economy, it may seem unimportant to discuss the presence of developing economies in the global environment. However, the incremental growth of large firms from developing countries is noteworthy. The growth of these firms demonstrates the economic evolution of these countries. In the discussion of FDI, you should recall the importance of FDI into developing countries for economic development. Eventually, these countries develop to a point where they have the economic strength to build global firms, usually through acquisition. The result is globally competitive firms. Looking again at changes in the Global 500 between 2002 and 2005, we can see that the developing countries with the largest increases in the number of Global 500 firms were Taiwan and Brazil (150 percent increase for each), India (700 percent increase), South Africa (200 percent increase), and Saudi Arabia (300 percent increase). Although the actual number of Global 500 firms from each of these countries is small, the trend is very clear. More and more large, globally competitive firms will be from developing countries, all of which have very different cultures, political and legal environments, and business practices. For the international negotiator, the complexity of the international business environment increases with each country that enters the picture. The growth of large firms from developing regions has become such an important factor in the global economy that along with the Global 500, the *Financial Times* compiles the Eastern

Europe 100, the Latin America 100, and the Asia 100. Each of these lists indicates the largest firms in the respective region. Thus, the international business manager can follow the economic trends and changes within the growing regions of the developing regions of the world.

Regionalization

Historically, the natural flow of trade would begin with neighboring countries and expand to other countries usually within relatively close proximity. The main impetus for this trade path was logistics; distance was a limiting factor in the export of products. Transportation was not as advanced as it is today and, therefore, limited the distance over which products could be transported. With each technological advancement in transportation and communication, trade with distant countries has become more physically and economically feasible.

Also looking from a historical perspective, governments traditionally protected their enterprises from foreign competition through the creation of laws that were detrimental to foreign companies. However, over the last 60 years, the trend has been to strengthen cooperation between countries by reducing or eliminating barriers to cross-border trade. Beginning with the General Agreement on Tariffs and Trade in 1947 (now the World Trade Organization), trade between countries has been substantially liberalized. Regionalization has been a logical outcome of trade liberalization. Many firms look to expand internationally within their own geographic region before moving to other regions of the world. There are several factors influencing this type of strategy. First, country cultures are generally more similar within a region than with countries from other regions of the world. The movement of people from one country to another is more likely to happen when countries are in closer proximity. When people move, cultures move. Since cultures are more similar in neighboring countries (within a region), doing business in those countries is easier. It is easier to understand the laws, the business practices, and so forth. In many regions, such as Latin America, many countries speak the same language.

A second factor for regionalization is economics. Transporting goods to closer countries is cheaper than transporting goods to countries farther away. Plus, as there are some similarities in culture, demand for similar products is more likely. Finally, it is easier for companies to manage business when it is closer to headquarters than when it is farther away. Although communication and transportation technologies today make it much easier to manage foreign operations anywhere in the world, the perceived difficulty of managing at a distance is still great.

Understanding how the world looks region by region provides a starting point for understanding differences in cultures, business practices, and negotiating strategies. The United Nations Conference on Trade and Development divides the world into several regions for monitoring and reporting economic activity. The tables included in this section provide a general overview of the population and gross domestic product (GDP) of each country within a region. Also included is the GDP per capita, which illustrates the purchasing power of the people of that country. GDP and GDP per capita are in U.S. dollars. From viewing these tables, you can see the size and economic strength of each country within the region.

Table 2.5   Population and Economies of Non–European Union Developed Countries

	Population	*GDP*	*GDP/Capita (USD)*
Western Europe			
Gibraltar	0.028 m[a]	0.8 B[a]	27,900
Iceland	0.3 m	9.4 B	31,900
Malta	0.4 m	7.2 B	18,200
Norway	4.6 m	183.0 B	40,000
Switzerland	7.5 m	251.9 B	33,800
North America			
Canada	32.8 m	1,023.0 B	31,500
United States	295.7 m	11,750.0 B	40,100
Other			
Australia	20.1 m	611.7 B	30,700
Israel	6.3 m	129.0 B	20,800
Japan	127.4 m	3,745.0 B	29,400
New Zealand	4.0 m	92.5 B	23,200

SOURCE: Central Intelligence Agency, n.d.
[a]m = million, B = billion $

Table 2.6   Population and Economies of South, East, and Southeast Asia

	Population	*GDP*	*GDP/capita (ppp)* (USD)*
Afghanistan	29.9 m[a]	21.5 B[a]	800
Bangladesh	144.3 m	275.7 B	2,000
Bhutan	2.2 m	2.9 B	1,400
Brunei Darussalam	0.37 m	6.8 B	23,600
Cambodia	13.6 m	26.99 B	2,000
China	1306.3 m	7.3 B	5,600

Hong King, China	6.9 m	234.5 B	34,200
India	1,080.3 m	3,319.0 B	3,100
Indonesia	241.97 m	827.4 B	3,500
Laos	6.2m	11.3 B	1,900
Macao, China	0.45 m	9.1 B	19,400
Malaysia	23.95 m	229.3 B	9,700
Maldives	0.35 m	1.3 B	3,900
Mongolia	2.8 m	5.3 B	1,900
Myanmar	42.9 m	74.3 B	1,700
Nepal	27.7 m	39.5 B	1,500
Pakistan	162.4 m	347.3 B	2,200
Philippines	87.9 m	430.6 B	5,000
Republic of Korea	48.4 m	925.1 B	19,200
Singapore	4.4 m	120.9 B	27,800
Sri Lanka	20.1 m	80.6 B	4,000
Taiwan Province of China	22.9 m	576.2 B	25,300
Thailand	65.4 m	524.8 B	8,100
Vietnam	83.5 m	227.2 B	2,700

SOURCE: Central Intelligence Agency, n.d.
[a]m = million, B = billion $
*ppp = purchasing power parity

Table 2.7   Population and Economies of West Asia

	Population	GDP	GDP/capita (USD)
Bahrain	688.3 t[a]	13.0 B[a]	19,200
Republic of Cypress	780.1 t	15.7 B	20,300
North Cypress		4.54 B	7,135
Iran	68.0 m[a]	516.7 B	7,700
Jordan	5.6 m	25.5 B	4,500
Kuwait	2.3 m	48.0 B	21,300
Lebanon	3.8 m	18.8 B	5,000
Oman	3.0 m	38.1 B	13,100
Qatar	863.0 t	19.5 B	23,200
Saudi Arabia	26.4 m	310.2 B	12,000
Syria	18.4 m	60.4 B	3,400
Turkey	69.7 m	508.7 B	7,400
United Arab Emirates	2.6 m	63.7 B	25,200
Yemen	20.7 m	16.3 B	800

SOURCE: Central Intelligence Agency, n.d.
[a]t = thousand, m = million, B = billion $

Table 2.8   Population and Economies of the Pacific

	Population	GDP	GDP/capita (ppp)* (USD)
Fiji	893.4 t[a]	5,173.0 M[a]	5,900
Kiribati	103.1 t	79.0 M	800
New Caledonia	216.5 t	3,158.0 M	15,000
Papua New Guinea	5,545.3 t	11,990.0 M	2,200
Samoa	117.3 t	1,000.0 M	5,600
Solomon Islands	538.0 t	800.0 M	1,700
Tonga	112.4 t	244.0 M	2,300
Vanuatu	205.8 t	580.0 M	2,900

SOURCE: Central Intelligence Agency, n.d.
[a]t = thousand, M = million $
*ppp = purchasing power parity

Table 2.9   Population and Economies of Central Asia

	Population	GDP	GDP/capita (USD)
Armenia	2.98 m[a]	13.7 B[a]	4,600
Azerbaijan	7.9 m	30.0 B	3,800
Georgia	4.7 m	14.5 B	3,100
Kazakhstan	15.2 m	118.4 B	7,800
Kyrgyzstan	5.1 m	8.5 B	1,700
Uzbekistan	26.9 m	47.6 B	1,800

SOURCE: Central Intelligence Agency, n.d.
[a]m = million, B = billion $

Table 2.10   Population and Economies of Central and Eastern Europe

	Population	GDP	GDP/capita (ppp)* (USD)
Albania	3.6 m[b]	17.5 B[b]	4,900
Belarus	10.3 m	70.5 B	6,800
Bosnia and Herzegovina	4.0 m	26.2 B	6,500
Bulgaria	7.5 m	61.6 B	8,200
Croatia	4.5 m	50.3 B	11,200
Czech Republic[a]	10.2 m	172.2 B	16,800
Estonia	1.3 m	19.2 B	14,300
Hungary	10.0 m	149.3 B	14,900
Latvia	2.3 m	26.5 B	11,500
Lithuania	3.6 m	45.2 B	12,500
Poland	38.6 m	463.0 B	12,000
Republic of Moldova	4.5 m	8.6 B	1,900
Romania	22.3 m	171.5 B	7,700
Russian Federation	143.4 m	1,408.0 B	9,800

Serbia and Montenegro	10.8 m	26.3 B	2,400
Slovakia	5.4 m	78.9 B	14,500
Slovenia	2.0 m	39.4 B	19,600
TFYR Macedonia	2.0 m	14.4 B	7,100
Ukraine	47.4 m	299.1 B	6,300

SOURCE: Central Intelligence Agency, n.d.
[a]Countries in italics are members of the European Union.
[b]m = million, B = billion $
*ppp = purchasing power parity

Table 2.11   Population and Economies of Latin America

	Population (2005 est.)	GDP (2004 est.)	GDP/capita (ppp)* (USD)
Argentina	95.5 m[a]	483.5 B[a]	12,400
Belize	0.3 m	1.8 B	6,500
Bolivia	8.6 m	22.3 B	2,600
Brazil	186.1 m	1,492.0 B	8,100
Chile	16.0 m	169.1 B	10,700
Colombia	43.0 m	281.1 B	6,600
Costa Rica	4.0 m	38.0 B	9,600
Dominican Republic	9.0 m	55.7 B	6,300
Ecuador	13.4 m	49.5 B	3,700
El Salvador	6.7 m	32.4 B	4,900
Guatemala	14.7 m	59.5 B	4,200
Haiti	8.1 m	12.1 B	1,500
Honduras	7.0 m	18.8 B	2,800
Jamaica	2.7 m	11.1 B	4,100
Mexico	106.2 m	1,006.0 B	9,600
Nicaragua	5.5 m	12.3 B	2,300
Panama	3.0 m	20.6 B	6,900
Paraguay	6.3 m	29.9 B	4,800
Peru	27.9 m	155.3 B	5,600
Uruguay	3.4 m	49.3 B	14,500
Venezuela	25.4 m	145.2 B	5,800

SOURCE: Central Intelligence Agency, n.d.
[a]m = million, B = billion $

Table 2.12   Population and Economies of Caribbean Basin

	Population	GDP	GDP/capita (ppp)* (USD)
Antigua and Barbuda	68,722	750.0 M[a]	11,000
Aruba	71,566	1,940.0 M	28,000
Bahamas	301,790	5,295.0 M	17,700

(Continued)

Table 2.12   (Continued)

Barbados	279,254	4,569.0 M	16,400
Bermuda	65,365	2,330.0 M	36,000
British Virgin Islands	22,643	2,498.0 M	38,500
Cayman Islands	44,270	1,391.0 M	32,300
Dominica	69,029	384.0 M	5,500
Grenada	89,502	440.0 M	5,000
Guyana	765,283	2899.0 M	3,800
Haiti	8,121,622	12,050.0 M	1,500
Jamaica	2,731,832	11,130.0 M	4,100
Netherlands Antilles	219,958	2,450.0 M	11,400
St. Kitts and Nevis	38,958	339.0 M	8,800
Saint Lucia	166,312	866.0 M	5,400
Saint Vincent and The Grenadines	117,534	342.0 M	2,900
Suriname	438,144	1,885.0 M	4,300
Trinidad and Tobago	1,088,644	11,480.0 M	10,500

SOURCE: Central Intelligence Agency, n.d.
[a]M = million $
*ppp = purchasing power parity

Table 2.13   African Countries

Algeria	Gambia	Senegal
Angola	Ghana	Seychelles
Benin	Guinea	Sierra Leone
Botswana	Guinea-Bissau	Somalia
Burkin Faso	Kenya	South Africa
Burundi	Lesotho	Sudan
Cameroon	Liberia	Swaziland
Central African Republic	Madagascar	Togo
Chad	Malawi	Tunisia
Comoros	Mali	United Republic of Tanzania
Congo	Mauritania	Uganda
Côte d'Ivoire	Mauritius	Zambia
Dem. Rep. of Congo	Morocco	Zimbabwe
Djibouti	Mozambique	
Egypt	Namibia	
Equatorial Guinea	Niger	
Ethiopia	Nigeria	
Gabon	Rwanda	

SOURCE: Central Intelligence Agency, n.d.

❖ SMALL- AND MEDIUM-SIZE FIRMS

Much discussion of the global business environment typically focuses on the large multinational corporation. When we look at FDI, the majority of activity involves large corporations, and the majority of revenues derived from foreign activities come from these multinational corporations, as can be seen from the Global 500 rankings. While this category of companies deserves the attention it attracts, there is another category of firms critical to a full understanding of the global environment: small- and medium-size firms (SMEs).

SMEs vary in size and definition from country to country. Because many of these firms are not publicly traded firms, there is less consistency in measures across countries. The Organization for Economic Cooperation and Development (OECD, 2005)[2] provides a useful definition for understanding an SME: "SMEs are generally considered to be non-subsidiary, independent firms which employ fewer than a given number of employees" (OECD, 2005, p. 18). The upper limit in terms of number of employees used to designate an SME for most countries is 250 employees. European Union countries use this limit. Some countries set an employee limit of 200 to designate an SME. At the upper level, the United States defines an SME as a firm with fewer than 500 employees.

Within the general category of SMEs, firms are further segmented into three groups based on the number of employees and the financial assets of the firm. Again, while the specific limits setting each group vary, there are three general categories of SMEs: medium-size firms, small firms, and microfirms. Using the parameters set by the European Union, we can see how SMEs are segmented. Medium firms employ between 50 to 250 people and should have a turnover of no more than 50 million euros. Small firms employ 10 to 49 people with a turnover limit of 10 million euros. The third category, microfirms, employs fewer than 10 people and reach annual turnover rates of no more than 2 million euro (OECD, 2005).

For SMEs from most countries, firm size is important. Governments set policies that can be more beneficial to firms of specific sizes. For example, in the United States, small businesses receive some preferences in attaining government contracts. The definition of a small business in these cases varies by the industry in which the firm operates. For the European Union, the definition given previously is used for funding and business aid programs.

SMEs play a particularly important role in most countries in terms of employment. In OECD countries (Table 2.14 lists OECD member countries), SMEs and entrepreneurial activity "account for over 95 percent of enterprises, generate two-thirds of employment and are the main source of new jobs" (OECD, 2005, p. 15). Firms of these sizes are responsible for most net job creation in member countries. Discussion of SMEs and their roles in the global environment is not complete without some mention of entrepreneurship. Entrepreneurship is the catalyst behind

SMEs. Entrepreneurship, as defined by the European Commission, is "the mindset and process to create and develop economic activity by building risk-taking, creativity and/or innovation with sound management" (OECD, 2005, p. 22). In the United States, entrepreneurship is defined as "the process of creating something new with value by devoting the necessary time and effort, assuming the accompanying financial, psychic, and social risks, and receiving the resulting rewards of monetary and personal satisfaction and independence" (Hirsch, Peters, & Shepherd, 2005, p. 8). While these definitions differ, a common thread exists. Creating new activities that add value to the individual and the system within which it operates underlies both definitions.

Table 2.14   OECD Member Countries

Country (year joined)	Country (year joined)
Australia (1971)	Korea (1996)
Austria (1961)	Luxembourg (1961)
Belgium (1961)	Mexico (1994)
Canada (1961)	Netherlands (1961)
Czech Republic (1995)	New Zealand (1973)
Denmark (1961)	Norway (1961)
Finland (1969)	Poland (1996)
France (1961)	Portugal (1961)
Germany (1961)	Slovak Republic (2000)
Greece (1961)	Spain (1961)
Hungary (1996)	Sweden (1961)
Iceland (1961)	Switzerland (1961)
Ireland (1961)	Turkey (1961)
Italy (1962)	United Kingdom (1961)
Japan (1964)	United States (1961)

SOURCE: http://www.oecd.org/

For many developing countries, entrepreneurship and SMEs are critical to economic development. The needed economic and legal policy changes to move these countries forward occur slowly, and it is difficult for state-run or larger firms to adapt their mindset to market-oriented economic development and entrepreneurial activity.

Internationalization of SMEs can present many challenges. According to the OECD, SMEs are underrepresented in the international environment. All the factors that add to the challenge of internationalization—political and legal environment, culture, and so forth—are difficult for SMEs to overcome. SMEs are limited in their human and capital resources due to their size, especially when compared to multinational corporations. As a result, building a knowledge and experience base in foreign markets may be slow.

However, SMEs are realizing the need for global expansion in order to maintain competitive position and to grow. Several factors have influenced the growth of SMEs in the international environment, including worldwide consumer demand for more specialized and sophisticated products, the advancement of manufacturing that allows more flexible manufacturing, shortened product life cycles, and the convergence of consumer tastes and preferences (Knight & Cavusgil, 1996; Rennie, 1993). Additionally, advances in technology have made it easier to access information about business practices in other countries, gain knowledge about other countries, transport products, and manage from a distance. Small firms that internationalize have a growth advantage over their domestic-only competitors in that they tend to grow faster (Andersson, Gabrielsson, & Wictor, 2004; Rennie, 1993). As a result of the factors mentioned previously, a growing number of SMEs are internationalizing their activities early in the firm's existence. These firms are frequently called *born global* firms.

A born global firm is defined as "a company which from or near its founding, seeks to derive a substantial portion of its revenue from the sale of its products in international markets" (Knight, 1997, p. 1, as cited in Moen, 2002). Traditionally, firms have followed a more gradual approach to internationalizing, typically by building a solid domestic base before venturing into foreign markets. Born globals typically have regarded foreign markets to be as or more attractive than the domestic market and tend to follow a niche strategy (Knight & Cavusgil, 1996; Moen, 2002) that they use in multiple countries. They tend to have a stronger global orientation also. Specifically, leaders of these firms have a strong international vision (they perceive foreign markets to have a high potential for exports), are proactive in seeking international markets, and have a customer orientation in how they respond to market forces (Lloyd-Reason, Damyanoc, Nicolescu, & Wall, 2005; Moen, 2002; Moen & Servais, 2002). CEOs and other firm leaders also tend to be younger (Andersson, Gabrielsson, & Wictor, 2004) and have more international experiences (Reuber & Fischer, 1997).

SMEs from developing countries face a variety of motivations for internationalizing early. Some of these motivations include the need to accumulate hard currencies, geographic proximity of foreign markets, approach from foreign partners, and a falling domestic market (Lloyd-Reason et al., 2005). Because developing countries typically do not have a high number of large firms, the majority of firms in these countries face these issues. Especially important for developing-country SMEs is the accumulation of hard currencies. Currencies of developing countries are typically not easily exchanged for other, especially hard, currencies. Therefore, their own currencies are good only in their respective countries. Exporting products to other countries allows an SME to collect hard currency for payment, which can then be used to buy other foreign products or services to be used in their activities and operations. In a study looking at SMEs from some of the Eastern European countries, Lloyd-Reason et al. (2005) found that the CEO's international orientation influenced the propensity for internationalization of the firm. Internationally oriented CEOs not only had a greater degree of international experience, but they also encouraged their key employees to gain international knowledge (languages) and experience (travel to other countries). Through international experiences, the CEO and his or her firm develop an international network, which facilitates international growth.

Because of the size of SMEs, especially small and microfirms, the CEO is many times the person leading the negotiation in the foreign market. A CEO of a small- or medium-size firm may or may not be trained in business. Therefore, it would follow that training in business negotiation may be even less likely. Although the research cited in this section indicates that internationalized SMEs tend to have leaders with more international experience and interest in the international environment, the breadth and depth of knowledge needed to function effectively in the international environment, and particularly in an international negotiation, can be vast. Nevertheless, in most countries, SMEs are the hope for the future.

❖ TECHNOLOGY

A final consideration for gaining a worldview perspective is the role technology plays in the international business environment. When we think of technology, the first thing most people think of is the Internet. Although the Internet has been very valuable in improving access to people, information, and markets, it is only one piece of the technology contribution to globalization. If we go back a few decades, we can see how, even before the Internet, technology influenced the rapid pace of globalization. One of the most important technological advances to the global environment has been the development of satellite communication.

Prior to the ability to send and receive data via satellite, countries were able to control information in and out of their borders. With satellite communication, however, that control was lost. As a result, country governments that had strictly controlled information could no longer do it. Satellite allowed real-time transfer of information virtually around the world. No longer could one country prevent its citizens from learning about how people in other countries lived, leading to an increase in cross-cultural influences.

The Internet has provided an organized and focused channel to access information and communicate with others potentially anywhere in the world. Once a relationship has been developed, interaction via the Internet helps maintain the connection between the parties involved. The Internet helps us gather information about other countries, cultures, products, markets, and so forth. However, it is extremely important to remember that the Internet can never substitute for the personal relationship developed between the people involved in international business transactions. The United States is one of the most individualistic cultures in the world. However, the United States and the other individualist countries remain a minority of the world's population. Relationships still count. They are so important, especially in the global environment where there are so many variables that affect a business decision, that the personal relationship between the parties involved in a transaction can become the anchoring link. For most SMEs, relationship development is crucial to international success.

❖ THE BIG PICTURE

The elements of the global environment discussed in this chapter provide a big-picture view of the world in which international business transactions take place. The most important thing to remember is that you now have a snapshot of the global environment, but that the world is dynamic and continually changes. Thus, it is important for managers working in the global environment to continually learn and update their knowledge base from which decisions are made. For negotiators, once a strategy is determined for a specific country or region, it may be necessary to modify that strategy as the country grows politically, legally, and economically. The ability to readily adapt to the changing environment will be essential for long-term success as a global manager and negotiator.

Guidelines for Understanding the Global Environment

When entering into a negotiation with a firm from a foreign country, it is important to understand the environment of that country, and, in many cases, the region of the world in which that country is located. The following guidelines help accomplish this. Just as it is important to understand the company and the offerings of the party with which you are negotiating, it is also important to understand the global context of the firm's location.

1. Learn about the economic, political, and legal history and policies of the country.

2. Understand the current economic, political, and legal condition of the country (and region).

3. Identify the largest trading partners of the country.

4. How involved is government with business?

5. Understand the role of FDI in the economic development of the country and the industry in which you operate. In other words, is the country dependent on FDI for economic growth? If so, what industries are given preferential treatment by the government (governments tend to favor business activities in targeted growth areas).

6. Know the country's relationship with economically integrated areas. The country could be a member of an economically integrated area or it may be part of other types of trade agreements.

7. If you are doing business with an SME, know what incentives might be available to that company through its government.

❖ DISCUSSION QUESTIONS

1. As an international business negotiator, why is it important for you to have a strong understanding of the global environment?

2. FDI drives economic growth in many countries. What is FDI and why is it important in the global economy?

3. As an international business negotiator, how would you balance the goals of your company and the goals or needs of a developing country when negotiating with a firm in that country? Is it

your responsibility as a business to balance these goals? Why or why not?

4. Why are SMEs important in the international business environment? How might negotiating with an SME be different from negotiating with a large firm?

5. Looking at the tables that provide population and economic data for regions of the world, how would you assess the "state" of the global environment today?

❖ NOTES

1.   Although the internal focus for economic development did not help advance the economic growth of the Soviet Union, it should be noted that the way its political policies and ideologies were carried out compounded the economic difficulties.

2.   The Organization for Economic Cooperation and Development is a multilateral organization where the governments of member countries cooperatively address economic, social, and governance challenges of today's global environment. The OECD is well known for its publications and statistical compilations and analyses.

❖ REFERENCES

Andersson, S., Gabrielsson, J., & Wictor, I. (2004). International activities in small firms: Examining factors influencing the internationalization and export growth of small firms. *Canadian Journal of Administrative Sciences, 21*(1), 22–34.

Bartlett, C., Ghoshal, S., & Birkinshaw, J. (2004). *Transnational management.* Boston: Irwin/McGraw Hill.

Central Intelligence Agency. (n.d.). Country reports. *World factbook.* Retrieved May, 2006, from www.cia.gov/

The global 500. (2005). *Financial Times.* Retrieved May, 2006, from www.FT.com/

Hirsch, R., Peters, M., & Shepherd, D. (2005). *Entrepreneurship* (6th ed.). Boston: McGraw-Hill/Irwin.

Knight, G. A., & Cavusgil, S. T. (1996). The born global firm: A challenge to traditional internationalization theory. *Advances in International Marketing, 8,* 11– 26.

Lloyd-Reason, L., Damyanoc, A., Nicolescu, O., & Wall, S. (2005). Internationalization process, SMEs, and transitional economies: A four-country perspective. *International Journal of Entrepreneurship and Innovation Mangement, 5*(3–4), 206–226.

Moen, O. (2002). The born globals: A new generation of small European exporters. *International Marketing Review, 19*(2–3), 156–175.

Moen, O., & Servais, P. (2002). Born global or gradual global? Examining the export behavior of small and medium sized enterprises. *Journal of International Marketing, 10*(3), 49–72.

OECD. (2005). *OECD SME and entrepreneurship outlook 2005.* Paris: OECD Publishing.

Population Reference Bureau. (2004). *Transitions in world population.* Retrieved May, 2006, from www.prb.org/

Porter, M. E. (1990, March–April). The competitive advantage of nations. *Harvard Business Review,* 73–93.

Rennie, M. (1993). Global competitiveness: Born global. *The McKinsey Quarterly, 4,* 45–52.

Reuber, R., & Fischer, E. (1997). The influence of the management team's international experience on the internationalization behaviors of SMEs. *Journal of International Business Studies,* 807–825.

Spending spree leaves Beijing nerves frayed. (2005, March 8). *Financial Times,* p. 5.

UNCTAD. (2004). *World investment report: 2004: The shift toward services.* Geneva: United Nations.

World Bank Group. (2005). *Data and statistics: Country classification.* Retrieved May, 2006, from http://www.worldbank.org/data/countryclass/coutryclass.html

3

A Geocentric
Negotiation Process

Global trade can encompass many different types of business deals. International trade, technology transfer, franchising, coproduction agreements, service agreements, mergers, and joint ventures are just some of the growing opportunities of today's marketplace. All these business transactions require some degree of negotiation. Negotiation is the process in which at least two conflicting, interdependent parties attempt (through the communication process) to reach a mutually satisfying agreement. The attempts to reach agreement are manifested in the communication strategies and tactics the parties select to employ. Many scholars have focused their research on the selection and impact of various negotiation strategies. (Buttery & Leung, 1998; Drake, 2001; Parnell & Kedia, 1996). Most of this research has focused within cultural transactions. Although there has been a good deal of research on intercultural communication (Gudykunst, 2005), most of it has been cultural or country specific (i.e., U.S. versus

Japan). Recently, however, scholars have recognized the need to examine the complexity of integrating the issues of culture, negotiation, and communication. Specifically, there is a need to understand intercultural global negotiations from a communication perspective.

❖ A GEOCENTRIC APPROACH TO NEGOTIATION

Fisher and Ury (1981) and others have long advocated that to maximize the possibility of completing a successful negotiation requires knowledge of the other side as well as knowledge of your self. This requirement for success applies across the board, from negotiating with one's family members to complex business transactions. However, the concept of knowing the other party and knowing one's self, when applied to intercultural, international transactions, requires additional factors to be considered. Many of the past negotiation research has focused on negotiating with others within your culture. It is not uncommon for writers to give examples such as negotiating with your next-door neighbor or your boss of 20 years. These examples and discussions are helpful if we remain ethnocentric; however, they provide little help for those interested in the international setting.

A geocentric approach to the international business transaction requires negotiators to have knowledge about themselves and the other party in terms of culture, subculture, language, and communication style, in addition to all the other issues pertinent to knowing one's self and the other party. Negotiators who share common culture, language, and communication styles may not need to spend as much time or effort learning about these factors, compared to the international negotiator. Gaining a better understanding of the other party increases the opportunity for common ground to be established and thus maximizes the potential for successful agreement to be achieved.

Most negotiation researchers have embraced Fisher, Ury, and Patton's (1991) argument that knowledge about both parties' underlying interests, as opposed to a focus on positions, is key to attaining the best possible agreement. This is especially true for global negotiations in which perception and meaning may vary a great deal. In addition, knowing one's cultural biases, one's communication style, and the conditions under which the negotiation can maximize profits is essential in today's growing global economy.

This chapter contains a discussion focusing on the negotiation process for a geocentric approach. The key underlying premise for the influencing factors in the geocentric negotiation is communication. Specifically, the global business negotiation is presented by using a four-stage model that is embedded in a communication perspective. The four stages contain key elements to facilitate global negotiation success, or GNS. These components vary in importance and stature depending on many factors, including the type of business, the cultural background of the parties, the subject of negotiations, and the individual negotiators' style and skill. The order in which they are discussed is sequential in time, to mirror a typical international business negotiation. We believe that performing the elements in each of the four stages will maximize the probability of attaining GNS.

❖ PRENEGOTIATION → NEGOTIATION PROCESS → AGREEMENT → RENEGOTIATION

The four major stages are (a) prenegotiation activities and planning, (b) the negotiation process itself, (c) the negotiated agreement, and (d) renegotiation. The first three stages are presented in this chapter. The fourth, renegotiation, is included in the following chapter on alternative dispute resolution. First, we begin with the prenegotiation stage.

❖ PRENEGOTIATION STAGE

A. Know the Other Party
   1. Know the Other Party's Culture
   2. Intranational Regionalism Cultures/Subcultures
   3. Organizational Culture
   4. The Individual
   5. The Other Party's Options

B. Know Thyself
   1. Who Am I?
   2. What Are My Options?
   3. What Is My Communication Style?
   4. What Is My Negotiation Approach?
   5. What Is My Organizational Culture?

C. Contextual Factors
   1. Ripeness
   2. Role
   3. Negotiation Team

In global negotiations, perception and meaning, or reality, may vary a great deal. The prenegotiation stage is often the most important stage of the negotiation. What happens at this stage influences or may determine whether any negotiation occurs at all. If you learn as much as you can about the other party, you increase your chance for a successful agreement that can be attained in an efficient amount of time. In general, we suggest that for every hour you spend in a negotiation, you should spend a minimum of two hours outside preparing for that one hour. This formula increases exponentially if you are unfamiliar with the other party's culture, organization, and individuals in the negotiations. Preparation is key to success in any negotiation, especially an international transaction. Prenegotiation research, preparation, and planning is not the stage to skimp on time or resources.

How people find meaning in messages is related to our culture, regional culture, and individual style as well as contextual elements unique to our interests. People rely on this information to effectively communicate during the negotiation. Each of the major areas of gaining knowledge is discussed below. First, we focus on what negotiators need to know about the other party followed by a discussion of what we should know about ourselves before entering a negotiation. Last, critical contextual factors related specifically to the negotiation are discussed. As discussed next, truly obtaining accurate knowledge of these three elements involves more than may first appear.

A. The Other Party

Knowing the other party includes information concerning the other party's culture, the organization and its culture, any pertinent regional or subcultural information, the individual or negotiating team, and the other party's options. Some knowledge of the legal system is essential. Of course, the overriding goal is to gain an understanding of the other party's major interests, goals, and needs.

1. Knowing the Other Party's Culture. Culture defines one group of human beings from all others. Culture has been defined as "the socially transmitted behavior patterns, norms, beliefs and values of a given community" (Salacuse, 1998, p. 222). Salacuse also identifies possible effects culture can have on international negotiations, including creation of misunderstandings in verbal communications and physical actions. Culture can also affect the form and substance of the deal and the negotiation strategies employed by the parties (Salacuse, 1998, 2005). Culture includes history and religion, customs, mores, and communication styles.

Culture can affect negotiations in many ways. Culture can affect a person's perception of reality. It can serve to block out information inconsistent with one's own culture, and create misunderstandings of actions and words (Martin, Mayfield, Mayfield, & Herbig, 1998).

Researchers have made attempts to categorize cultures in the pursuit of enhancing intercultural communications. Cultures can be categorized by the characteristics of masculinity, power distance, uncertainty avoidance, and individualism (Hofstede, 1991).

Masculinity cultures emphasize work, self-achievement, and assertiveness, whereas feminine cultures emphasize empathy and quality of life for all (see Chapter 4 for further discussion). The implication is that masculine cultures may be more appropriate for power negotiating or win-lose, whereas feminine societies may be more receptive to Fisher and Ury's principled negotiation strategies, emphasizing the win-win approach.

Power distance refers to people's acceptance or rejection of authority and the structure of the hierarchy in society. This has implications for the appropriate negotiation strategy selection. For example, typically in business negotiations in the United States, negotiators quickly address each other by their first names regardless of the position level held within the company. This informal address is viewed as a form of communication designated to associate equality and informality, promoting a "team effort" approach to negotiating. However, in cultures such as Japan's the power distance is acknowledged and honored as part of the structure of conversation. Communication that fails to abide by the hierarchical power distance structure is considered inappropriate and disrespectful. Thus, addressing one by his or her formal name and title is an important factor when negotiating with Japanese companies but less so with U.S. companies.

Individualistic cultures emphasize the task at hand, whereas collectivist cultures make relationships a priority. The United States and the United Kingdom are in the individualist category, whereas some Latin American and Asian societies are collectivists.

Uncertainty avoidance deals with the degree to which a culture is willing to assume risk, especially if the risk involves new and unknown endeavors. High risk avoidance cultures may be reluctant to share information or work to create mutually beneficial options, two tenets of integrative, win-win negotiation strategies.

Salacuse (1998, 2005) created a tool for international business executives to use as a guide in international negotiations. The author created 10 trait categories and examined how countries varied according to these categories.

The traits include the following:

Negotiation Goal—Contract or Relationship?

Negotiation Attitude—Win/Lose or Win/Win?

Personal Styles—Informal or Formal?

Communications—Direct or Indirect?

Time Sensitivity—High or Low?

Emotionalism—High or Low?

Agreement Form—Specific or General?

Agreement Building—Bottom Up or Top Down?

Team Organization—One Leader or Consensus?

Risk Taking—High or Low?

SOURCE: From Salacuse, J. W. (1998).

Companies may find this checklist useful for beginners in international negotiation business transactions. It is important to remember to think of these 10 factors on a continuum rather than as dichotomous variables. That is, negotiators will vary by degrees toward one direction on the continuum. For example, are Japan and Germany considered equal in their formality of communication style? Most practitioners would argue that both are more formal than Chile. However, when comparing Japan to Germany, Japan is considered more formal in communication style. Thus, the relativity to what is your comparison culture is critical in the assessment of how to interpret Salacuse's work.

We get cultural information from a variety of sources: formal training, research, stories from our peers and colleagues, media portrayals (although the accuracy is often incorrect), and the individual interactions or experiences with others from another culture. Most of us have limited experience or schemas to rely on when we begin intercultural negotiations. A significant amount of intercultural training occurs in the United States. Most training, however, remains ethnocentric and one-dimensional (i.e., United States negotiating with Japan) or even more general, such as Westerners negotiating with non-Westerners. Corporate in-house training often addresses the intercultural negotiation more specifically as corporate culture. This basic knowledge can act as the foundation, but one cannot or should not expect this to provide enough knowledge for actually negotiating in the global market.

There are two significant points that are important for international negotiators to keep in mind when preparing for an intercultural business negotiation. The first point is that negotiators have an obligation to become familiar with the culture of the people with whom they are going to interact. Once you are off the plane and have stepped on the foreign ground, it is too late to prepare. Cultural training must take place prior to the actual face-to-face negotiation and preferably before the initial contact. Why? The importance of first impressions is a critical factor in determining whether there is another interaction.

Ignorance of others' history, traditions, rituals, communication styles, and ways of conducting business is the first step in ruining a relationship. In some cultures, one's lack of preparedness is viewed as an insincere attempt to do business. Often talks are ceased with no explanation.

The second point of developing an understanding of the other party's culture is assessing your bias and attitudes about the other's cultural beliefs and behaviors. The significance of this is that not knowing your own self can result in harm being done during negotiations that may hinder the goal of reaching GNS (more on this is discussed in the upcoming "Know Thyself" section).

Culture and nationality are often used synonymously. In the modern world, that is often inaccurate. Homogenous cultures are rarely prevalent throughout an entire country. Virtually any country in the world can serve to illustrate this point. Examples include the United States, Iraq, Russia, and India. Japan until the early 1980s was considered by some to be a homogenous culture with little influence from outside the country. However, within the last decade, the Japanese culture is seeing the influence of United States' culture on their youth. Japanese teens have taken on many of the styles and behaviors of the U.S. teens. Some people in Japan have responded negatively to the U.S. media impact on their youth because it has resulted in a loss of homogeneity. The global information explosion has resulted in fewer cultures being able to protect their "oneness" or cultural "pureness." This globalization effect has forced the once steadfast homogenous cultures to become responsive and adaptive to the intercultural influences.

The relationship between China and the United States is another example of how quickly views of another culture can become obsolete or irrelevant as changes occur in political, economic, or market structures. It is truly amazing to consider that until President Nixon made his historic visit to China in 1972, there was virtually no trade or economic interaction between the two countries. A mere 30 years later, the economic activities between the countries are vast, and the cultural exchanges are similar in significance. The opening of trade with China provided new opportunities for U.S. businesses to sell and source their goods. However, most U.S. companies knew little about the practices of business negotiations with Chinese. U.S. views of the Chinese culture were limited to a political bias, which served little value in trade negotiations.

2. Intranational Regionalism Cultures/Subcultures. In many countries, nationality is less helpful in determining negotiation style and behavior than regional or subcultural knowledge. Knowing national and regional cultures and being able to distinguish them from one another is important for the global negotiator. Many have found the key to success is in the ability to communicate within the confines of the regional culture and understanding how regional cultures fit under the national umbrella. Regionalism influences management style, structures, and processes (Adler, 2002). Multinational corporations are often a conglomeration of several different regional cultures combined with the corporate culture. Regionalism can easily cut across several national cultures. For example, India has many different regions within one nation that have different beliefs, practices, and rituals. Understanding the specific region or subculture that represents the area where you are conducting business is essential to avoiding costly negotiation mistakes.

In addition, there may be very distinct dialects and word meanings by region. For example, Wengrowski (2004) studied the People's Republic of China, where distinct dialects in one region were very different from those of another although the written symbols were universally understood.

The importance of regionalism cannot be overlooked. Often, businesses assume that because they have negotiated with a company in one region of a country, they can easily do business in another area. This may be far from accurate. Furthermore, there may be different cultures within the same country or region based on different industries.

3. Organizational Culture. Educate yourself on the organizational culture of the other party. Every organization has a culture that is unique. The organizational culture is influenced by many factors beyond national culture. For example, Griffith and Harvey (2001) concluded that we must consider factors such as the diversity of the workforce, the compatibility of policies with subsidiaries and the parent company (especially for international companies), and governmental regulations. Some organizational cultures are heavily bureaucratic while others appear supportive (Chaisrakeo & Speece, 2004). Bureaucratic organizations typically are rule intensive, noncooperative, and less creative, whereas supportive organizations tend to adapt more easily to the marketplace, allow negotiators a wider range of decision making, and maintain a flexible work environment that can quickly adjust to the marketplace. These differences may have impact in intracultural negotiations, but in intercultural negotiations these issues and having knowledge of them can prove to be critical to reaching GNS.

The negotiator comes to the workforce with a cultural background that is usually well developed before that person reached his teens. However, the workplace culture defines the strategies, values, and goals of how the negotiator is to operate and represent the organization. The accepted and promoted norms, attitudes, and behaviors of the organization are learned and embraced by members of the organization and are demonstrated daily in business transactions. Knowing at least the basics of the opposing party's organizational culture should be an important part of planning your global negotiation.

Being cognizant of your culture, as well as your organizational culture and that of the opposing party, helps clarify the communication strategy choices available. For example, if you are from the United States, a relatively direct, aggressive, individualistic culture, and work for a company that values aggressive, direct communications and supports the use of threats if needed, you are likely to use communication strategies in the negotiation process that reflect both the organizational culture and the culture of the United States. The same can be said for the opposing party with respect to their corporate and national or regional culture. The possible communication behaviors in a negotiation that are available to you are direct request for what you want, direct intimidation, possible threat of going elsewhere or threat of ending the negotiation process, and the use of direct questions requesting reasons why your proposal is rejected. There are many others, but these strategies were selected specifically because they are not viewed as appropriate ways of conducting business for a culture such as South Korea. In South Korea, where face is an important aspect of any communication interaction, strategies that might threaten one's face should be avoided. Therefore, a negotiator from South Korea whose company culture is similar to the national culture (valuing harmony and respect) would not have the same repertiore of strategies available nor would they easily understand or appreciate the use of them by the U.S. negotiator.

Of course, it is possible to have an organizational culture that is quite different from the national culture. Indeed, the prevalence of multinational corporations creates this situation more and more often. Assume the organizational culture of the company in the United States is based in the deep southern part of the U.S. but is Japanese owned and has a workforce that is predominately from Mexico. The organization has embraced the collectivistic value of work. This company has several cultural layers that influence the way in which they may negotiate. The negotiation in this instance is a very difficult dynamic because of the subcultural and regionalism influence. Those entering into an international negotiation with this company must look at the regional and subcultural influences, not just the culture of the United States.

Neuliep (2003) offers a model for explaining the contexts that affect organizational culture. He proposed that organizational culture is made up of six factors or dimensions: cultural, sociorelational, environmental, perceptual, intercultural relations, and verbal and nonverbal codes. These represent any organization across any culture.

Briefly, culture context is similar to Hofstede's dimensions of culture: individualism/collectivism, high/low context, value orientations, high/low power distance, and uncertainty avoidance. These most often represent the national culture. *Sociorelational* context refers to group memberships, ingroups/outgroups, muted groups, and perceptions of men and women. An example of this might be the family corporate culture where nepotism is practiced or the different treatment of women as influenced by culture. *Environmental* context deals with information load, privacy, and the overall orientation to nature. Market forecast may be viewed as something that cannot be predicted because it is simply nature and not controllable by the organization. *Perceptual* context refers to how we categorize, stereotype, and process information. Neuliep suggests that Americans tend to rely on logical thinking whereas Asians rely on intuition. *Intercultural relations* refer to such dynamics as power distances, male and female differences, relational orientations, and marriage and divorce rates. Finally, *verbal and nonverbal codes* simply refer to how we use language, touch, body movement and gestures, and smell and eye gazing that affect the intercultural organizational culture.

This model is a general model for intercultural communication. However, this model can be helpful in understanding the role organizational culture plays in the global negotiation process. Using Neuliep's six contextual factors model is important to the global negotiator's planning and processing for meaning. The better equipped the global negotiator is in each of these contexts, the more likely he or she is to communicate appropriately and effectively, thus increasing his or her intercultural communication competency.

4. *The Individual (the other person).* Knowing the individual(s) you will be meeting with is more important than knowing the culture. Although

research is conflicting about the importance of culture versus individual, the most current research indicates the more important contributor is the individual across the table.

John Graham (1996) wrote in his article titled "The Importance of Culture in International Business Negotiation," "In most places in the world, personalities and substance are not separate issues and can't be made so" (p. 86). The idea that a human being sitting across the negotiation table is insignificant to the issues of negotiation seems rather strange to most of the international market. In Western cultures, such as the United States, Fisher, Ury, and Patton's (1991) principle of separating the people from the problem has become a widespread belief for conducting business. The concept calls for negotiators to focus on substantive issues as joint problem-solvers, rather than spending time and energy dealing with personalities of the negotiators. These two approaches to negotiation may both work given the right context. For example, in cultures where individuals are trained and evaluated based on how well logic and argument persuade, the benefit of Fisher Ury, and Patton's principle is an important one. Business negotiations where short-term gains are the primary goal may benefit from viewing the problem separate from the person. This allows the parties to focus on the issues and not individual bias, prejudices, or positions.

However, most international negotiations are long-term investments. Considering that in many cultures (e.g., Asian, African, and Middle Eastern), individuals are socialized and rewarded for considering the value of sincerity, trust, and face honoring, viewing the individual as part of the issues can help in building a lasting business relationship that will bring harmony and wealth, in the form of GNS.

Getting to know the other person with whom you are negotiating will reduce the uncertainty about how he or she is likely to respond to your offers. Research has found that reducing the uncertainty about another individual is an important factor in establishing a negotiating relationship. According to Berger and Calabrese's (1975) uncertainty reduction theory, people initiate communication with strangers in order to reduce their anxiety about that person. That is, people use communication to find common ground or interests so that they can better predict the other's behavior. Berger and Calabrese identify three strategies individuals use to reduce their uncertainty about others, including passive (observe), interactive (initial actual conversation), and active information-seeking strategies.

The amount of uncertainty individuals are willing to experience varies according to cultures and personalities. For example, many Japanese and Chinese prefer to reduce the uncertainty about who the other party is before proceeding into formal negotiations. In addition, certain types of individual traits (e.g., communication apprehension, adaptability) contribute to higher uncertainty levels. (See Chapter 5 for further discussion.)

In most instances, the opposing party may not be just one person, but a team of negotiators. It is imperative to gather as much information as possible about the team, including the names and positions of the team members, the authority levels of the team members, their titles and backgrounds, and each person's role on the team. It is also necessary to determine, if possible, the relationship between the team and the opposing party. Is the team composed of high-level people? If not, why not? What is the authority level of the team? This can be critical.

Ultimately, knowing the other party as a person first will enrich the opportunities for business. Several scholars have found that the individual negotiator and the organizational culture are more important than national cultural factors in determining the success of a negotiation (Kanter & Corn, 1994). This new phenomena may be a result of new information technology. People from all over the world now interact with people from a variety of cultures. In addition, this new age of worldwide media brings into many households across the globe a view (often distorted) of different cultures. Perhaps, as we move from a world driven by dominant cultural values to a place of individual differences, we will find the common ground of humanity, thus ultimately changing the study of international negotiation from a purely intercultural communication perspective to a more individualistic perspective.

5. *The Other Party's Options.* Fisher, Ury, and Patton (1991) discuss the importance of developing and identifying alternatives to successfully negotiating an agreement with the other party. Gaining information about the other party's *best alternative to a negotiated agreement* (BATNA) as well as the *worst alternative to the negotiated agreement* (WATNA) is critical information. This information provides a range for compromising and collaborating to develop workable agreements. If we are able to have a clear understanding of the other negotiator's BATNA, we can use this information, along with our BATNA, to construct a joint bargaining range.

The initial bargaining range helps formulate one's strategies and helps in understanding the other's limitation in offerings. This range may change as the negotiation process proceeds. Often the range is a beginning point and should not be confused with a fixed range. Rather, external influences, such as a change in the market structure, political changes, or social changes, may cause considerable fluctuation in the initial bargaining range. However, the most likely cause for change in the initial bargaining range is the negotiation process itself. The result of collaborative negotiation is that parties often move from a fixed sum (distributive approach) to an expanded pie (integrative approach). Searching for creative alternative solutions to problems may result in positive negotiation outcomes for both parties, rather than having one winner and one loser. Using a win-win or collaborative approach permits the parties to reevaluate their original BATNA comparisons and redevelop their bargaining range. The important point to remember about options is that we need to know the other party's options and our own options, and be cognizant of how these options will change as we progress through the negotiation process. This is especially true for the international trade market, where flexibility and change are key characteristics of the business trade.

B. Know Thyself

1. Who Am I? How do you feel about knowing the other person before discussing business? Is this a waste of time? What if the other party is continually late? When is someone considered late? All these questions raise issues that reflect different cultural practices. There is no right or wrong; rather, people live and conduct their lives in a variety of ways. Knowing what those ways are will save the international business negotiator much energy and confusion.

What cultural and individual biases do you bring to the table? Most of what we read about intercultural negotiations is related to understanding cultural differences. Although this information is important, we need to examine our own cultural and individual biases that can affect the way we negotiate in the international business transaction. The ethnocentric approach to negotiation is in part a result of not looking inward before judging outward. We become better international negotiators by simply examining our perceptions as subjective views, analyzing our cognitive processing as a means to assess reality, and gaining knowledge about our communication predispositional traits and skills.

Victor Friedman and Ariane Berthoin Antal (2005) posit that "a person's cultural repertoire not only offers a range of responses to its members, it also constrains the range of responses available to an individual" (p. 74). They suggest that to be interculturally competent, individuals must be willing to expand their cultural repertoire to allow for new behaviors and responses that are appropriate for intercultural interactions. These authors describe three critical beliefs to negotiating reality: all people are equally important and worthy of respect; people are different because they have different repertories of viewing the world; and each view of the world is equally right (p. 77). An essential skill for international business negotiators is to learn how to stop their automatic thinking process or their unconscious tapes that prevent them from seeking an awareness of the world around them. The issue is to avoid framing the other party's communication and behaviors from your own cultural perspective. Otherwise, the opportunity to find and create mutually advantageous solutions is limited and opportunities for relationship development are lost.

The cognitive thinking that "my culture is better than your culture" must be replaced with an integrative, multicultural view. Often those who have successfully integrated their cognitive processing to a multicultural level may find it difficult to identify with their homeland culture. As we move into this geocentric approach to interacting, the egocentric form of cultural identity will be replaced with a more complex, multifaceted view of who we are and interpretation of how we see others. The future holds a changing world of negotiators who will not settle for simple adaptation to other cultures but rather integration. With this change, communication will be more about the individuals rather than the culture.

2. What Are My Options? Much research has focused on developing your best position so that you are negotiating from a position of power. We agree that you should avoid going into a negotiation with little power compared to your opponent. The negotiation process is most likely to achieve a satisfying agreement if it is approached from a relative power balance of the parties (Wilmot & Hocker, 2001). Therefore, you need to know what your BATNA and WATNA are as well as those of your opponents. Developing your options so that they become viable alternatives if the negotiation fails helps to establish a better position in the negotiation.

Generally, the stronger the BATNA is for a given party, the more power that party has. Logically, then, it makes sense to do everything possible not just to identify the BATNA, but also to improve your BATNA before and during the negotiations. If the other party knows that you have little choice or few alternatives except to reach an agreement with them, they have a power position and will be less likely to consider concessions. The second important option factor to know is the WATNA. One of the critical points to keep in mind when deciding when to enter into the negotiation is gaining an accurate assessment of your options and the attractiveness of those options. These should be weighed against the options of the opposing party to determine the relative power positions of the parties.

3. What Is My Communication Style? Critical to the success of the international business negotiator is the influence of an individual's predispositional communication traits on the negotiation process. Although many scholars and professionals have acknowledged the important role of negotiator communication style, few have looked for answers beyond strategy choice. We believe negotiator strategy choice is heavily influenced by the communication traits the person brings to the table.

Our model of the global negotiator examines negotiation by viewing one's regional and national culture, organizational culture, and individual communication traits as antecedent variables that influence the communication style used in geocentric business negotiations. Communication behavior is largely a result of one's education, environment, and predispositional communication traits. Training programs can teach the negotiator about another's culture, company, or region, but understanding one's own propensity to behave in a preferred manner is critical for those entering new global negotiation territory. That is, if we understand what we are likely to say, we can then understand how our individual behavior may help or hurt the negotiation. We can become sensitized to our own traits and adjust our behavior to maximize the potential for successful outcome. The combination of education and individual communication traits creates the best chance for global negotiation success, or GNS.

These communication traits (discussed in Chapter 5) contribute to the competent global negotiator. Specifically, there are five major characteristics that affect individual negotiators' behavior and communication strategy choice in negotiating with others in intercultural business settings: argumentativeness, verbal aggression, self-monitoring, communication apprehension, and intercultural communication competency. These predispositional traits directly affect the appropriateness and effectiveness of the negotiator's communication in the negotiation environment. Therefore, spending adequate time assessing our own style and communication influences will ultimate impact our success or failure in the international market.

4. What Is My Negotiation Approach? Two predominant approaches to negotiation are often cited in the negotiation literature. Historically, negotiation was dominated by win-lose/competitive/distributive tactics and strategies. This long-used negotiation approach features confrontation, threats, power plays, gambits, delays, and the withholding of information. It is still alive and well throughout the world. The seminal work of Fisher and Ury (1981) created a negotiation process featuring a win-win/cooperative/integrative approach. This negotiation process features a joint problem-solving approach by the parties, who focus on underlying interests rather than positions. It also features sharing of information early and often. It has gained much acclaim and widespread use.

The win-lose approach to negotiation is dominated by aggressive tactics. The Chinese have a saying that describes the competitive approach: *"Shang chang ru zhan change,"* which means, "The marketplace is a battlefield" (Zhao, 2000, p. 217). As the Chinese saying implies, a competitive approach requires a negotiator to be a good defensive player as well as offensive. (By the way, this is not the predominant approach for most Chinese negotiators.) This requires withholding information to gain an upper hand, using aggressive, sometimes threatening, tactics to gain an edge over one's opponent. The win-lose approach is characterized as using distributive strategies to reach agreement. For the winner, using this approach may attain significant short-term gains compared to using a collaborative approach. However, the negotiating relationship usually suffers under this process, and ultimately one's gain may be very short-sighted. This may work well within some cultures that are expecting this approach. However, cultures that embrace the cooperative approach are likely to be offended and withdraw from the negotiation playing field.

The win-win approach is a cooperative, integrative perspective. Win-win approach has led to integrative problem solving, which results in mutual gain outcomes and long-term relationships. Problem solving is the often-described characteristic of the win-win perspective. Listening for points of shared interest, willingness to make fair concessions, and openness to persuasion of a good argument are critical communication behaviors for this approach. The advantages of win-win are that creative solutions occur, relationships are enhanced, and parties are often able to reach greater mutual gains. There may be disadvantages in that it sometimes takes longer to negotiate using win-win. The collaborative approach works when both parties are willing to engage in this type of negotiation. Fisher and Ury and others suggest tactics to get a reluctant opponent to participate in win-win negotiations. Tactics such as questioning the other party's theory or reasoning for their offer, seeking the other party's advice on what he or she should do, or looking behind the other party's position to what may be motivating the other party to engage in hard bargaining may help move negotiators from distributive to collaborative, or win-win, negotiations. Although some cultures are more versed in this approach to negotiation, all have to some degree a problem-solving view (Chaisrakeo & Speece, 2004).

Sunanta Chaisrakeo and Mark Speece, in their 2004 article, suggest that the approach you use is influenced by your inherent personality characteristics. Thus, we are reminded that strategy selection is influenced by culture and the individual negotiator's traits, at least initially.

5. What Is My Organization? A consideration in examining the organizational culture is how much time is given to negotiating internally to make the intercultural negotiation work. If your organization is unrealistic about what can and cannot be accomplished at the international negotiation table, you will spend a great deal of time trying to convince your organization of the reality you face in reaching a deal. The more isolated your organization is from the international community, the more difficult your job becomes as the representative in the market. Experience is often the best teacher of international negotiations. Assessing the impact that the organization culture has on your ability to reach an agreement is a powerful tool in determining which marketplace to enter.

In international negotiation, the selection of the negotiator or the negotiation team is critically important. Some cultures will take it as a serious insult if the opposing negotiators hold a lower position in the organization than their negotiators.

C. Prenegotiation Contextual Insights

1. Ripeness. When is it best to enter into a negotiation? Parties should enter into international business negotiations when the potential is greatest to impact on gain or loss of gains. Although ripeness has been conceptualized and discussed predominantly in the diplomatic arena, that research is easily adapted to the international business marketplace. Two conditions are necessary for meaningful negotiation to occur in international business transactions (Donohue & Hoobler, 2002; Zartman, 2000). The first consideration is the *mutually enhancing opportunity*, or MEO. In the global business setting, MEO is conceptualized as an opportunity, such as a joint venture, for two or more companies to develop an agreement that would enhance all parties' businesses. The second consideration developed by Zartman is MHS, or *mutually hurting stalemate*. MHS occurs when not doing business with the other party is more costly than going to the negotiation table.

For example, Zco Corporation manufactures toys that require a specific type of nontoxic paint. Zco Company has a small plant that manufactures the paint for its internal use only. Although it is rather costly for Zco to produce the paint internally, they have still been able to make a profit overall thanks in part to the governmental tariffs that have kept several competitors from entering the national market. Therefore, Zco has avoided buying paint from Jobob in Brazil even though Jobob can make the paint for much less than Zco can. However, due to new foreign policy, the tariff is being lifted and foreign competitors will be able to sell their toys for less than Zco Corporation can. Zco has reached an MHS point. It is now more costly to avoid negotiating with other paint manufacturers such as Jobob because Zco will no longer be able to compete if it continues to manufacture its own paint internally. Thus, MHS coupled with MEO creates a "ripe" time for negotiations to occur between Zco and Jobob Corporation. Many times, the economic pressures create the ripeness of interest in negotiating.

2. Role. A significant amount of research has investigated the role of buyer and seller in the international marketplace (Drake, 2001). How this role is perceived is influenced by the larger culture and the organization. Cai and Donohue (1997) concluded that the role of buyer and seller determined what facework strategies (strategies that preserve a positive self-image) were used more than culture did. In addition, the role of buyer or seller carries with it certain status and power that influence the expected behavior of each. For example, in China, the status of the seller is generally lower than that of the buyer (Zhao, 2000). In Western cultures, the buyer and seller are viewed as similar in status, and if a competitive approach is used, the buyer and seller are expected to make very high demands on price with the understanding that someone will win and the other will lose. Ghauri (1986) suggests that in some Arab countries, the seller's personality is more of an influence in reaching an agreement than is the quality of the product.

3. Negotiation Team. Rarely is international negotiation composed of two individual negotiators sitting across the table from one another. Most often, companies are represented by several individuals with different expertise needed to negotiate a specific contract. Teams vary in terms of size, composition, and authority. These variations enhance the complexity of reaching a settlement. Size of the team can often be construed as overpowering the other side. For example, China's negotiation team is typically twice as large as U.S. negotiation teams (Zhao, 2000). Given that China generally requires consensus in their decision making, it is not surprising that they would want to have representation of all interested parties at the table to hear the issues discussed. Compare that to the United States, where the decision maker is generally one person who receives advice from key people who are often part of the negotiation team.

Although we discuss international business negotiations as bilateral, often they are multiparty negotiations (Graham, Mintu, & Rodgers, 1994). For instance, two companies may be involved in the actual exchange of goods or services but key governmental agents or regulatory advisors may also be required parties in some cultures.

Who is really making the decision to accept or reject the agreement? It depends on the culture, the organizational culture, and the role of the negotiator. One of the difficulties some international negotiators face is determining if they are meeting with the final decision maker. For example, China typically sends the technical staff to the negotiation table to do the initial data gathering. It is not until the end of the negotiation that the CEO appears to accept or reject the agreement.

James Sebenius (2002) stated, "Understanding both formal decision rights and cultural assumptions in less familiar settings can be vital" (p. 79). Often what makes the agreement work is not simply the signing of the contract. He further reminds us that in many countries, other influential parties can cause a negotiation agreement to stall, fail, or succeed. For example, in Japan it might be the industrial groups referred to as keiretsu or in Germany the labor force that is well connected to various boards and financial institutions.

Ghauri (1986) noted that in Eastern Europe, negotiation teams are often replaced by new negotiation teams on a daily basis, thus allowing the teams to remain fresh. This can be very confusing to Westerners, who typically maintain one team for the duration of the negotiation.

It is recommended that the negotiators at the table have broad authority to make financial and legal commitments for the principal. Either the corporate officers should actually attend the negotiations, or they should be willing to delegate significant authority to those who are present. In most situations, it is a hindrance to reaching agreement if the people for both sides who have authority to commit to the agreement are not present.

❖ NEGOTIATION PROCESS STAGE

Introduction and Relationship Development

This first stage of communication with the other party may occur over a period of time. Initially, someone makes contact via e-mail, telephone, letter of interest, or through the introduction by a third party. Third-party intermediaries are often helpful in initiating beginning discussions, especially in countries such as China, Japan, Korea, and Mexico. Knowing which introductory method is preferred can often determine whether you actually get to the negotiation table. It is customary in Japanese organizations to send the highest-level individual to represent the company to make initial personal contact before beginning the negotiation (Susskind, 2004). In the United States, the CEO usually is not present until the agreement is ready to be signed. The level of the negotiators who begin the process can be viewed as a gesture of insincerity in desiring to work with the other. This can undermine any further discussions. A lack of knowledge concerning cultural relationships can lead to unkind reputations. For example, Graham (1996) found in his research on U.S. and Japanese negotiations that Japanese are often considered the best negotiators because they spend their time getting to know their opponents, whereas the Americans were viewed as the worst because they are ethnocentric in their thinking.

Whether you are exchanging business cards, greeting the other individual, or writing an invitation to begin discussions, it is imperative that negotiators understand differences and respectfully display the appropriate communication messages. Wengrowski (2004) gives important advice about the exchange of business cards. He suggests that one side should be in English and the other side in the host national language. In addition, he points out the importance of keeping your card in your front pocket, not in your back pants pocket. The location represents that "the person carrying the card considers the other person important enough to make a presentation from the heart" (p. 27). Always take a few minutes to read the card when it is presented to you. This indicates a sense of respect and consideration for the other person.

Social meetings and dinners are often used as a method for developing relationships. In some parts of the world, this informal meeting time is the most important part of the negotiation (Ghauri, 1986; Zhao, 2000). Two most popular ways for relationship building are holding social meetings at a restaurant and sending gifts, followed by sending proposals.

United States-based companies complain about the long time it takes for Chinese to begin discussing the business issues. Typically, negotiators from China, Japan, and Korea are more comfortable discussing business after a good relationship has been established. Given that China tends to view business agreements as long-term ventures, it is not surprising that relationships would come first and substantive issues second. Perhaps Americans could reframe the time spent on developing a relationship as a cost savings in the end because it may prevent problems in the future.

Does similarity help in the development of a relationship? Negotiator similarity may not be as important as we once thought. Nancy Adler and John Graham (1989) suggest that similarity is not as important as behavior reciprocity in the negotiation process is to producing a good outcome. Rather, sensitivity to others and their differences is more important. Susskind (2004) reported that the philosophy of "when in Rome, do as the Romans do" is not necessarily the best approach for successful international negotiations. Such an attempt to assimilate may be viewed by the other party as insincere. For example, an American negotiating with an Arab oil company may have received training to make very little direct eye contact in an attempt to assimilate into the Arab culture. The Arab negotiator has been told that the Americans make regular eye contact as an expression of their honesty. If the American begins the negotiation by looking away from the Arab opponent when the latter attempts to make eye contact with him, this may be very confusing to the negotiator from the Middle East. He does not know whether the American is dishonest or genuine. The result is a miscommunication and potential breakdown in the negotiation if it is not cleared up. It is better to be yourself and appreciate the differences in eye gazing than to attempt behaviors that have not been internalized as part of who you are.

International negotiators are most successful when they exhibit an acceptance of others' differences. However, global negotiators may incorporate their international negotiation experiences into their identities, thus resulting in a multicultural identity that cannot be characterized by their home countries. Ultimately, we would expect more and more people to achieve this multicultural identity as world trade grows.

Discussion of Issues and Exchange of Information

After introductions and relationships have been established, negotiation parties can begin to discuss their business interests. Relationship development will continue as negotiators continue to conduct business. However, several important issues arise as one begins the substantive issues discussion. The sequential order of issues to be discussed, how issues are discussed, how information is shared and exchanged, the influence of roles, the issue of questioning and interruptions, and how negotiation goals emerge in the negotiation process are essential factors as parties begin the discussion of issues and interests.

Order of Issues

There are three predominant methods for discussing issues in the negotiation: sequencing, general, or packaging. Discussing issue by issue is referred to as *sequential* discussion of items. Each issue is discussed and negotiated as an individual item relatively independent from other issues. *General discussion* is a conversation about principles and general premises without referring to specific issues. Within these general areas lie specific issues; however, using a general approach reframes the discussion of specifics. *Packaging* issues is presenting a combination of issues together. Different groupings of issues are presented in different packages. This type of discussion of issues is often used when issues are highly interdependent and not easily separable.

All three of these methods may emerge as a viable negotiation process structure for international business transaction. General discussion of principles allows negotiators to gain a sense of agreement in principle before moving onto specific tasks of individual issues. The benefit of this method is that if agreement is achieved in principle, then the specific issues are just a matter of problem solving. Oftentimes, once agreement is reached on general principle, a successful outcome is just around the corner. Some cultures prefer general discussion of issues, whereas others prefer sequential. For example, Chinese, Japanese, and Koreans generally prefer to agree on general principles before proceeding into specific issues (Graham, 1996). Often African and Middle Eastern negotiators present information in a circular manner, allowing several issues to be discussed conceptually first, before the specifics are addressed (Wengrowski, 2004). "Chinese are more likely to compromise on specific issues after first gaining a sense of the broader purposes of their opponents" (Cai, 1998, p. 107). On the other hand, Germans, Americans, and Norwegians generally prefer to discuss the issues in sequential order, taking one issue at a time, reaching agreement, and then moving on to the next issue. The method creates a building momentum that helps the negotiators move on to achieve GNS, built upon the momentum of the past agreements.

Sometimes negotiators package issues. Packaging issues allows parties to link several issues together and allows for the discussion of several issues simultaneously (Moore, 2003). One of the benefits of packaging issues is that the process allows parties to maintain a sense of power or leverage as they work through the negotiation process.

A general rule, if one exists, is that major, contentious issues should not be addressed first, regardless of which method of discussion is used. Attempts to hit a home run on the first day of negotiations by tackling the major, most contentious issue is not recommended. If the attempt fails, the negotiation is over on the first day. Successfully agreeing on smaller, less contentious issues first builds the relationship and gathers momentum to continue the negotiation process.

Determining which method of discussing issues to use is an important step in the negotiation process. Negotiators may want to prepare for a variety of methods. However, trying to negotiate using two different approaches is not advised. It is difficult to maintain a flow of communication when the method for discussion of the issues is not shared and agreed upon. Miscommunication is likely to occur.

Approaches for Information Sharing

Drake discusses two common themes related to how negotiators share information. The first is a distributive negotiation (win-lose) approach. This type of information-sharing approach creates an opportunity for "fixed sum error" to occur. Negotiators do as little sharing as possible. The *fixed sum error* (FSE) is described as "a negotiator's assumption that each side prioritizes the issues identically, so that mutually satisfying outcomes do not exist" (Drake, 2001, p. 319). The distributive negotiator discloses information only as a method for gaining information. However, when information is exchanged, it is direct and with purpose. United States negotiators are often characterized as using this approach. Given the preference of some cultures to negotiate sequentially, issue by issue, there is a greater likelihood of FSE occurring. As Drake points out, the potential integrative solutions may go unnoticed because negotiators are making judgment errors about their opponent's priorities. The result is lower profits, based on missed opportunities (Thompson & Hastie, 1990). The integrative approach to information sharing should minimize these lost opportunities.

The integrative approach is contrary to the distributive form of exchanging information. This is a cornerstone of Fisher and Ury's win-win negotiation strategy. Information is freely shared in pursuit of the shared goal of problem solving. Drake characterizes this method as the "heuristic trial and error or HTE." This approach often involves packaging several issues simultaneously as offers. Once the offers have been made, they continue to be discussed and revised until both parties find them acceptable (Drake, 2001; Tutzauer & Roloff, 1988).

A culture that generally prefers to work collectively would tend to use HTE, or heuristic trial and error method. HTE requires negotiators to consider the dynamics of several issues and their importance when presenting them to the other party. Negotiators who are unfamiliar with this approach may need to revisit their priority of issues so as not to lose advantage when revising the package. Therefore, global negotiators must be aware of their preference and the preference of the other party.

The Manner in Which Information Is Shared. In addition, one must consider the manner in which information is shared. Some cultures tend to be more direct and straightforward in their messages whereas others communicate their information indirectly, using subtle language and manner. Often, negotiations break down because of misperceptions about information sharing.

For example, Americans typically communicate directly and do so with the assumption that the other party will reciprocate. Japanese, on the other hand, approach information sharing by indirect communication. Negotiation between Americans and Japanese may fail in part because the Americans were unable to detect the significance of the subtle, indirect information sharing.

Research supports that information sharing and building relationships results in higher joint gains (Hendon, Roy, & Ahmed, 2003; Olekalns & Smith, 2000). Reciprocal information sharing results in parties sharing their interests versus their positions. Parties who are willing to share information increase their opportunities for establishing common ground and developing ways to help each other. Thus the agreement is based on the uses and needs of their requests (interests) rather than just simply what they want (positions). Ultimately, information sharing moves negotiation from simply a persuasion process to a problem-solving process.

Use of Questions for Information Exchange. Questions play a critical role in negotiations. Good questioning techniques versus careless questions can make or break a deal. Confrontational questioning is generally considered acceptable behavior in most Western cultures. Examples such as, "What will it take to make this deal happen?" "What is your lowest figure you can offer me?" and "How did you derive that price?" are typical U.S. inquiries for closing a deal. However, Asian cultures would find these aggressive communication messages distasteful at best, if not offensive.

In many cultures, such as Chinese or Japanese, questions are used differently. Often, Japanese and Chinese negotiators use questioning to reduce uncertainty about the other party and develop a relationship before any specific issues are discussed. "Chinese tend to ask leading questions in a positive way to preserve harmony and friendship" (Ulijn &

Verweij, 2000, p. 224). They report that negotiators start with open-ended questions about the opponents' needs as a way of developing a relationship and then move to more direct questions.

Clearly, questions play a critical role in obtaining information regarding the underlying interests of the opposing party. Proper questions yield information. But improper questions may close the door to information sharing. Types of questions, depending on the structure, may restrict the amount of negotiation range and outcome opportunities. If questions occur too early in the negotiation, before a relationship has developed, the questioning behavior can prevent any further negotiation. This is a challenge for negotiators who desire a quick agreement and place less value on reducing the other party's uncertainty.

If we keep in mind the issue of intent of questions (Is the question attempting to meet instrumental goals or relationship goals?), we are more likely to maximize our profits in the end. As Jan Ulijn and Maurits Verweij (2000) noted, "Experienced negotiators never say what they have in mind without being invited to do so" (p. 223). The art of asking the right questions in the right manner can pave the way for successful negotiations.

Interruptions. Chinese as well as Spanish negotiators interrupt more frequently than those in many Western countries. Arab, African, and Latin cultures tend to overlap in conversations, whereas Germans and Americans prefer linear turn taking. Interruptions are often style differences and have no reflection on power and disrespect.

In the United States, interruptions are viewed as inappropriate conversational etiquette. However, depending on the status of the interrupter, it may be viewed differently. If the person interrupting is higher in status than the person who is being interrupted, the violation is viewed as less severe. Similarly, if a low-power person interrupts a superior, a greater violation has occurred. However, in other cultures, such as Spain and Chile, interruptions are considered part of the conversational dynamic and no violation has been committed.

Interruptions are but one of many conversational rules that are governed by cultural rules. It is easy to see how miscommunication can occur when we consider the dynamics of attributing meaning from conversational structure.

Types of Goals

Much of what happens in the negotiation process is directed by the goals of the parties. There are four general types of goals: instrumental goals, self-presentation goals, relational goals, and transactional goals (Wilmot & Hocker, 2001). Not all goals are equally important. Depending on the complexity of the task, one type of goal will take precedence over the others (Cai, 1998). For example, in the relationship-building stage of negotiation, relational and self-presentation goals may be more important; whereas during discussion of issues and concession stages, transactional and instrumental goals may emerge as the primary focus. What specifically are these goals and how do they affect the negotiation process?

Instrumental goals are usually the content goals. They are what we want. Typically, in business negotiations, instrumental goals are the goods we wish to buy, or the dollar amount we want for our services, or the contract for a fair agreement. Negotiators must be able to coordinate the management of several instrumental or task goals in a given negotiation. Prioritizing these goals is important and can help in the packaging and concession making of possible proposals.

Self-presentation goals are the images we want others to see of ourselves. This is referred to as "face" (Goffman, 1959). Examples of face goals in business negotiations are being viewed as trustworthy, honest, credible, or perhaps powerful.

Relational goals refer to the interpersonal relationship we would like to obtain or maintain with the opposing party. Examples of relational goals might be to establish a friendly working relationship with the other party or to develop a trusting relationship between friends or business partners. If the relationship has been established in a previous negotiation, the relationship goals are less in the forefront than if this is a first-time intercultural interaction.

Transactional goals (Wilmot & Hocker, 2001) are goals formulated during the negotiation process that influence how the negotiation may fluctuate because of the communication and information shared during the negotiation process. Transactional goals cannot be preplanned but rather emerge during the negotiation process. They are an outcome of the interaction experience. No one is ever sure what exactly will be said, what the response will be, or what effect a particular strategy or tactic may have on the other party. For example, in 1980 Camp David talks, President Jimmy Carter's request for Sadat's autograph for his grandchildren led to Sadat's reentry to the negotiation process with Begin.

We must constantly be aware that although expectations, cultural attitudes, organizational goals, and preplanned strategies come to the table, they may be overridden by the discourse that emerges from the negotiation interaction. Negotiators must therefore be able to adjust to the current discourse in the negotiation. Bush and Folger (2005) argue that transformation of conflict occurs when parties experience recognition of other and self-enlightenment. These require that the negotiator move beyond his or her agenda and into the relationship and ultimately into an unforeseen business agreement that brings not only profit but also a new outlook on conducting business beyond our own backyard.

Concessions

A concession is a critical issue that may affect both the substance of a negotiation and the relationship between the parties. Several key factors may influence concessions. First, negotiators use concession-making behavior for different reasons. Concessions can indicate a willingness to work with the other party. They can often be viewed as an offer of good will. United States negotiators are known for making concessions first before their Asian counterparts. However, because the U.S. negotiator makes concessions before the issues have fully been discussed, which is the Asian style, U.S. negotiators may suffer in the amount of gains compared to their Asian negotiation partners.

A second consideration in concession making is the rate at which concessions are made and who initiates the first concession. Buyer-seller negotiation research indicates that first concessions and rate are often determined by the role of the negotiator. The rate and timing of concessions can aid the negotiation process or disrupt the process and limit the range of possible outcomes. That is, if you make concessions too early before a full discussion has occurred, you may find fewer options for bargaining later.

Furthermore, early concessions may create suspicion and distrust. As discussed earlier in this chapter, some cultures wait until the end of the negotiation to make concessions, whereas others tend to make them throughout the process. The difference in rate and timing of concession making can influence possible gains. In addition, there is a distinct difference among intercultural negotiators regarding the timing of concessions. For instance, U.S. negotiators tend to make small concessions often and expect concessions to be reciprocated, whereas Chinese and Japanese negotiators often wait until the end to make concessions and may make rather large ones if they are satisfied with the general principles of the agreement. A result of U.S.-Japanese negotiations is that Japanese negotiators often fare better in the agreement because the U.S. team has already conceded much of what they had available (Graham, 1985; Menger, 1999). This is also true for U.S.-Chinese business negotiations (Zhao, 2000).

In general, it is best to make small concessions at first and wait for reciprocal moves before offering another concession. Trade-offs are an important part of the concession process. Also, keep in mind that some concessions are likely to come late, so leave yourself room for movement in the final stages of the agreement. Deadlines will influence the rate of concession making. As one approaches a deadline for agreement, concession behavior may increase.

The use of *logrolling* often results in achieving a positive integrative outcome. Shapiro and Rognes (1996) found that integrative settlements were achieved for parties who "logrolled (i.e., conceded on issues of lesser importance in exchange for concessions on issues of greater importance)" (p. 89). By trading off issues based on priority, negotiators were able to avoid simply trading concessions, which often results in a compromise solution. Logrolling can allow for negotiators to obtain what is most important to them and successfully reach an agreement.

Always calculate your concessions. Rinehart and Page (1992) suggest to determine your concession level by "multiplying the importance of the issue by the degree of concession made on that issue and summing the products for all the issues that were negotiated" (p. 21). By calculating the concession levels of each party, negotiators can then assess the value of their agreement. However, the perception of importance is subjective, and therefore misrepresentation could result. Having said this, calculating your concession level is an important tool to gauge the negotiation process.

Finally, know that concessions are critical for the agreement and the long-term relationship. If people feel beat up at the end of concession making, they are likely not to do business with you again. Short-term gains for giving little and getting lots at the expense of the relationship is short-sighted. Long-term partnerships in the international market are worth achieving, and concessions are necessary.

❖ AGREEMENT

Agreements have different interpretations around the world. For example, many cultures in the world place tremendous importance on verbal agreements. Indeed, verbal agreements, if proved in court, are legally binding in most countries. This concept may be totally foreign to a U.S. negotiator accustomed to the legal requirements in the United States for signed contracts. However, even under U.S. law, verbal agreements are legally enforceable in many situations, such as after physical performance of the agreement has been commenced by one or both parties. Advice to business executives is that verbal commitments should not be made unless and until they are willing to perform the commitments. Otherwise, both serious relationship problems and legal issues may quickly arise.

It is recommended that all agreements for international transactions be in written form, signed by authorized representatives from each side. Verbal agreements are not to be relied on in international commerce for a variety of reasons, including difficulty proving the existence of the agreement and potential disputes of what the terms may be absent any writing.

Certain minimum requirements of the agreement are recommended. The agreement must clearly identify the product(s) or services that are being bought and sold, and the quantities involved. Furthermore, the agreement must identify what law shall govern the contract and where disputes will be resolved. For example, if a U.S. company is importing machines from Germany, is the contract governed by German law or U.S. law? If there are quality problems with the equipment, will that be litigated in a U.S. or German court, or some third location? Those basic questions should be answered in the written contract agreement itself, and these issues should be part of the negotiation.

The written agreement should also outline a process for managing the process of changes and dispute resolution during the performance phase of the transaction. "Chinese view negotiation as a process for achieving a long-term cooperative relationship and mutual benefit rather than just a written contract" (Zhao, 2000, p. 233). It is suggested that all international trading partners adopt this view.

❖ CONCLUSION AND DEVELOPMENT
   OF A NEW DYNAMIC

The creation of the "third culture" has been discussed in the past readings as being a result of shared meaning and empathy. Broome, building upon Casmir's (1993) idea of third culture, argues that the third culture emerges because of the interaction of two cultures that create through communication a shared interdependency of meaning, worldview, interpretation, and reality. During the interaction process, the individuals create a new understanding that was not present before the negotiation began. Similar to how Bush and Folger talk about transformation in mediation, the third culture is the transformation of individuals' shared meanings that is a direct result of the communication process during negotiation.

Negotiation is the framework that disputing parties work within to reach an effective and satisfying agreement. Communication discourse is the means by which disputing parties create solutions and wise agreements. This exchange and mutually influencing process is a transactional communication process. That is, each message is dependent to some degree on the previous message and the shared meaning that is derived from this exchange. The intercultural communication experience cannot be understood by simply looking at cultural influences, or the individual expectations, the organizational goals, or the professional role one assumes. Rather, these antecedent influences, or prenegotiation factors, influence the likelihood of successful outcomes. From a communication perspective, cultural factors are important, but one must not ignore the communicated meaning that is uniquely derived from the discourse of the negotiation process. The negotiation is a dynamic process that is created by the parties' discourse. This unique discourse is created during the negotiation process. We cannot prescribe the exact exchange that occurs because of the uniqueness of human communication during the problem-solving process. It is important that as global negotiators we plan our communication strategies *and* be willing to move from prescriptive communication to a transactional process that is created because of our interactions with someone who is different from us.

As we learn new ways of negotiating in our global economy, we will experience the benefits of a new discourse. The success of our communication essentially determines our success in global negotiation.

We conclude this chapter with the following guidelines for reaching GNS.

❖ GUIDELINES FOR GLOBAL NEGOTIATION SUCCESS

1. The most important factor in international business negotiation is the prenegotiation stage. This is the only point in the process that you have complete control over managing. Research the other party and understand who the person is, his or her culture, his or her organization, the region of his or her homeland, and the BATNAs available to him or her.

2. Know your own strengths and weaknesses as a person, as an organization, as an opposing negotiation partner, and as a

communicator. Seek advice from others and invite criticism from your colleagues. It will give you insight and make you a better negotiator.

3. Realize that your assumptions about the negotiation process are less than accurate. Be flexible and adaptable in how issues are addressed, including how time is used and how communication occurs. Global business negotiators use the past as experience, not a forecast for the future.

4. The agreement reached today is tomorrow's renegotiation issue. International business transactions are long-term investments that will continue to emerge and hopefully grow with the changing market. Make today's agreement a foundation for future relationships and prosperous outcomes.

❖ DISCUSSION QUESTIONS

1. How do regional cultures and sub-subcultures affect international business negotiations?

2. What impact do global corporations have on international business negotiations?

3. How does your national, regional, and ethnic culture influence your ability to be a successful negotiator?

4. What critical factors are important to consider in creating a negotiated agreement?

5. Why is it important to view international business negotiation from a geocentric perspective? A communication perspective?

❖ REFERENCES

Adler, N. J. (2002). *International dimensions of organizational behavior* (4th ed.). Cincinnati, OH: South-Western.

Adler, N. J., & Graham, J. L. (1989). Cross-cultural interaction: The international compassion fallacy? *Journal of International Business Studies, 20*(3), 515–537.

Berger, C. R., & Calabrese, R. (1975). Some explorations in initial interaction and beyond: Toward a developmental theory of interpersonal communication. *Human Communication Research, 1,* 99–112.

Bush, R. A., & Folger, J. P. (2005). *The promise of mediation: The transformative approach to conflict.* San Francisco: Jossey-Bass.

Buttery, E. A., & Leung, T. K. P. (1998). The difference between Chinese and Western negotiations. *European Journal of Marketing, 32*(3/4), 374–389.

Cai, D. A. (1998). Culture, plans, and the pursuit of negotiation goals. *Journal of Asian Pacific Communication, 8*(2), 103–123.

Cai, D. A., & Donohue, W. A. (1997). Determinants of facework in intercultural negotiation. *Asian Journal of Communication, 7*(1), 85–110.

Casmir, F. (1993). Third-culture building: A paradigm shift for international and intercultural communication. *Communication Yearbook, 16*, 407–428.

Chaisrakeo, S., & Speece, M. (2004). Culture, intercultural communication competence, and sales negotiation: A qualitative research approach. *Journal of Business & Industrial Marketing, 19*(4), 267–282.

Donohue, W. A., & Hoobler, G. D. (2002). Relational frames and their ethical implications in international negotiation: An analysis based on the Oslo II negotiations. *International Negotiations, 7*, 143–167.

Drake, L. E. (2001). The culture-negotiation link: Integrative and distributive bargaining through an intercultural communication lens. *Human Communication Research, 27*(3), 317–349.

Fisher, R., & Ury, W. (1981). *Getting to yes, negotiating agreement without giving in.* Boston: Houghton Mifflin.

Fisher, R., Ury, W., & Patton, B. (Eds.). (1991). *Getting to yes, negotiating agreement without giving in* (2nd ed.). New York: Penguin Books.

Friedman, V. J., & Antal, A. B. (2005). Negotiating reality: A theory of action approach to intercultural competence. *Management Learning, 36*(1), 69–87.

Ghauri, P. N. (1986). Guidelines for international business negotiations. *International Marketing Review, 4*, 72–82.

Goffman, E. (1959). *The presentation of self in everyday life.* Garden City, NJ: Doubleday.

Graham, J. L. (1985). The influence of culture on the process of business negotiations: An exploratory study. *Journal of International Business Studies, 16*(1), 81–96.

Graham, J. L. (1996). The importance of culture in international business negotiations. *International Business Communications,* 78–91.

Graham, J. L., Mintu, A. T., & Rodgers, W. (1994). Explorations of negotiation behaviors in ten foreign cultures using a model developed in the United States. *Management Science, 40*(1), 72–95.

Griffith, D. A., & Harvey, M. G. (2001). Executive insights: An intercultural communication model for use in global interorganizational networks. *Journal of International Marketing, 9*(3), 87–103.

Gudykunst, W. B. (2005). *Theorizing about intercultural communication.* Thousand Oaks, CA: Sage.

Hendon, D. W., Roy, M. H., & Ahmed, Z. U. (2003). Negotiation concession patterns: A multi-country, multiperiod study. *American Business Review, 21*(1), 75–84.

Hofstede, G. (1991). *Cultures and organizations: Software of the mind.* London: McGraw-Hill.

Kanter, R. M., & Corn, R. I. (1994). Do cultural differences make a business difference? Contextual factors affecting cross-cultural relationship success. *Journal of Management Development, 13*(2), 5–23.

Martin, D., Mayfield, J., Mayfield, M., & Herbig, P. (1998). International negotiations: An entirely different animal. In R. J. Lewicki, D. M. Saunders, J. W. Minton, & B. Barry, *Negotiation* (4th ed., pp. 340–354). Boston: McGraw-Hill/Irwin.

Menger, R. (1999). Japanese and American negotiators: Overcoming cultural barriers to understanding. *Academy of Management Executive, 12*(4), 100–101.

Moore, C. W. (2003). *The mediation process.* San Francisco: Jossey-Bass.

Neuliep, J. W. (2003). *Intercultural communication: A contextual approach* (2nd ed.). Boston: Houghton Mifflin.

Olekalns, M., & Smith, P. L. (2000). Understanding optimal outcomes: The role of strategy sequences in competitive negotiations. *Human Communications Research, 26*(4), 527–557.

Parnell, J. A., & Kedia, B. L. (1996). The impact of national culture on negotiating behaviors across borders. *International Journal of Value-Based Managements, 9,* 45–61.

Rinehart, L. M., & Page, T. J., Jr. (1992). The development and test of a model of transaction negotiation. *Journal of Marketing, 56,* 18–32.

Salacuse, J. W. (1998). Ten ways that culture affects negotiating style: Some survey results. *Negotiation Journal, 14*(3), 221–240.

Salacuse, J. W. (2005). Negotiating: The top ten ways that culture can affect your negotiation. *Ivey Business Journal, 69*(4), 1–6.

Sebenius, J. K. (2002). The hidden challenge of cross-border negotiations. *Harvard Business Review, 80*(3), 76–85.

Shapiro, D. L., & Rognes, J. (1996). Can a dominating orientation enhance the integrativeness of negotiated agreements? *Negotiation Journal,* 81–90.

Susskind, L. (2004). What gets lost in translation? *Negotiation,* 3–5.

Thompson, L., & Hastie, R. (1990). Social perception in negotiation. *Organizational Behavior* and *Human Decision Processes, 47,* 98–123.

Tutzauer, F. E., & Roloff, M. E. (1988). Communication processes leading to integrative agreements: Three paths to joint benefits. *Communication Research, 15,* 360–380.

Ulijn, J. M., & Verweij, M. J. (2000). Questioning behaviour in monocultural and intercultural technical business negotiations: The Dutch-Spanish connection. *Discourse Studies, 2*(2), 217–248.

Wengrowski, B. S. (2004). The importance of culture and bargaining in international negotiations. *Defense AT&L, 33*(5), 26–29.

Wilmot, W. W., & Hocker, J. L. (2001). *Interpersonal conflict* (6th ed.). Boston: McGraw-Hill.

Zartman, I. W. (2000). What I want to know about negotiations. *International Negotiation, 7,* 5–15.

Zhao, J. J. (2000). The Chinese approach to international business negotiation. *Journal of Business Communication, 37*(3), 209–237.

4

Influence of Cultural Goals and Values

The foundation of who we are as individuals and as members of a group is initiated at birth and continues to be developed throughout our lives. This foundation is our culture. It guides how we think, what we believe, how we behave, and how we react. It is one of the main ingredients in our development as a member of our local as well as the global society.

What complicates cultural understanding is its stealthlike nature; we know it is there, because it manifests itself in our behaviors, but we can't see the internal workings or engine that creates those behaviors. Cultural learning occurs at a subconscious level. Norms and behaviors are absorbed through subconscious interaction with others within one's environment. In most cultures, families are the initial and primary teachers of culture. From an early age, we learn appropriate behaviors for interacting with others, what is considered to be right or wrong, and how to behave in a variety of situations. Unless consciously challenged to cognitively think about the "whys" of our behaviors, most people do not question them.

From a business perspective, our behaviors are guided by the country's cultural behaviors as they are interpreted and manifested by the culture within a business organization. Individuals who work within an organization usually adapt their business-related behaviors to fit the organization's culture. Thus, when dealing with culture as it affects business interactions, two levels of culture must be considered: the individual's culture and the organization's culture. Within a country, cultural adjustment takes place primarily at a subconscious level—we imitate others. Crossing cultural boundaries, however, creates a more complicated challenge and requires cognitive understanding, awareness, and flexibility at both levels.

Research in the area of cultural differences between countries is substantial and covers both the macro and micro aspects of cultural variation. From a macro perspective, research identifies general differences between cultures. The micro level looks at differences relating to specific situations, environments, and interactions. This chapter will address both levels. While some of the information presented may seem basic and dated, it is important for understanding culture, especially as it relates to the international business environment. It is important for building a foundational understanding of cultural differences. Just as learning one's own culture is evolutionary, understanding similarities and differences between cultures is the same. Your knowledge, understanding, and awareness of cultural norms and behaviors across countries and cultures is an evolutionary process that builds on past knowledge and experience.

❖ IMPORTANCE OF CULTURE

Culture represents our mental programming that directs and guides our behaviors (Hofstede, 1989). Our beliefs about right and wrong, good and bad, and so forth make up our values. Our norms dictate the appropriate behaviors for exemplifying those values. National culture (Hofstede, 1989) typically consists of a group of people with similar values and norms. Communication within this group or society is considered intracultural communication. Communication between cultural groups is considered intercultural communication.

Our ways of communicating are formed as part of our cultural development. Within a culture, we have little difficulty communicating as long as we interact with others from our culture. However, in an increasingly global environment, remaining isolated from other cultures becomes impossible. Once we start crossing over and interacting with people from other cultures, communication becomes more challenging.

Cognitive awareness and understanding of cultural values and norms is key to meeting the challenges of intercultural interactions. This requires an understanding of the elements that form the foundation of culture and the ability to assess each of these elements in terms of specific cultures. In addition, cognitive and affective integration of the understanding of various cultures is necessary for successful intercultural interaction. In other words, understanding the foundational elements of each individual culture is not sufficient for effective intercultural interactions; one must be able to assimilate the knowledge of one culture with another (or several others) in order to determine the most effective way to interact and communicate. In many situations, a "third" culture is developed that integrates elements of both/all cultures in order to enable more effective interactions.

As stated, developing an awareness and understanding of cultures and their differences involves both a cognitive and affective component. Cognitively, one must learn what elements/components make up culture and how these elements are defined and interpreted (differently) by cultures. This can be accomplished through the study and comparison of cultures. In today's global environment, there are numerous sources for learning about differences between cultures for personal, business, and other types of situations. This process will result in a high level of awareness and knowledge of cultural differences.

While the cognitive component of an intercultural interaction is important, the affective component is also necessary for effective and successful intercultural interactions. Affective understanding requires an experiential approach to learning. It is only through the experience of interacting with different cultures that one can develop a strong affective understanding of other cultures. The process is gradual and requires conscious attention to normally subconscious processes. As will be discussed in Chapter 5, individuals with certain personality traits may have a greater propensity for developing the skills needed for competency in intercultural communication.

❖ CULTURE AND BUSINESS

Culture underlies all interactions, including business interactions. Business interactions involve two levels of culture, the individual cultures of the people involved in the interaction and the organizational culture of the businesses involved. Culture influences most areas of business, as illustrated in David Ricks' book, *Blunders in International Business* (1993, 1999). Ricks describes numerous failures in business situations, such as the laundry detergent company that created a print ad to sell their detergent in a Middle Eastern country. In order to overcome the language issues, the company used only pictures in the ad. Unfortunately, they placed the picture progression of dirty clothes, laundry detergent, and clean clothes from left to right. In many Middle Eastern languages, people read from right to left (p. 53). Another example illustrates the danger in assuming one's own culture is universal. In a negotiation between an American businessman and a Malaysian businessman, the American assumed that the more informal structure of American business practices would suffice in Malaysia. After being introduced to his Malaysian counterpart, the American addressed him by a shortened version of what the American thought was his first name (Rog for Roger). The American later learned that the Malaysian businessman was introduced to him as *rajah*, a title of nobility, not the first name Roger (Ricks, 1993, p. 93), but the insult had already occurred and the relationship between the two men was at risk. No matter how skilled the American was in negotiating, the lack of understanding of the Malaysian culture caused the interaction to fail. Clearly, a lack of cultural understanding contributed to each of these cases.

Business negotiations take place at a variety of levels. A negotiation can be formal, such as a negotiation of a manufacturing contract, or it can be more informal, such as the day-to-day interactions with coworkers. Our cultural values and norms influence how we communicate and how we react to communication from others. Without a solid cognitive and affective understanding of the culture with which we are negotiating, the potential for misinterpretation and misunderstanding increases. Numerous research studies have identified cultural misunderstandings as a primary cause of failure in business transactions (Hall & Hall, 1987).

Based on earlier work, Adler and Graham (1989) helped to categorize the types of obstacles faced by international business negotiators. Four levels of culture-related problems that affect international business negotiations were identified. Each subsequent level represents more serious challenges to effective international business negotiations. The four levels are (a) language, (b) nonverbal behaviors, (c) values, and (d) thinking and decision-making processes. The macro-oriented discussion of culture in the remainder of this chapter is organized according to this typography. As we progress through these levels of cultural challenges, we will move from obvious differences to more subtle differences, helping us to see the complexity of the topic.

Language

Understanding of and adaptation to one's national culture or home culture begin at birth. There are several components of one's culture. The most obvious component is language. Verbal language differences immediately separate two cultures, making communication difficult or impossible. In today's global business environment, English is usually the language of business, although some countries, such as Saudi Arabia, require the host country language for business negotiation and contracts. However, English as a second language is not the same as English as a native language. Although having the ability to communicate in English during a business transaction may help in meeting the immediate business objective, it does not add to the cognitive knowledge and understanding of another culture. Many times, because a negotiation is conducted in English, other aspects of cultural differences may be ignored or assumed to be the same as one's own culture.

Interpreters

Language obstacles remain one of the most obvious cultural differences. Even though more and more businesspeople around the world speak English, most people are more comfortable speaking in their native language. Thus, including an interpreter as part of your negotiating team is a wise decision. Ideally, interpreters working in the area of international business will also have some formal academic training in business. This allows the interpreter to help interpret the words of the foreign party in the context of business and business practices for his or her negotiating team. Using an interpreter also displays respect for the foreign negotiating team. Without an interpreter, the foreign team would be forced to use its non-native language as the negotiation language as well as for all other communication. If the foreign party has an interpreter (and you don't), they may feel obligated to allow their interpreter to interpret for both sides, which would overload the interpreter. The workload for only one interpreter is overwhelming and very difficult for one person to effectively perform. Interpreting is a mentally demanding and tiring job and having only one interpreter does not allow time for rest. It also can put one of the two negotiating teams at a disadvantage, especially if the interpreter is from the culture of the other negotiating team. The team without an interpreter who has home-country business knowledge is at a disadvantage because a host-country interpreter may be less familiar with the home-country's customs and business practices, and therefore less able to accurately interpret dialogue in the home country context.

Even when English is used as the negotiating language, an interpreter can be useful in getting clarification from the foreign party when the English dialogue is not clear. Clarification in a native tongue is usually most effective. Language difficulties also occur in verbal understanding. Most non-native speakers of a language learn a formal form of the language. Native speakers tend to use a less formal form of their language. Native speakers tend to use idioms, slang phrases, and shortened versions of the language. When negotiating in your native language with a foreign negotiating team where your language is their second or third language, using formal language is important.

In his research, Tompenaars (1994) observed that translators (interpreters) play different roles depending on culture. In individualist cultures, translators play a neutral position; they simply translate the words being spoken. For collectivist cultures, translators are more involved and may add cultural interpretations to what is being said by the negotiators.

Translators

A unique component of language when negotiating in the international business environment is the need for written translation. Even when English is used as the verbal negotiating language, documents may be required in each team's native language. Translators and translation is a factor in all negotiation planning except when the negotiation occurs between two parties whose native languages are the same. Both sides of a negotiation should provide their own translator.

Written translation is also an important component of the negotiation process. Even if negotiations occur in a common language, written agreements are usually needed in both (or all) native languages. The translation process can be long and complicated and costly. In all cases, translation should include two steps for each iteration of the translation. A document should be translated from the original language to the second language, then back-translated to the original language by a different person. This is necessary for all drafts of the documents. Through translation and back-translation of written documents, language differences (e.g., word meanings), as well as differences in the understanding of what has been agreed upon, become more obvious.

If the back-translated version is identical to the original version, the translation can be considered a success.

Nonverbal Behaviors

In addition to differences in verbal language between cultures, there are also differences in nonverbal languages between cultures. According to Hall and Hall (1987), "80–90 percent of a culture is reflected in its non-verbal messages. These are usually taken for granted and are transmitted unconsciously" (p. 3). The unconscious or subconscious nature of nonverbal language amplifies the challenge of cognitive understanding.

A number of researchers have contributed to our understanding of nonverbal cultural differences. Most notable in the context of international business is Edward T. Hall. His work provides a solid framework for understanding nonverbal differences across cultures.

The context, information that surrounds the event and is integrated into the meaning, in which we communicate is not standard across cultures. On a continuum, cultures can vary from high to low context (Hall & Hall, 1976). In high-context cultures, much of the communication occurs outside of the written or spoken word. Internal knowledge as a result of a strong relationship between the individuals accounts for a large part of the communication (Hall, 1976). Higher-context cultures include Asian, Middle Eastern, Latin European, and most Latin cultures. High-context managers have a network of coworkers who all share information and confer together when making decisions. Not only are the words important in high-context communication, but also important is the situation and environment in which the communication takes place. "Reading between the lines" is a normal part of the interaction.

In low-context communication, the majority of information is contained in the explicit code of the message (Hall, 1976). Low-context managers face decisions in a linear fashion, compartmentalizing the information used for each decision. European and North American cultures are lower-context cultures. These cultures focus on the words and tend to ignore the situation (context) of the interaction. Reading between the lines is not typically practiced.

Misunderstanding arises when high-context and low-context cultures try to communicate. In their research comparing cultural differences between Japanese and American business culture, Hall and Hall (1987) noted that high-context Japanese might interpret the wordiness of American businesspeople as being condescending due to the American low-context practice of providing very detailed information, much of which would be assumed in the context by the high-context

Japanese. In this same situation, the Americans may interpret the Japanese high-context dialogue as providing insufficient information and, therefore, may feel left out, creating a lack of trust. As business relationships develop, finding the appropriate level of context is important for long-term success. It is not an easy task and requires a substantial amount of time to build a trusting relationship and comfortable level of communication.

The Silent Languages

Through his research as a cultural anthropologist, Hall (1976) identified five silent languages that affect business communication in the international environment. They are the silent languages of time, space, friendship, things, and agreements. Thirty years after these silent languages were identified, they still play an important role in understanding and assessing cultural differences in international business practices.

Time

Understanding how a culture defines or relates to time enhances our understanding of the culture. Time is not something we consciously think about in terms of its meaning; we think about it in terms of its effect on our lives, usually in a subconscious manner. Hall (1976; Hal & Hall, 1987) categorizes cultures into two main groups, the monochronic and polychronic time-oriented cultures. The prefixes of the terms help to understand their meanings: mono—single, and poly—many. When trying to compare one culture to another, it helps to think of these two categories as the anchors of a continuum. All cultures will have a varying degree of monochronic and polychronic characteristics, and these characteristics may vary by situation (e.g., business vs. social) within a culture.

Monochronic cultures relate to time in a linear fashion. Typically, people from monochronic cultures do one thing (single) at a time and use the clock to direct when to begin and end a specific task. Monochronic cultures tend to be more task oriented than polychronic cultures. They typically prefer to have an agenda for a meeting, follow the agenda, and complete each item on it. The leader of the meeting will remain aware of the time in order to be able to complete all the items on the agenda. Punctuality is also related to time. In a monochronic culture, individuals will arrive on or before the scheduled time of the meeting. Depending on the strength of the monochronic culture, the amount of time one arrives prior to a meeting will vary. Punctuality for the Japanese is so important that they will schedule delays into their time schedules if they are dealing with cultures that are known to be less punctual (i.e., most other cultures worldwide).

Polychronic time relates to time in a more abstract fashion. Polychronic cultures do not perceive time to be as important in directing their activities as monochronic cultures. Polychronic cultures are considered to be more multitasking; they are involved in more than one thing at a time. The main focus of most interactions in a polychronic culture is the process and interaction with others. The clock is there as a source of information, not as a taskmaster. Polychronic cultures tend to be less concerned about punctuality. However, the degree of concern varies by culture. Some polychronic cultures, like France and Italy, consider arriving for a meeting 10 to 15 minutes after its scheduled starting time to be acceptable. Of course, the more important one is in the hierarchy of the organization, the later he or she is allowed. If you use the same rule for meetings in many parts of Latin America, the potential for frustration increases. In Mexico, beginning a meeting 30 minutes after its scheduled start time is not unusual. Additionally, completing a meeting without interruptions is less likely in a polychronic culture than in a monochronic culture, as is completing all the items on an agenda.

When Monochronic and Polychronic Meet

The seemingly logical differences between monochronic and polychronic time orientations can cause high levels of frustration, especially for businesspeople unaware that such differences exist. Even with the cognitive understanding of the differences in time orientations, it is difficult to have no reaction. While collecting data for their research, Hall and Hall (1987) found that "it is hard not to respond viscerally when your own time system is violated. Our intellectual understanding did not mitigate our feelings of frustration" (p. 27). People from a monochronic time orientation can experience a high level of frustration when interacting with people from polychronic cultures who typically arrive sometime after the scheduled time of a meeting. For polychronic-time-oriented individuals, the punctuality of monochronic-time-oriented people is more of a bewilderment than a frustration. After all, they are not the ones who have to wait for their counterparts to arrive. They are busy interacting with others.

The time it takes to make a decision can also cause frustration between monochronic and polychronic negotiating teams. Decisions by collectivist cultures (many of which are polychronic) tend to take longer than decisions by individualist (usually monochronic) cultures

(Trompenaars, 1994). This difference tends to try the patience of the individualists and confuses the collectivists regarding the capabilities of their opponents. Along the same lines, collectivists tend to appreciate silence during a negotiation as it allows them to consider the points of the negotiation. They have learned to use silence as a tactic when negotiating with impatient individualists. The cumulative effect of these types of interactions can result in the deterioration of the relationship between the two parties if those involved are not aware of these fundamental and subconscious differences.

Space

The spatial relationship, or personal territory occupied by people, significantly influences communication within a culture as well as between cultures. The appropriate spatial relationship between people varies by the type of relationship (personal, business, etc.) and by their cultures. In most Western cultures, the appropriate spatial distance is arms length. The space created by the arms-length circle around an individual is considered personal space. When meeting someone, one stretches out his or her arm to shake hands as a form of greeting that protects this personal space from uninvited intruders. Western cultures understand and respect the size and scope of their personal space. Many non-Western cultures have a closer spatial relationship than Western cultures. Some cultures, such as Middle Eastern cultures, regard personal space to be very limited. It is quite common for interactions to occur at a distance of only a few inches. The spatial relationship between individuals from Latin and Latin European cultures is more distant than that of Middle Eastern cultures and closer than that of Western cultures.

Misunderstanding the spatial relationship of cultures can jeopardize building a constructive relationship between negotiating partners. When the spatial distance is farther apart than the cultural norm, it could be interpreted as a lack of trust. When the spatial distance is closer than the norm, an interpretation of being too aggressive is possible from the party accustomed to a larger distance. To further hinder the relationship, when a counterpart unknowingly steps into a personal space, the natural reaction of the person whose personal space was "violated" may be to step backward in order to recreate the appropriate personal space, sending the unintended message of distrust and dislike. In either case, the relationship between the two parties is usually weakened if the issue is not addressed directly.

Other aspects of the nonverbal language of space influence business interactions. Differences in workspace make it more difficult to assess the hierarchical importance of individuals. In Western cultures, privacy is an important aspect of the workspace. This complies with their individualistic nature. Most managers expect to have a private office. For employees who work in a more open area, such as telemarketers, partial walls or modular cubicles are typically erected in order to create some level of privacy.

Many Asian cultures prefer a more open (collective) plan for workspace organization. Managers, although they may have private offices, prefer working in an area with other managers. This way, they are able to maintain their relationships with coworkers as well as stay abreast of the most current information (Hall & Hall, 1987). For staff workers such as engineering technicians, it is common to work in a large room with rows of desks and computer stations, but no privacy barriers between the desks. Each chair is occupied and employees all work independently, yet together.

In the late 1980s, Bridgestone Corporation, a Japanese tire company, bought Firestone Corporation, an American tire company. When Bridgestone sent a number of Japanese managers to the United States, both sides faced a number of cultural challenges when adjusting to working together. One of these challenges was the configuration of workspace. The Japanese preferred their large open work area, whereas the Americans were more comfortable with their individual personal spaces. Another challenge focused on work effort. Americans were perceived as being lazy by the Japanese. Assessment of work behavior helps to understand the misunderstanding. Because of the importance of building relationships in Japanese culture, it was not unusual that Japanese businessmen would socialize most evenings with colleagues and other business relations. This helped to build the long-term trust relationship. Americans did not spend as many hours in the office or socializing as the Japanese, thus appearing lazy to the Japanese.

Material Things

Possessions and other material goods provide a visible display of what is important to that culture. These are used when assessing individuals from that culture. For cultures in which material possessions are important, people are assessed by the clothes they wear, the houses in which they live, the size of their office, and so forth. Individualistic cultures tend to consider material possessions important. Collective cultures tend to put a greater emphasis on the relationships between people and less on the ownership or presence of material things. As with most cultural norms and behaviors, the assessment of these elements usually takes place at the subconscious level. Before we cognitively realize a difference, our subconscious minds may have formed an impression based on the material context of the individual, but using our own cultural criteria for interpretation of the situation. This impression can influence the way in which we interact with the other person, either positively or negatively.

The material culture of the West has long been perceived as valuing material things as a visible sign of status and position. As developing economies grow, the adoption of material symbols becomes more apparent. In Eastern European countries, signs of success can be seen. More and more people are driving foreign cars, which command a premium price due to import regulations and taxes, and are building large single-family homes in areas where apartment living has always been the norm. These outward material adaptations to others' cultural behaviors can cause a false sense of cultural understanding. It may "look" like a foreign culture is changing based on their material culture, but the indigenous values and norms remain intact.

Friendship

Collective cultures value relationships with others as one of the most important aspects of their cultures. These relationships form the foundation for business transactions. The level of trust in these relationships is high, and therefore business transactions have a greater potential for success. For these cultures, friendship becomes almost a prerequisite for doing business. A certain level of trust must be developed in order for business to take place. When you think about the high-context nature of collectivist cultures, friendship is a logical element. Friendships facilitate high-context interactions.

Individualist cultures tend to separate friendships from business transactions—business is business. Friendships are perceived as personal and are compartmentalized (Trompenaars, 1994). Individualist countries, being low-context communicators, expect that detailed agreements (i.e., contracts) will communicate the needs and expectations of each side. These contracts also help to depersonalize the interaction and the transaction and remove personal responsibility from the individual to the company.

Agreements

Although not as directly important as it has been historically, the way cultures perceive agreements still differs. Historically, many countries viewed a handshake as more important than a contract (Hall,

1976). However, today, as countries strive to become economically stronger, they have adapted to the Western practice of using contracts to seal an agreement. Thus, the contract could be considered the primary form of agreement in international business transactions today. The developing world understands the need for Western involvement in their development, and thus the need to adapt to Western practices in terms of agreements. This does not mean that all cultures will interpret the meaning and importance of the contract equally. In low-context cultures, the contract is interpreted as being specific and detailed. It is expected that a contract will be carried out explicitly. Some high-context cultures view the words of a contract similarly to how they view the words of a communication; the contextual surroundings of that communication influence the meaning. Likewise, the contextual surroundings of the contract could affect its meaning, and if the context changes, then the contract may change as well.

Also embedded in agreements is the personal responsibility taken by the individuals involved in the transaction. For individuals from collectivist countries, responsibility tends to be more personal. In Japanese history, there are many examples of individuals performing hara-kiri as a result of failure. Although this person may not have been the only one involved in causing the failure, the personal responsibility taken by the individual resulted in shame and, therefore, death. A business failure brings disgrace to the Japanese businessman.

Individualist cultures tend to take a more distant and representative approach to the responsibility embedded in an international business transaction. Individuals act as representatives of their home company and do not necessarily feel the same depth of responsibility as individuals from collectivist cultures. A business failure to a U.S. businessperson, for example, is viewed in terms of a lost competitive event and used to develop better strategies for future negotiations; it is part of business.

Values

The third level of Graham's (1996) categorization of cultural obstacles faced by international negotiators involves values. Values form the foundation through which we assess and interpret our surroundings and through which our communication behaviors with others are guided (Ting-Toomey, 1999). Our values are developed throughout our lives and are influenced by a variety of elements within our societies. Some of the general elements that influence our value systems are briefly discussed in this section.

Institutions

There are a number of institutions that are common to most cultures. The difference lies in the relative importance and strength of each institution within a culture. The values and norms of an institution will reflect the values and norms of the culture within which it operates. The institution of the family is prominent and the greatest influence on values in most cultures. What differs is how the family is defined. In most of the Western cultures such as the United States, Canada, Britain, and Australia, the family is generally defined as the immediate family: the father, mother, and their children. In Asian and Latin European cultures such as China, Malaysia, and Spain, the family is extended to include grandparents. Middle Eastern countries typically extend the family even further to include aunts, uncles, cousins, and so forth. Thus, the term family has different interpretations in different cultures.

Educational institutions also play an important role in most cultures. The structure and control of educational systems within a national culture impose great influence on its citizens' cultural development. For example, educational curriculum in France is controlled at the national level. Students in a specific grade will all learn the same material at the same time across the country. In the United States, the majority of educational curricula is determined at the state level, following national guidelines. In this structure, there is the potential for greater variation between states in meeting national guidelines. In Taiwan, students wear uniforms throughout K–12. Until a few years ago, when entering the junior year of high school, girls were required to cut their hair to shoulder length or shorter. These differences relate to the level of conformity expected within a culture. With higher levels of conformity, there should be greater consistency within cultural behaviors. Other institutions also play a role in molding a country's culture. Social and civic institutions, government, and economic institutions influence culture. The influence of each type of institution will vary by country, based on the social and political structure of the country.

Another important institution within most cultures is religion. Religion strongly influences cultural values in terms of what is considered right or wrong. Religious institutions play a stronger role in some cultures than in others. In Russia, religious institutions were forbidden throughout its communist era. In France, approximately 85 percent of the population consider themselves Catholics. However, less than 25 percent are practicing Catholics. Historically, the high percentage of Catholics in France increased its cultural conformity.

The increase in immigration from developing to developed countries has created greater variation in religious values and norms within a country. Whether the influence is religion or race, there has been an increase in the potential for value conflict. In most cases, immigrants tend to hold lower economic positions within the society and can be perceived as being discriminated against. In late 2005, France experienced an intense period of civil unrest in its capital city of Paris. Violence throughout the city during a period of several weeks resulted in fire, riots, vandalism, and some deaths. The areas affected most were occupied by Muslim immigrants. In France, immigrants made up about 10 percent of the country's population. According to the BBC ("Fresh Violence Hits Paris Suburbs," 2005), these immigrants, most of whom were Muslims, had the highest rate of unemployment and experienced hostile relations with the French police. When situations like this occur, it is difficult to rule out the influence of cultural differences and lack of understanding and acceptance of these differences as playing a role in the conflicts. In Islamic countries, religious beliefs are the basis of their legal system; thus religion dictates appropriate behaviors.

Aesthetic Component

The aesthetic component is especially important when addressing the nonverbal language of culture. As discussed earlier in this chapter, friendship is an important aspect of doing business in many cultures. In order to develop the long-term relationship needed to be successful in the international environment, it is necessary to invest time and effort into building a strong and sincere relationship with your foreign counterpart. In most cases, this involves social interaction. Aesthetic elements are especially important in the social development of this relationship.

Aesthetic elements of a culture give it its appreciation for beauty and other things pleasing to the cognitive and affective senses of an individual. Beauty is defined differently among different cultures—not just how we look, but also our fashion styles, the design and decor of our homes, our commercial architecture, and our landscape design. Elements such as color, symbols, and textures also play a role in defining the aesthetics of a culture. Art forms such as painting, music, and dance are also incorporated into the aesthetic framework of a culture. Although the aesthetic component of culture may not have a direct bearing on a negotiation, it can influence the way one evaluates the environment in which one is operating. For example, it is well known that gift giving is an important part of the Japanese culture. However, it is inadvisable to give a gift that is a set of four of something, such as a set of four glasses, or four candles. Although a set of four in the United States and other countries is quite common, in Japan, the word for *four* is very similar to the word for *death*, and thus elicits a very negative interpretation. Gifts in Japan also tend to be more symbolic and should be the same for all involved, implying equality. However, in more individualist countries, a more valuable gift for someone "higher-up" is expected.

Color can also complicate communication. It is generally understood that black is the color of mourning in most Christian-based countries and that white is the color of mourning in Islamic-based countries. However, it is more difficult to find information on other, more subtle and specific, uses of color. For example, in France, bringing flowers to a dinner party is not as common as in other Western countries. However, many Americans do not realize this and thus bring flowers to the host of the dinner. What is not clear is that certain types and colors of flowers could be insulting. According to Platt (1994), chrysanthemums are only for graveyards, carnations imply bad luck, and yellow flowers given to a hostess send a message that her husband is deceiving her (p. 181).

Gaining knowledge of the aesthetic components of a culture is important for building relationships. As you will see in Chapter 9, knowing about the art, music, wine, and other cultural aesthetics contributes to success in the international business environment. Knowledge in these areas shows that you have a sincere interest in the people with whom you are negotiating.

Thinking and Decision-Making Processes

Graham and Adler's final level of cultural challenges involves the deepest level of cultural differences facing international business negotiators. Thinking and decision-making processes play a role in the national culture as well as organizational culture. The following discussion of Hofstede's work provides a framework for understanding cultural differences that influence these processes. Additionally, Trompenaars (1994) has done extensive research on the effect of culture on management. A brief overview of his work is also presented. These are by no means the final word on cultural differences, but they do provide food for thought as to why people from different cultures behave differently in similar situations. From this, the international negotiator can begin to develop an intercultural understanding that can be used to modify negotiation strategy to fit the foreign environments in which he or she may be operating.

The Dimensions of Culture

While working for IBM, a multinational corporation, Geert Hofstede (1983) developed a model consisting of four dimensions of culture. The four factors, or dimensions, accounted for 50 percent of the variance in the factor analysis used to analyze the data. Hofstede's research shows the relative position of one culture to another and how these differences could influence how individuals might interact with each other in the business setting. While there have been numerous studies subsequent to his work, Hofstede's seminal work provides a base for understanding cultural differences, especially in terms of relative differences between countries.

Individualism/Collectivism

The first dimension, individualism/collectivism, has been referred to earlier in this chapter. It addresses how individuals within a country relate to each other. Cultures near the individualist end of the continuum hold individual freedoms as critically important. Individualists look after themselves and their immediate families, and relationships between people outside of the family do not carry as strong a bond as those from collectivist cultures. Individualism and economic wealth of a country were shown to be statistically related; the higher the wealth of a country, the more individualist the culture (Hofstede, 1983).

Collectivist cultures showed different traits. The bond of a relationship was very strong. The groups to which people belonged were predetermined through the social structure of the country. India, with its caste system, is a good example of this. People in India are born into their group and, for the most part, remain in that group throughout their lives. Group well-being is paramount to individuals within the group, and decisions are made based on what is best for the group and not the individual. By necessity, most developing countries fall toward the collective end of the continuum. Collectivist behaviors are a means of economic survival. As countries develop economically, shifts along the continuum toward individualism tend to occur. One needs to look at the increase in demand for material goods in China for an illustration of this trend. One of the most expensive apples in the world is the Katayama apple. Between 2003 and 2005, the amount of these apples exported to China (the largest apple producer in the world) increased from 2 to 20 tons (Faiola, 2005). In 2005, Katayama apples were sold for $17 per apple in China, a higher price than in Japan, which has long been considered one of the costliest markets for specialty fruit. The demand for specialty items implies that Chinese consumers, especially those at higher economic levels, are looking for ways to differentiate themselves from others, thus becoming more individualistic. While this illustration may be somewhat superficial, it shows the direction of change in a very collective developing country.

Power Distance

Power distance addresses the issues of power distribution among people of a culture. It relates to how centralized and autocratic power is within a culture. Hofstede (1983) argues that countries with a high level of centralization and autocratic rule have been "mentally programmed" (p. 81) so that people at all levels of society expect and are comfortable with the structure. People at the lower end of the hierarchy are dependent on those at the higher end to make decisions. These cultures would have a relatively high power distance. At the opposite end of the continuum are cultures with a relatively low power distance. In these cultures, there is more interaction among the levels of hierarchy within an organization. For example, in the United States, a subordinate would likely provide input into a decision, whereas in France (larger power distance than the U.S.), a subordinate may provide data for use in the decision but would not offer a position (opinion) on a specific decision. In the French culture, it is expected that decisions will be made at the top.

From a communication standpoint, it is important that negotiators from individualist cultures frame their communication in a manner that shows the benefit of their propositions to the group and not the individuals of a collective culture. In a team setting, this can be especially confusing. Individualist cultures, especially those with a large power distance, are accustomed to a distinct hierarchy of authority and importance on a negotiating team (or most types of business teams). Each individual has his or her specific responsibilities and positions. In countries that are more collectivist, although there may be a large power distance, it is difficult for the individualist to determine the hierarchy of authority. The tendency of the individualist team is to identify the decision maker of the opposing team and communicate directly to that person. However, in a collectivist culture, all team members should be treated collectively and equally; one team member should not be singled out as being more important than another even though a distinct hierarchy exists.

An interesting combination of power distance and space can be seen in this example. Power distance is relatively large in China, but there are variations. On crowded streets in Chinese cities, people have very small personal space; the streets are crowded and people are accustomed to walking close together. However, when a Westerner walks down the street, the Chinese provide him or her a larger personal space. To illustrate the strength of power distance in that country, one only has to look at the space given to law enforcement people. When walking down the street, a police or military officer will typically have a significantly larger (empty) space around him than either a Chinese citizen or a Westerner.

Uncertainty Avoidance

The continuum of uncertainty avoidance (strong or weak uncertainty avoidance) deals with how a culture handles the risk of tomorrow. Countries with strong uncertainty avoidance want to reduce the amount of uncertainty in the future. Through technology, law, and religion, a country can develop a sophisticated framework through which they can better predict, and thus reduce the risk and subsequent consequences of, various events. Technology provides protection and security (e.g., homes, airport screening, medical diagnostic equipment). Laws help ensure the consequences of nonconformity, which provides a certain level of behavioral expectations for most people. Religion provides a hope of bigger things in the face of uncertainty, making it easier to cope with the unexpected and the uncertainty of day-to-day life. Uncertainty is addressed in more detail in Chapter 6.

Masculinity/Femininity

The fourth dimension, masculinity/femininity, addresses the role of the sexes in society. Countries at the masculine end of the continuum tend to be more patriarchal, with clear divisions between what is considered a male role and a female role. The most masculine of cultures in Hofstede's studies was Japan (1983). In Japan, there is a clear distinction between sex roles. Until recently, men held all upper-level management positions in Japanese firms. Women held support positions in companies, but were not given the opportunity to move into managerial positions. Traditionally, for many positions, women wore specific colored uniforms that indicated the level and type of position held. In masculine cultures, according to Hofstede (1983), more masculine traits such as showing off and being competitive are considered more important than the nurturing feminine traits.

Feminine cultures have a more nurturing, human approach. Helping people, especially those less fortunate, is an important value for both men and women. Roles of males and females are not as clearly defined. Women have more opportunity to participate in the management of corporations, cities, and families. The countries closest to the femininity end of the continuum include the Nordic countries and the Netherlands. Latin American countries, Middle Eastern countries, and many of the Asian countries tend to be more masculine.

The masculinity/femininity of a culture seems to relate to the acceptance of female international managers and negotiators. Adjustment to and acceptance of women in these positions would be more difficult in cultures with strong masculine orientations. And even though Western women (American, British, etc.) are more accepted in foreign countries, women still face greater hurdles than men when negotiating in Middle Eastern, Latin American, and some Asian countries. Further, while more masculine-oriented cultures are becoming more accepting of foreign women as international managers and negotiators, that trend does not typically apply to home-country women.

Cultural Dichotomies

As an extension of earlier work (Kluckhohn & Strodtbeck, 1961) and based on more than a decade of research on the effect of culture on management, Trompenaars (1994) developed seven dichotomies of culture. Cultures can be distinguished by the manner in which they resolve specific problems. Trompenaars places these dichotomies into three categories: problems arising from our relationships with other people, problems relating to the passage of time, and problems relating to the environment. The dichotomies related to relationships include: the rules of relationships, the group versus the individual, expression of emotion, involvement, and status. The remaining two dichotomies focus on attitudes toward time and attitudes toward the environment. As you read through this section, you should notice some commonalities among Trompenaars, Hofstede, and Hall while at the same time identifying their different perspectives.

Five of Trompenaars's dichotomies relate to relationships with people. The dichotomy between universalism and particularism relates to the degree to which a culture "follows" rules. A universalist perspective is common in a rules-based culture, where rules are expected to be followed regardless of the circumstances. Particularist cultures tend to view appropriate behavior as depending on the circumstances of the situation. According to Trompenaars (1994), particularist cultures put relationships before rules and will bend rules when needed to support strong relationships.

Contracts can be interpreted quite differently between universalists and particularists. Rules-based universalists would view a contract as needing all details of an agreement included and followed. Particularists would view this type of document as communicating a lack of trust. They would view the relationship between the parties as communicating commitment and trust, and therefore there would be no need for detailed contracts; the particularist party would behave in a manner that would be beneficial to the universalist party. This type of situation also relates to Hall's (1976) silent languages of relationships and agreements discussed earlier.

The particularist/universalist dichotomy can also affect the perception of time. Trompenaars (1994) advises universalist-oriented businesses to take more time than they would in another universalist country when in particularist countries, where building relationships is important. This concurs with Hall's silent language of time, where monochronic cultures tend to be more linear and time oriented and polychronic countries more interested in the development of relationships.

Trompenaar's dichotomy of individualism and collectivism is similar to Hofstede's dimension of culture and does not need further definition. The different perspectives between individualists and collectivists can have an effect on negotiation. In individualist cultures, a single negotiator with authority to make decisions would be considered acceptable. In a collectivist culture, however, negotiating teams would be considered more typical. If negotiations move to unexpected (or unplanned for) topics, individualists would be comfortable making decisions whereas collectivists would expect to communicate with superiors not at the negotiation table (Trompenaars, 1994).

The extent of emotional expression varies by culture and is conceptualized by the neutral versus emotional dichotomy. Neutral cultures tend to carefully control their emotions, whereas emotional cultures outwardly express their emotions. Trompenaars (1994) found that Japan exhibited the most neutral culture and the United States, France, and Italy tended to be more emotional. The use of humor falls into this category because humor is used to elicit an affective response. Humor is very culturally based, and its use in a professional setting varies greatly across cultures. It requires a deep and fluid understanding of language that many foreigners may not have. The same issue arises when using colloquialisms and comments meant to be sarcastic, or other emotionally evoked comments. Typically, it is not advisable to use these in an international setting.

Communication behavior also relates to the affective dichotomy. People from different cultures speak at different rates. Some cultures, such as the United States and many Western European countries, are uncomfortable with silence and tend to respond/talk when others are silent. Contrary to this, many Asian cultures view silence as a form of respect, allowing time to consider the words of others. Silence is also an issue for many low-context monochronic cultures. Because low-context cultures rely on the written and spoken word for communication, silence may imply a break in communication. A natural response to silence for a low-context individual is to speak. High-context cultures, such as Japan and Taiwan, have learned to use the discomfort with silence of low-context cultures, like the United States, to their advantage. They realize that the longer they remain silent, the more likely others will talk and give concessions in the negotiation. The monochronic component of culture relates to silence in that many low-context cultures tend to be monochronic; these cultures are linear and silence interrupts the linear flow of the communication. Additionally, when communicating across cultures, tone will vary. Asian languages tend to maintain a constant neutral tone, whereas Latin countries tend to use a tone that frequently changes from excited to calm (Trompenaars, 1994). When neutral and affective cultures interact in a negotiating setting, it becomes a challenge to interpret affective responses and behaviors of the other party.

The level and depth of involvement in relationships defines the dichotomy between specific-oriented cultures and diffuse-oriented cultures. In specific-oriented cultures, individuals segment relationships based on the type of involvement. Their public space tends to be larger than their private space, and relationships are developed somewhat superficially and based on common interests. For diffuse-oriented cultures, private space is larger and the level and hierarchy of interactions tend to be more consistent over all activities. For example, in a specific-oriented culture, the relationship between a boss and subordinate at work may be quite hierarchical whereas that relationship in a church setting may be more egalitarian. In a diffuse-oriented culture, the boss-subordinate hierarchy would follow through all interactions. Americans tend to be more specific oriented, whereas many Asian and African countries tend to be more diffuse oriented (Trompenaars, 1994).

You should see a clear connection between this dichotomy and Hall's silent language of friendship. Countries that lean toward being diffuse oriented also view strong relationships as an important part of doing business. Thus, building a relationship with someone from a diffuse-oriented culture implies that the relationship will spread across all aspects of their lives. This may be a challenge for specific-oriented cultures like the Northern European and North American cultures.

Since these cultures build compartmentalized relationships that relate to only specific interactions, it may be frustrating when interacting with people from a diffuse-oriented culture, where building a wider and deeper relationship takes more time than what would normally be expected. Further, the level of self-disclosure is usually greater than what two specific-oriented parties would expect.

Let's look at the dinner interaction to try and illustrate the point. Specific-oriented Americans view dinner with business partners as an alternative venue to continue business discussions. Eating is secondary to the potential to "do business." Time spent on relationship development is usually minimal and superficial. Specific-oriented cultures focus on the specific task at hand. If it is successful, future agreements can take place, eventually leading to a wider, more general, relationship. Contrast this with the Japanese diffuse-oriented culture. Dinners with business partners, or potential partners, occur frequently. They tend to be longer and do not involve any discussion of business. The purpose of these dinners is to build a strong and deep relationship. As relationships grow, business interactions become easier because both sides want to do what is best for all parties involved, and it is understood (high-context) that business together will take place. In this case, diffuse-oriented cultures begin with a general relationship (agreeing to do business), then move to specific tasks. Unfortunately, it is difficult for specific-oriented cultures to adjust to the more relationship-focused, diffuse-oriented cultures, and vice versa.

The issue of status also has two sides. In some cultures, status is earned or achieved, whereas in other cultures, status is assigned. Factors that influence status include elements such as gender, social position, education, and professional position (Trompenaars, 1994). In countries where achievement is important, education and professional attainment are very important in determining status. Cultures that assign status give more importance to elements such as family (who we are), age (seniority), and gender, and status is determined by these factors.

In a negotiation situation with a team from an achievement culture, in which status is earned, and a team from an ascriptive culture, in which status is assigned due to specific factors, misinterpretations may occur. In many cultures, such as Asian cultures, Arab cultures, and Latin cultures, position and status are determined by seniority (age as well as length of time with a firm). These cultures also tend to be more collectivist than cultures in which achievement determines status. North American and Northern European cultures tend to be oriented toward achievement as a means for assigning status. Thus, factors such as age and time with a firm may not necessarily play a role. The misunderstanding or misinterpretation of the negotiating setting can occur as a result of using one's own cultural norms to interpret the makeup and behavior of the opposing negotiating team. For example, it would not be unusual for a negotiating team from an achieving culture such as Norway (Northern European) to include relatively young managers, especially those with specific competencies (such as information technology) on a negotiating team. For negotiators from an ascriptive culture, this could be interpreted that the firm from the achieving culture is not as serious about the partnership. The ascriptive-oriented culture team would expect the members of the negotiating team to be more senior, implying a greater status and therefore greater authority, adding more importance to the negotiation.

Also embedded in this dichotomy is the issue of decision-making authority. Achieving-oriented cultures give decision-making authority to individuals who have earned it regardless of factors such as age, gender, and so forth. For ascriptive-oriented cultures, decision making is determined by status based on age, seniority, and so forth. Again, frustration and misinterpretation can occur in a negotiation setting. Achieving-oriented negotiating teams may expect their ascribing-oriented counterparts to be able to make decisions. However, the ascribing-oriented negotiators would expect to take decisions to a higher level than those at the negotiating table.

The differences in behaviors in this dichotomy relate to the context of the cultures as well as the importance of relationships. Achieving-oriented cultures also tend to be more low-context oriented, where relationships typically are not as important as for other cultures. Ascribing-oriented cultures tend to be higher context and relationship oriented. Thus, it would make sense that the ascribing-oriented negotiating team would not be as concerned about decision-making authority because their primary purpose in the negotiation is to build a stronger relationship. The details of the negotiation are secondary to the relationship, because once the relationship is developed, the details are simple.

Trompenaars's final two dichotomies involve how people relate to time and to their environment. The time dichotomy follows Hall's (1976) classification of polychronic and monochronic time orientations. Synchronic (polychronic) time orientation involves synchronous (at the same time) activities. Contrast this with sequential (monochronic) time orientation, in which activities occur one at a time, or sequentially, and it should be easy to see the potential conflicts between the cultures.

The final dichotomy is related to the level of internal or external control a culture perceives itself as having over the environment. Individuals from internally controlled cultures consider themselves to have a substantial amount of control over what happens. They are responsible for their own successes and failures. At the other end of the dichotomy, externally controlled cultures perceive themselves as having less control over their environment (external forces have greater influence).

In his research regarding the internal/external dichotomy, Trompenaars measured the response to the statement, "What happens to me is my own doing" (1994, p. 138), and found that for the majority of countries, over 50 percent of respondents for each country responded that they believed that what happens to them is their own doing. This included countries that would be considered individualist countries as well as collectivist countries. If you think about the differences in perspectives between individualist and collectivist cultures, the similarity in response to the internal/external dichotomy should become clear; the same response could be due to different reasons. For the more individualist countries such as the Western European and North American countries, this response could be explained by the individualist nature of the cultures. However, the same response could be expected from collectivist countries, such as Japan or Indonesia, but for different reasons. Individuals in collective cultures would take responsibility for their circumstances, especially negative circumstances, in order to protect other members of their group (so others could save face). From a management or decision-making perspective, internally oriented cultures would be more comfortable making and implementing decisions whereas externally oriented cultures may see a greater power distance between levels in an organization and expect directives to come from higher levels within the organization.

❖ ARE GENERALIZATIONS ENOUGH?

The discussion of cultural similarities and differences presented in this chapter may tempt us to generalize cultural characteristics by regions of the world. It is human nature to create "rules" for making decisions; they help reduce the complexity of the decision. Thus, it would seem reasonable to view Asian countries as collective, Western countries (North America, Western Europe) as individualistic, Latin American countries as polychronic, and so forth. Although these generalizations help us grasp the relative position of one country/region to another on specific factors influencing cultural behaviors, they do not provide sufficient knowledge about cultural differences on a country-by-country basis. This macroperspective of cultural differences is a necessary first step for intercultural understanding. What is also needed is a micro-oriented perspective of cultural differences as they relate to international business negotiations. To this end, numerous bilateral or multilateral studies have explored differences in negotiating behaviors between countries. It is the cumulative knowledge gained from these studies that helps the international negotiator gain a geocentric perspective to cultural behaviors in the context of international business negotiations.

Table 4.1 lists some of the studies that have looked at country-specific cultural differences in international business negotiation. The countries/cultures compared appear to have no systematic at justification for the comparison. However, each study adds perspective to the microdifferences between cultures in regard to international business negotiations.

❖ INTERCULTURAL CHALLENGES AND ISSUES

In this chapter, we have attempted to provide you with some of the most commonly accepted work in the area of culture and cultural differences. Two things are certain: it is not an exact science and it is a dynamic area. The challenge to the negotiator is to identify cultural similarities as well as differences in order to understand how the other culture communicates and behaves. For long-term success in building a relationship with the foreign partner, this cannot be a superficial attempt at understanding foreign culture. It requires an investment in time and self to truly learn about, understand, accept, and respect the values and norms of another culture.

The changing international business environment also presents dynamic challenges to the international negotiator. Negotiations may take the traditional bilateral structure in which the negotiation involves individuals from only two cultures. However, with the continued growth of economic integration and other forms of strategic alliances (discussed in Chapter 7), international business negotiators may find themselves more frequently involved in negotiations with more than one other cultural group. And, as the interaction among different cultural groups grows, new hybrid cultural behaviors develop, complicating and confusing the ability to culturally adapt to the situation based on the foundation of knowledge developed. Thus, it is up to the negotiator to use his or her knowledge and experience regarding cultural differences, and independently apply them to each international business interaction. The ultimate goal in the majority of international business interactions and negotiation should be the strengthening of the long-term relationship, both business and personal, between the parties involved. The following guidelines should help the international negotiator learn about and assess the cultural environment of his or her foreign counterpart.

Table 4.1 Selected Research in Cross-Cultural Negotiation

Author(s)	Year of Publication	Regions/Countries Compared	Elements Compared	General Findings
Hendon, Roy, & Ahmed	2003	U.S., Canada, UK, Australia, New Zealand, South Africa, Kenya, Thailand, Hong Kong, Taiwan, Singapore, Malaysia, Indonesia, India, Philippines, Papua New Guinea, Mexico, Peru, Chile, Uruguay, Brazil	Price concession patterns	More similarity between regions regarding patterns disliked than in concession patterns liked; All regions are different in the way they make price concessions
Hise, Solano-Mendez, & Gresham	2003	U.S., Mexico	15 cultural traits	U.S. executives assigned higher levels of importance to cultural dimensions than Mexican executives; U.S. and Mexican executives agreed on which cultural dimensions were important
Elahee, Kirby, & Nasi	2002	U.S., Canada, Mexico	National culture's influence on trust	Intra- and intercultural differences in negotiation behaviors involving Mexican negotiators but not with U.S. and Canada

(Continued)

Table 4.1 (Continued)

Author(s)	Year of Publication	Regions/Countries Compared	Elements Compared	General Findings
Fraser & Zarkada-Fraser	2002	Greece, Russia, UK	Level of cultural awareness; Approaches to negotiation	Level of awareness of other cultures was high; No systematic differences in negotiation approach found
Osman-Gani & Tan	2002	Chinese, Indian, Malaysian (working in Singapore)	Negotiation styles in a multicultural, multiethnic environment	Culture/ethnicity significantly influences negotiating styles of Asian managers from the cultures studied
Palich, Carini, & Livingstone	2002	U.S., China	Logic frameworks on negotiating approaches (non-empirical)	Recommends guidelines for U.S. firms negotiating with Chinese firms
Volkema & Fleury	2002	U.S., Brazil	Negotiation tactics	U.S. and Brazil differed in their use of several negotiation tactics in a cross-cultural setting
Shi & Wright	2001	China	Negotiator profile	Negotiator profile traits are strongly influenced by cultural backgrounds

Author(s)	Year of Publication	Regions/Countries Compared	Elements Compared	General Findings
Zarkada-Fraser & Fraser	2001	Australia, U.S., UK, Japan, Russia, Greece	Morally acceptable tactics used in sales negotiations; Decision-making frameworks	Moral acceptability of specific practices vary (e.g., use of gamesmanship)
Mintu-Wimsatt & Gassenheimer	2000	U.S., Philippines	Use of problem-solving approach between high- and low-context cultures	Significant difference in the use of PSA; No gender differences found
Ulijn & Verweij	2000	Netherlands, Spain	Asking questions as part of an international negotiation	Dutch ask significantly less questions than Spanish; Question differences appear language and culture bound; Type of information needed to become more confident depends on communicator's personality rather than cultural background
Gelfand & Christakopoulou	1999	U.S., Greece	Judgment accuracy of other's priorities; Own vs. other's goals	Americans had less judgment accuracy than Greeks; Americans claimed more value to themselves throughout negotiation; Greeks perceived that they had more concern for Americans than vice versa

(Continued)

Table 4.1 (Continued)

Author(s)	Year of Publication	Regions/Countries Compared	Elements Compared	General Findings
Kumar	1999	U.S., Japan	Communicative goals in first interactions	Developed model, but did not empirically test
Paik & Tung	1999	U.S., S. Korea, Japan, China	Negotiating styles	Differences found between cultures in logic, preparations, resolution, and motivation for the negotiation
Brett & Okumura	1998	U.S., Japan	Negotiation outcomes of intracultural and intercultural negotiations; Understanding of other party priorities	Lower joint gains in intercultural than intracultural negotiations; Less understanding of other party priorities in intercultural negotiation than in intracultural negotiation
Lituchy	1997	U.S., Japan	Intercultural and intracultural negotiation behaviors	Intracultural Japanese negotiations were integrative; Intracultural American negotiations were distributive; Japanese/American negotiations were distributive

Author(s)	Year of Publication	Regions/Countries Compared	Elements Compared	General Findings
Graham, Mintu, & Rodgers	1994	U.S., Canada, Mexico, UK, France, Germany, (former) USSR, Taiwan, China, Korea	PSA framework; Attractiveness; Role of negotiator	Importance of each varied by culture
Francis	1991	U.S., Japan, Korea	Level of adaptation to other culture	Some cultural adaptation is beneficial to negotiation; Substantial cultural adaptation may be less beneficial
Adler & Graham	1989	U.S., Japan, Francophone Canadians, Anglophone Canadians	Cross-cultural vs. intracultural interactions in negotiation behaviors	Negotiators adapt behaviors in cross-cultural interactions
Graham	1988	Japan, Korea, China, Taiwan, France, UK, Germany, Canada (anglo- and francophone), Mexico, Brazil, U.S.	Buyer/seller profits and cultural context; Power distance; Status/rank of seller	Power distance had no effect; High-context cultures tended to achieve higher profits than low-context cultures; Status was important between buyers' and sellers' profits for some of the cultures
Graham	1985	U.S., Japan, Brazil	Verbal and nonverbal behaviors	Differences observed between the three cultures

❖ GUIDELINES FOR GLOBAL NEGOTIATION SUCCESS

1. Using secondary sources, learn about the cultures (and other aspects, such as legal and political environment) of the country and region you will be visiting and negotiating in. Learn about the elements of culture as well as the nonverbal and organizational aspects of the cultures.

2. Talk to others, including other noncompetitive firms, who have visited and done business in the area to which you are planning to go. Ask about their experiences and perceptions. Remember that this is just information gathering and should not be considered the "final word."

3. Assess how the culture you are learning about is different from your own cultural values and behaviors. Determine differences that may require you to adapt your behaviors and attitudes in order to adjust to your counterpart's behaviors. For example, do you and your counterpart define *on time* in the same way? If not, how should you adjust your expectations?

4. When planning your trip to the foreign country, add 2 days to the beginning of the trip (i.e., arrive early) in order to give yourself time to adjust to the environment and recover from jet lag. Also, keep your schedule as flexible as possible in the foreign country. It is advisable not to schedule anything too important immediately after your scheduled return time in case it is necessary to modify your travel plans.

5. Determine if you need an interpreter and/or a translator and make arrangements.

6. Be sure to have the appropriate number and types of gifts for the country you are visiting.

7. After each meeting with your foreign counterparts, debrief with your team and assess your cultural interactions and responses. What went well, and what didn't? Adapt your strategy for the subsequent meetings (typically, on a foreign visit, there is more than one meeting scheduled).

❖ DISCUSSION QUESTIONS

1. Summarize the cultural frameworks of Hall, Hofstede, and Trompenaars. Identify the similarities and differences among the three frameworks.

2. Summarize Adler and Graham's four levels of culture-related challenges in international negotiation. Discuss a strategy you would use to overcome each challenge.

3. What is the difference between an interpreter and a translator? How would you use each?

4. Assess your own perception of time for business and for social situations. Thinking about past experiences, how do you react to others whose time perception is different from your own?

5. For each stage of the negotiation process, identify and discuss how culture influences international negotiation.

❖ REFERENCES

Adler, N., & Graham, J. (1989). Cross-cultural interaction: The international comparison fallacy? *Journal of International Business Studies, 20*(3), 515–537.
BBC. Fresh violence hits Paris suburbs. (2005, November 3). Retrieved May, 2006, from http://news.bbc.co.uk
Brett, J., & Okumura, T. (1998). Inter- and intra-cultural negotiation: U.S. and Japanese negotiation. *Academy of Management Journal, 41*(5), 495–570.
Elahee, M., Kirby, S., & Nasif, E. (2002). National culture, trust, and perceptions about ethical behavior in intra- and cross-cultural negotiations: An analysis of NAFTA countries. *Thunderbird International Business Review, 44*(6), 799.
Faiola, A. (2005, December 15). $17 Japanese apples for a ka-ching dynasty: China's newly rich gobble boutique-fruit exports. *Washington Post Foreign Service,* p. D01.
Francis, J. (1991). When in Rome? The effects of cultural adaptation on intercultural business negotiations. *Journal of International Business Studies, 22,* 403–428.
Fraser, C., & Zarkada-Fraser, A. (2002). An exploratory investigation into cultural awareness and approach to negotiations of Greek, Russian, and British managers. *European Business Review, 14*(2), 111–127.
Gelfand, M., & Christakopoulou, S. (1999). Culture and negotiator cognition: Judgment accuracy and negotiation processes in individualistic and collectivist cultures. *Organizational Behavior and Human Decision Processes, 79*(3), 248–269.
Graham, J. (1985). The influence of culture on the process of business negotiations: An exporatory study. *Journal of International Business Studies, 16*(1), 81–96.
Graham, J. (1988). Deference given the buyer: Variations across twelve cultures. In F. Contractor & P. Lorange (Eds.), *Cooperative strategies in international business* (pp. 473–485). Lexington, MA: D.C. Heath.
Graham, J. (1996). The importance of culture in international business negotiations. In J. D. Usunier & P. H. Ghauri (Eds.), *International Business Communications.* Oxford: Elsevier Science.

Graham, J., Mintu, A., & Rodgers, W. (1994). Explorations of negotiation behaviors in ten foreign cultures using a model developed in the United States. *Management Science, 40*(1), 72–95.

Hall, E. T. (1976). *Beyond culture.* New York: Anchor Books Doubleday.

Hall, E. T., & Hall, M. R. (1987). *Hidden differences: Doing business with the Japanese.* New York: Anchor Books Doubleday.

Hendon, D., Roy, M., & Ahmed, Z. (2003). Negotiation concession patterns: A multi-country, multiperiod study. *American Business Review, 21*(1), 75–83.

Hise, R., Solano-Mendez, R., & Gresham, L. (2003). Doing business in: Mexico. *Thunderbird International Business Review, 45*(2), 211.

Hofstede, G. (1983). National cultures in four dimensions: A research-based theory of cultural differences among nations. *International Studies of Management and Organization, 12*(1–2), 46–74.

Hofstede, G. (1984). *Culture's consequences: International differences in work-related values.* Beverly Hills, CA: Sage.

Hofstede, G. (1989). Organising for cultural diversity. *European Management Journal, 19*(4), 390–397.

Kumar, R. (1999). Communicative conflict in intercultural negotiations: The case of American and Japanese business negotiations. *International Negotiation, 4,* 63–78.

Kluckholn, F. & Strodtbeck, F., (1961) *Variations in Value Orientations,* Evanston, IL: Row, Peterson.

Lituchy, T. (1997). Negotiations between Japanese and Americans: The effects of collectivism on integrative outcomes. *Canadian Journal of Administrative Sciences, 14*(4), 386–395.

Mintu-Wimsatt, A., & Gassenheimer, J. (2000). The moderating effects of cultural context in buyer-seller negotiation. *Journal of Personal Selling & Sales Management, 21*(1), 1–9.

Osman-Gani, A., & Tan, J. S. (2002). Influence of culture on negotiation styles of Asian managers: An empirical study of major cultural/ethnic groups in Singapore. *Thunderbird International Business Review, 44*(6), 819.

Paik, Y., & Tung, R. (1999). Negotiating with East Asians: How to attain "win-win" outcomes. *Management International Business Review, 39*(2), 103–122.

Palich, L., Carini, G., & Livingstone, L. (2002). Comparing American and Chinese negotiating styles: The influence of logic paradigms. *Thunderbird International Business Review, 44*(6), 777.

Platt, P. (1994). *French or foe?* London: Culture Crossings.

Ricks, D. A. (1993). *Blunders in international business* (2nd ed.). Oxford: Blackwell.

Ricks, D. A. (1999). *Blunders in international business* (3rd ed.). Oxford: Blackwell.

Shi, X., & Wright, P. (2001). Developing and validating an international business negotiator's profile: The China context. *Journal of Managerial Psychology, 16*(5/6), 364–389.

Ting-Toomey, S. (1999). *Communicating across cultures.* New York: Guilford Press.

Trompenaars, F. (1994). *Riding the waves of culture: Understanding diversity in global business.* New York: Irwin Professional Publishing.

Ulijn, J., & Verweij, M. (2000). Questioning behavior in monocultural and inter-cultural technical business negotiations: The Dutch-Spanish connection. *Discourse Studies, 2*(2), 217–248.

Volkema, R., & Leme Fleury, M. T. (2002). Alternative negotiating conditions and the choice of negotiation tactics: A cross-cultural comparison. *Journal of Business Research, 36*.

Zarkada-Fraser, A., & Fraser, C. (2001). Moral decision making in international sales negotiations. *Journal of Business & Industrial Marketing, 16*(4), 274–291.

5

Communication Profile

Characteristics, Behaviors, and Skills

How we often act is based on what comes natural to us. Researchers periodically refer to these natural tendencies as traits, characteristics, styles, or cultural behaviors. To understand international business negotiation, we must embrace the individual effects and the interrelatedness of individual and cultural factors. This chapter discusses the role of the individual negotiator's communication characteristics, traits, and behaviors as influencing factors in global business transactions. The focus is on the *individual* communication characteristics that are critical to the negotiation process, especially in the international marketplace.

❖ OUR PERSPECTIVE

There are a number of competing perspectives about the origin of how we develop our communication style. For example, O'Keefe (1988) argues in her presentation of "Logic of Message Design" model that individuals may differ in their communication because they construct and interpret messages differently. Beatty, McCroskey, and Valencic (2001) propose a communibiological perspective, suggesting some communication behavior (e.g., verbal aggression) is tied to our personality traits, which are genetically derived. Others suggest a social learning perspective, positing that communication is a result of what we learn. Still others argue that communication behavior is contextually based.

And finally, there are those of us who view communication behavior as a factor of traits, learning, contexts, and motivation. We argue that at different times we may behave more trait-like whereas at other times we are influenced by the context. Thus, both trait and situation are factors that contribute to how one communicates and develops one's communication characteristics. We believe that individual negotiators exhibit preferred communication behaviors that can be thought of as characteristics. That is, these behaviors become a preference that captures the individuals' negotiation style.

We argue that one must be mindful that communication is a combination of our inherent nature and our environment. There is a need to integrate these contending perspectives in order to better understand the communication process in the international business negotiation. Therefore, this chapter attempts to answer, "What are the critical communication characteristics in international negotiation and how do certain communication behaviors contribute to the global negotiation success?"

❖ AN INTEGRATIVE COMMUNICATION APPROACH FOR INTERNATIONAL BUSINESS NEGOTIATIONS

The significance of examining individual factors (characteristics) has been largely ignored in explaining the intercultural negotiation context. Rather, extensive work on intercultural interactions has focused on the cultural level analysis (Gudykunst, 2005; Hofstede, 1980; Triandis, 1995). This alone is insufficient for understanding intercultural business transactions (Kim, Kim, Hunter, & Kim, 2001; Singelis & Brown, 1995).

With the advancement to an international marketplace, cultures reflect a more diversified makeup. Therefore, the cultural generalities that once guided us in conducting business across cultures have become blurred. This global change requires a fresh approach for communicating in business negotiations. It is imperative to consider how culture level and individual *communication characteristics* and *behaviors* affect the geocentric business transaction. Support for using a multilevel approach for understanding intercultural communication has surfaced.

For example, Gudykunst (1997) argues that understanding communication requires us to examine individual characteristics that influence our culture as culture influences us. In addition, he argues that in some cases individual factors explain more of the communication behavior than culture. Further support is provided by Kim, Kim, Hunter, and Kim (2001). They contend that many researchers are "supportive of an individual-level approach to theorizing about cross-cultural differences" (pp. 383–384). Interpersonal communication scholars also have concluded a need for examining communication characteristics to understand communication behaviors in social interactions (Beatty, McCroskey, & Valencic, 2001). Although researchers may disagree to what extent individual factors contribute to intercultural communication, all agree that the individual factors, or, as we refer to them, characteristics, are an important element of understanding intercultural interactions.

Several important communication traits and behaviors have been studied over the past several decades (e.g., communication apprehension) that influence the communication characteristics exhibited in international business negotiations. The communication characteristics, traits, and behaviors that may offer insight into the intercultural business negotiation process that cultural factors fail to explain are of particular interest. As we uncover what communication factors contribute to international business transactions, we can then create a better picture of the global business negotiation. There are four key communication traits or characteristics—argumentativeness, verbal aggressiveness, intercultural communication apprehension, and self-monitoring—that are influential in understanding how conflict is managed and agreements are reached in international business negotiations. What follows is a discussion of these communication characteristics and behaviors and their influence.

❖ ARGUMENTATIVENESS

Argumentativeness in its original conceptualization was considered a communication trait and later examined as an interactional concept (a result of trait and context). Argumentativeness is defined as "a generally stable trait which predisposes the individual in communication situations to advocate positions on controversial issues and to attack verbally the positions which other people take on these issues" (Infante & Rancer, 1982, p. 72). Individuals that are highly argumentative find arguing intellectually exciting, often feel invigorated after a discussion, and experience a sense of satisfaction and accomplishment resulting from discussing controversial issues. Whereas individuals low in the argumentativeness trait find potential communication situations where debate and conflict may occur uncomfortable and try to avoid arguments (Infante, 1982). The communication response of individuals in the middle range of argumentativeness depends to a great extent on the situation. That is, in some conflicts or differences, midrange trait argumentatives will respond, and in other situations, they will not, depending on their personal interests or the importance of the issue being presented.

Every negotiation has periods of argument or confrontation, persuasion, give and take, and active debate. Parties present their positions or interests and offer reasons and justifications for why they believe the other party should meet their expectations as part of the negotiation process. Usually the presentation of one's position is offered in the beginning of the negotiation process, often referred to as the information-sharing stage. However, presenting and promoting one's position continues throughout the negotiation as a style of discourse for resolving differences. Negotiators often present their arguments in a persuasive form to attempt to gain compliance or acceptance from the other party. This is clearly why understanding the impact of one's argumentativeness trait becomes an important factor in international negotiations.

Cultures vary widely in their view of how acceptable this form of negotiation is, and when it is appropriate to engage in the discussion of differences. For example, low-context cultures place a higher value on debate and open argument (e.g., the U.S., Greece), whereas high-context cultures (e.g., Japan, Korea) value a discussion of differences but only after they have developed a relationship with the other. Thus, culture may influence the value and appropriateness of the argumentative communication behavior.

We know the general parameters of how cultures view the exchange of persuasive attempts and debate, but we know little about the individual negotiator's characteristics (specifically argumentativeness) and how those characteristics influence the presentation of his or her position and the refutation behavior. As Avtgis and Rancer (2002) point out, "Researchers cannot assume that people from low-context cultures are similar in the degree to which they are influenced by context" (p. 193). Therefore, we must consider the cultural tendencies for open argument and debate as well as the individual tendency to argue when our goal is to understand and become effective global negotiators.

Argumentativeness in Global Business Negotiations

High Argumentativeness

The impact of an individual's argumentativeness can have a major influence in intercultural business negotiations. For example, the individual who characteristically is highly argumentative is likely to recognize controversial issues and advocate for his or her position by refuting the other party's proposal. The high-argumentative individual will strongly advocate his or her proposal by providing clear logical arguments for why his or her proposal is better and find fault with the opposing party's proposal. The high-argumentative negotiator does not attack or find fault with the other party. Rather, he or she is interested in the controversy of the issues and not in doing harm to the other party. There are several benefits of engaging in argumentation during a negotiation process. Some of those benefits are increased creativity, reduction in self-centered thinking, and an increase in better problem solving and decision making (Johnson & Johnson, 1974). It is easy to see how a high argumentative would be able to follow Fisher, Ury, and Patton's (1991) first principle of negotiation, "separate the people from the problem." Negotiators who are characteristically argumentative are inherently likely to be "hard on the problem and soft on the people."

High-argumentative individuals view arguing as a method for reducing conflict, whereas those low in argumentativeness see arguing as conflict and as something that should be avoided. (Rancer, Baukus, & Infante, 1985) Thus, a negotiator who inherently enjoys debate and has a sense of satisfaction about discussing controversial issues, such as a price agreement, would do well in negotiations with individuals who follow their cultural tendency of interpreting meaning from a low context and individualistic orientation.

However, in high-context and collectivism cultures, high argumentatives need to be more cognizant of their desire to debate and rely on less direct confrontational messages in order to avoid offending others who do not share the same belief about active advocacy. This is important for negotiators who typically communicate from a highly argumentative tendency. By considering their individual characteristics and the culture variables of the negotiation, they will be better prepared for a more effective negotiation.

Low Argumentativeness

Individuals who characteristically avoid engaging in arguments are often referred to as communicators who are low-argumentative individuals. Individuals who are typically low in argumentativeness trait try to prevent arguments from happening. If low argumentatives are forced into an argument, they feel uncomfortable and relieved when the argument is finished. Arguing is unsatisfying and is something that low-argumentative trait individuals try to avoid. This tendency to avoid arguments in some global business transactions can result in missed opportunities to persuade the other party. In some international negotiations, low argumentativeness can be viewed as a strength because it is a valued characteristic of the other party's culture. Obviously, this issue depends on the values and acceptable behaviors of the cultures engaged in the negotiation process.

How Can Argumentativeness Contribute to Global Negotiation Success?

High-argumentative trait individuals would do well in international negotiations in which negotiation is thought of as a communication experience where individuals will engage in debate, strongly advocate for their own position, and refute another's proposal. For example, in negotiations where open debate is frowned upon (i.e., Japan, China, Korea), an individual who prefers not to engage in aggressively advocating and refuting positions may be more successful in reaching an agreement. If negotiators have similar argumentativeness characteristics, they may find it easier to communicate because of their similarity. The important point for intercultural negotiations in regards to argumentativeness is that there are cultural tendencies (Hofstede, 1980) that may influence our individual style to openly communicate in an argumentative manner. This cultural influence coupled with our individual tendency to communicate can influence the negotiation process.

However, high-context, collectivistic cultures may value low-argumentative communication tendencies or style. Asian cultures would likely discourage open disagreement and view open disagreement or argument as an unfavorable communication process for resolving differences, especially in public. Negotiators low in argumentativeness may find conducting business in this type of setting productive. The low-argumentative negotiator who avoids controversial arguments during the negotiation may be viewed (especially in a high-context culture) as someone whose communication style is appropriate or culturally accepted. Thus, the perceived similarity to their culture reduces uncertainty, and trust and relationship development opportunities are enhanced, ultimately leading to efficient agreements.

For example, studies conducted by Prunty, Klopf, and Ishii (1990a, 1990b) concluded that Japanese, when compared to Americans, were less likely to approach argument situations and were significantly lower in the argumentativeness trait. Thus, an American business negotiator low in trait argumentativeness may find negotiating with a Japanese

businessperson more satisfying as well as productive. Open controversy exhibited by a highly argumentative individual would likely
offend a Japanese business negotiator (Barnlund, 1989; Kim et al., 2001).

Moderate Argumentative

The negotiator who characteristically is a moderate argumentative
is most likely to argue in response to the contextual cues. Infante and
Rancer (1996) posited that there are two types of moderates. The first
type of moderate, "conflict feeling," is motivated to argue when the
"probability of success is high and the importance of failure is low"
(p. 322). The second type of moderate argumentative, the "apathetic"
individual, argues when "the incentive of success is high, as they neither like nor dislike arguing and engage in it mainly for utilitarian reasons" (Infante & Rancer, 1996, p. 322). The importance of recognizing
the two types of moderates is that some will engage in argumentative
communication because they believe they can win or because arguing
serves some useful purpose.

Individuals characteristically moderate in argumentativeness may
be well suited for global negotiations because their communication is
dependent on the assessment of arguing successfully or because arguing serves some useful purpose in the negotiation. Thus, the accuracy
of the individual's assessment of "succeeding in arguing" or that
the arguing will present some "utility" or benefit to the negotiation is
important. For international business negotiation, moderate-trait individuals must see the usefulness in presenting and refuting arguments
or believe they will be successful or suffer little if they lose. Thus,
moderate-argumentative negotiators need to be educated in the usefulness and the outcome factors for them to engage in presenting and
refuting arguments. Moderates, regardless of the type, are more dependent on context and situation cues to determine the likelihood of communication behavior. This reliance on the situation cue to determine
whether to engage in advocating and refuting positions makes moderate argumentatives good candidates for international business transactions, especially if they are motivated to negotiate interculturally.

Samovar and Porter (1985) make a strong argument that to be a
competent intercultural communicator, one must have three factors:
knowledge, skill, and motivation. These same three factors hold true for
the global negotiation context, especially for the moderate-argumentative
individual who assesses the situational cues for behavior selection.
As discussed previously in Chapter 3, preparing for the negotiation is
critical to success.

Argumentativeness and International Business Negotiation

Communication researchers have examined argumentativeness from an intercultural perspective (Klopf, Thompson, & Sallinen-Kuparinen, 1991; Prunty, Klopf, & Ishii, 1990a, 1990b; Rahoi, Svenkerud, & Love, 1994).

The research suggests negotiators in cultures that are considered high-context cultures, such as Japan and Korea, are lower in argumentativeness than negotiators in the United States. For example, Prunty, Klopf, and Ishii (1990a, 1990b) looked at the differences in argumentativeness between Japanese and American students. They concluded that the Americans were significantly higher in argumentativeness than the Japanese. Americans were higher in argumentativeness than Koreans (Jenkins, Klopf, & Park, 1991). Fins and Norwegians are higher than the Americans in argumentativeness (Klopf, Thompson, Sallinen-Kuparimen, 1991; Rahoi, Svenkerud, & Love, 1994). These findings are indicative of what we know about the differences in high-context and low-context cultures. Therefore, if we are trying to match or accommodate the other party's communication style in the negotiation in order to facilitate the agreement process, the United States may want a negotiator that is low in argumentativeness or Korea may want negotiators that are higher in argumentativeness than is typical.

Part of the preparation for global business negotiation is assessing negotiating parties' communication styles. Once individuals become aware of their trait-like behaviors, they can develop a style that exemplifies a competent global negotiator. The argumentativeness scale developed by Infante and Rancer (1982) is a 20-item self-report measure for determining one's level of trait argumentativeness. (The 10-item short version is also used to measure argumentativeness and is included at the end of this chapter.) By completing this measure, negotiators can gain valuable insight into their trait behavior. For example, if you are high in argumentativeness, you want to be sensitive to environments where attacking and refutation communication is not going to serve you well in reaching agreement. You will need to adapt your behavior to refute less and develop other strategies for persuading the other party. If you are low in argumentativeness, and you are negotiating with a German company, you want to develop your ability to advocate and refute positions. If you are a moderate argumentative, your assessment of the negotiation is a critical component of your motivation to engage in controversial issues. Essentially, an individual's argumentativeness, whether high, low, or moderate, serves as an important factor in understanding the negotiation process. Even more important is the role that one's argumentativeness may play in interpreting the other party's messages.

The general cultural-specific research combined with the interpersonal knowledge of argumentativeness provides a richer understanding of the geocentric business negotiation. For example, let's assume Kimsu, headquartered in South Korea, is negotiating with company Nuve, headquartered in Norway. Based on the cultural knowledge, we might assume that the negotiator representing Nuve will be highly argumentative compared to the negotiator from Kimsu. Thus, we would expect that the negotiator from Nuve will present logical, rational arguments advocating why Kimsu should buy his or her product. Nuve would also expect that Kimsu would be persuaded by these arguments. However, Kimsu is rather offended by Nuve's need to refute Kimsu's position and responds with silence. If both parties are knowledgeable about their own traits, such as argumentative behavior, they can monitor more closely their tendency to respond in their typical fashion so that they do not alienate the other party. This situation requires that negotiators be cognizant of their general cultural behaviors as well as their individual argumentative communication characteristic to ensure successful communication in reaching an agreement.

Table 5.1   Argumentativeness

High	Moderate	Low
*Strongly advocates for his or her position *Engages in debate *Finds arguing invigorating *Recognizes other party's position and presents counterarguments	*Relies on situational cues *Importance of issues determines motivation to argue	*Avoids debate *Tries to prevent argument *Finds arguing unsatisfying

❖ VERBAL AGGRESSIVENESS

Unlike argumentativeness, verbally aggressive behavior is considered a destructive form of communication that results in attacking another individual's self-concept. The tactics that are used to persuade others during a conflict or disagreement are designed to gain compliance by communication attempts that do psychological harm to another. Most Western scholars view argumentativeness as a constructive form of communicating during disagreement, whereas verbal aggression is viewed as a destructive form. Verbal aggressiveness is defined as a pre-dispositional tendency to attack the "self-concept of another person in order to inflict psychological harm or damage" (Infante & Wigley, 1986). In addition, verbal aggression results in embarrassment, dis-trust, and hurt. Infante explains verbal aggressiveness as a subset of a more general trait—hostility. The destructive effect that verbally aggressive messages have on relationships in families and organiza-tions has been widely studied (Infante, Chandler, & Rudd, 1989; Infante, Myers, & Buerkel, 1994; Rudd & Burant, 1995). However, little research exists on verbal aggression in intercultural settings such as global business negotiations. Yet we know that verbal aggression is a frequent component of the communication process in the business transaction. Thus we believe that verbal aggression may also have a negative effect on global business negotiations.

Often people engaging in negotiation may approach negotiation in a predominantly aggressive manner that may result in exchanges that are verbally aggressive. The negotiation process is typically character-ized as having points of growing tension and even breakdowns. During these highly contentious periods, negotiators may feel frus-trated, if not angry, about such issues as the lack of movement in reaching agreement. Some negotiators respond to these periods by "blowing up," issuing "threats," "name-calling" or a myriad of other verbally aggres-sive destructive communicative messages (Fisher, Ury, & Patton, 1991). Negotiation scholars have written strategies for dealing with these periods. For example, Fisher, Ury, and Patton suggest "sidestepping" when an emotional outburst occurs. They offer "jujitsu strategy" as a strategy for getting parties to engage in win-win negotiation rather than win-lose negotiation. Although these strategies are helpful, we suggest that there is an underlying factor that helps explain why some people may engage in these periods of aggressive tactics—the trait of verbal aggressiveness and situational circumstances.

An individual whose communication is characterized as aggressive provides us with meaningful insight to a negotiator's style of handling periods of tension and disagreement. Not all individuals engaged in disagreements in the negotiation process resort to verbally aggressive messages. The reason may be partially explained by an individual's cul-tural perspective of the appropriateness of using these messages.

Common types of verbally aggressive messages include character attacks, competency attacks ("you are an idiot"), background attacks (derogatory racial comments), attacks on physical appearance ("you are too small to make that claim stick"), ridicule, threats ("I will ruin you"), profanity, malediction ("I hope you lose your job"), teasing ("come on, you girls talk it over and let me know"), and nonverbal emblems (using the middle finger) (Infante, 1987; Infante, Trebing, Shepard, & Seeds, 1984). Infante and Wigley (1986) developed the 20-item Verbal Aggressiveness Scale. This scale has proved to be valid across cultures (Sanders, Gass, Wiseman, & Bruschke, 1992). The 10-item short-version verbal aggressiveness scale is at the end of this chapter.

What Causes Verbal Aggressiveness?

Infante et al. (1984) conclude that there are four possible causes for verbal aggression: (a) psychopathological (transference of repressed hostility from an earlier time), (b) disdain for another person, (c) social learning (society conditions the person to be aggressive), and (d) argumentative skill deficiency (lacks the skills to argue constructively; see discussion of argumentativeness). It is believed that verbal aggression is aroused and energized by frustration (Infante, 1987). Infante goes on to suggest that there are two common sources of frustration: "having to deal with a disdained other and having the achievement of a goal blocked by another person" (p. 183). In addition, verbal aggression has been found to be a major factor in violence (Infante, Chandler, & Rudd, 1989; Toch, 1969). More recently, Beatty, McCroskey, and Valencic (2001) offer a communibiological explanation for verbally aggressive behavior.

High Verbal Aggressiveness

High verbally aggressive individuals are likely to use messages such as threats, character attacks, competency attacks, racial or ethnic attacks, profanity, or maledictions. The use of these messages during a disagreement results in less collaboration and a reduction in probabilities of maximizing a joint outcome. High verbally aggressive individuals in the United States are seen as less credible (Infante et al., 1992) and thus less trustworthy. The reduction of trust results in a damaged relationship and ultimately costs future negotiations or renegotiations.

Negotiators who have a combination of being highly verbally aggressive and low in argumentative skills are most likely to resort to verbally attacking their opponent during conflictual points of the negotiation process. Their choice of tactics and strategies may be limited to aggressive, domineering, and bullying forms as a means for gaining compliance. Keep in mind that highly argumentative individuals are interested in attacking the position of opposition, not the person, whereas the verbally aggressive individual will attack the person in order to do psychological harm. If an individual is low in argumentativeness and high in verbal aggressiveness, the communication tactics and strategies available to him or her are limited and thus the person may be quick to use verbal attacks aimed at the person and not the issues. This type of individual during contentious points in a negotiation communicates verbally aggressive messages in order to defend his or her position. If these verbally aggressive messages are viewed by the other party as personally attacking his or her self-concept, the opportunity for the conflict to quickly escalate can emerge, resulting in an abrupt end to the negotiation discussion.

Low Verbal Aggressiveness

Negotiators who are low in the trait verbal aggressiveness (or individuals who are less likely to use verbally aggressive messages) are not likely to resort to verbally aggressive messages during a conflict. Low verbally aggressive negotiators are more likely to walk away or avoid reciprocating the attack. Attacking someone's character, using threats, ridicule, swearing, profanity, or maledictions is not part of his or her general communication style in conflict. Negotiators who characteristically avoid using verbal aggressiveness are not likely to engage in these types of behaviors. Rather, they may attempt to continue the negotiation without reacting to the verbally aggressive outburst of the other party. Low verbally aggressive individuals may do very well in negotiating about highly intense issues. They can be trusted not to respond in a manner that might offend others.

For example, John (low trait verbal agression) rarely communicates in a verbally aggressive manner when negotiating with others regardless of the amount of conflict. On the other hand, Susan (high trait verbal agression) characteristically uses verbally aggressive messages to convince others of her position in negotiation situations. Both John and Susan enter into a negotiation with each other and quickly reach a stalling point in the negotiation. Susan has exhausted all of her clear arguments for why John should accept her deal. The following is a brief example of the interaction:

John: I just don't see your point.

Susan: I have told you every reason why I cannot accept that price.

John: I thought you understood that we couldn't go any higher.

Susan: Look, I have had it with you digging in your heels.

John: Why are you getting so angry?

Susan: Listen, you dumbass (*character attack*), I will take you down in this industry (*threat*). No one will ever want to do business with you or your company again (*threat*). I hope you lose your job over this (*malediction*). So get the hell (*swearing*) out of my office before I throw you out (*physical threat*).

John may even be surprised by Susan's outburst of aggression because John does not use verbally aggressive messages to gain compliance from another. Susan, however, may feel she has no other way to express her frustration or anger, so she resorts to her typical behavior and begins using verbally aggressive messages. If John is from a culture that highly values respect and formal communication, Susan's verbal aggression could cause a complete breakdown in the negotiation. However, if John is from a culture where aggression is part of everyday communication, Susan's outburst may be tolerated.

Moderate Verbal Aggressiveness

The situation/environmental factors often determine whether an individual who is characteristically a moderate verbally aggressive individual will use verbal aggression. That is, it depends a great deal on the situation whether a moderate verbally aggressive individual will use verbally aggressive messages. Essentially, the person who is moderate in the verbal aggressiveness trait has the ability to engage in attacking behaviors but may not, depending on how invested in the outcome he or she is or how he or she feels about the other person. As a result of this moderate characteristic, some negotiators will never be motivated to attack another verbally during a negotiation whereas in other situations (such as the family context), he or she may often become verbally aggressive. Thus, they are reactive to the contextual cues. The issues, the other party, or the situation greatly influence whether the moderate verbally aggressive individual engages in verbally aggressive messages.

Verbal Aggression and Culture

In the last decade, researchers have extended the study of verbal aggression to intercultural contexts. Most authors have focused their research at the cultural level of analysis looking for differences between cultures. There seems to be some disagreement among the initial studies in this area. For example, Prunty, Klopf, and Ishii (1990b) found no difference between Japanese and American men's verbal aggressiveness but found a significant difference in that American women's verbal aggression tends to be higher than that of Japanese women. A study of ethnic differences, conducted by Sanders et al. (1992), found Asian Americans more verbally aggressive than European Americans and Hispanic Americans. Ma (1990) reported that there are fewer examples of verbal aggression in high-context cultures. This is mainly due to the cultural influences on the communication rules of that culture. What is of particular interest to the global negotiator is the acceptability of the verbally aggressive message and the impact it has on reaching an agreement.

At this time, the intercultural research is limited in the area of verbal aggression. Perhaps a better explanation of verbally aggressive behaviors lies not at the cultural level, but rather at the individual level. This may prove particularly useful in the global business transaction. Therefore, global business negotiators must look beyond cultural tendency for understanding verbally aggressive behavior and consider the individual personality of the other party and of oneself.

❖ INTERCULTURAL COMMUNICATION APPREHENSION

Communication Apprehension

Communication apprehension is one of the most widely studied communication variables in the last several decades. The study of communication apprehension is of increasing importance in the intercultural setting. Because the intercultural relationship is so important in the global marketplace, understanding the effects communication apprehension has on the intercultural negotiation process is worth investigating. In general, relationships develop through communication. If one of the parties is apprehensive about communicating with the other party in a business negotiation, the opportunity for interaction is diminished substantially and the negotiation outcome may be affected. First, we will review communication apprehension in general, after which we will provide a summary of research on communication apprehension and culture and conclude with a discussion of its impact on global business negotiations.

McCroskey first conceptualized communication apprehension as a communication trait in 1970. In general, communication apprehension has been defined as "an individual's level of fear or anxiety associated with either real or anticipated communication with another person or persons" (McCroskey, 1977, 1978). More specifically, the intercultural context in which communication apprehension occurs has been conceptualized as intercultural communication apprehension. Neuliep and McCroskey (1997) defined intercultural communication apprehension as "anxiety associated with either real or anticipated interaction with people from different groups, especially different cultural or ethnic groups" (p. 152). Part of this anxiety is the lack of predictability about another's actions. Both trait communication apprehension and contextually based intercultural communication apprehension are relevant to the study of intercultural negotiation, although they may address different aspects of the anxiety experienced by an individual in the interaction. Knowledge of communication apprehension is particularly useful in planning what negotiation strategies will be most effective (see Chapter 3).

High Communication Apprehension

There are several types of behaviors exhibited by those high in communication apprehension. McCroskey (1997) proposed four behaviors that are likely to occur when an individual experiences an increased level of anxiety in a real or anticipatory social interaction situation. The high communication apprehensive person typically exhibits one or several of the following behaviors: avoiding the interaction (flight), withdrawing from the communication interaction (silence), behaving in disruptive communication patterns (incongruent thoughts expressed), or sometimes talking obsessively.

An example of flight might be someone leaving a place or situation in an attempt to reduce his level of anxiety. Withdrawal is similar to avoidance in that individuals may find themselves in a communication situation that they are very anxious about so they may use silence, shortened speech response, or partial responses to another's questions. A person who displays disruptive communication patterns may demonstrate disconnected verbal messages and unusual nonverbal behaviors. Obsessive talk is most often described as someone who does not allow for turn taking in a conversation. Individuals engaging in obsessive talk dominate through continuous speaking. They often move from one subject to another without considering the relevancy of their topic to the situation (McCroskey, 1997).

So let us explore how an individual's communication apprehension may affect an intercultural negotiation. For example, Mr. Ruiz (from Spain) is a high trait communication apprehension individual. Mr. Ruiz is negotiating a purchase agreement with Ms. Laubie, from Germany. Mr. Ruiz, upon meeting Ms. Laubie, senses a heightened increase in his anxiety. After the initial introductions, Mr. Ruiz is likely to (a) stop talking and experience an awkward silence, (b) use only short responses to Ms. Laubie's questions, (c) appear to be listening but provide irrelevant responses to Ms. Laubie's questions, or (d) start talking obsessively without allowing for Ms. Laubie to respond. The result of Mr. Ruiz's apprehension is likely to affect the relationship in a negative manner. Obviously, the behaviors of Mr. Ruiz may result in ineffective communication until one understands his apprehension. Of course, the magnitude of the damage is dependent on Ms. Laubie's view and her cultural norm of the appropriateness of Mr. Ruiz's behavior.

Low Communication Apprehension

An individual who is characteristically low in communication apprehension is likely to initiate conversations with strangers, talk more, be viewed as more competent, and experience low stress or anxiety in new situations. In Western cultures, low communication apprehension is considered a positive trait (Olaniran & Roach, 1994). Continuing with our example from above, assume Mr. Ruiz is a low communication apprehension individual. Upon meeting Ms. Laubie, he feels comfortable initiating conversation; he experiences little, if any, anxiety in getting to know Ms. Laubie even if Ms. Laubie is rather quiet. He is likely to respond to Ms. Laubie's request for more information immediately and confidently. Whether or not Ms. Laubie finds Mr. Ruiz's low communication apprehension a sign of competency is influenced by the German culture's view of Mr. Ruiz's communication as well as Ms. Laubie's individual perspective.

Contextually Based Communication Apprehension

Finally, those individuals who are neither high nor low in communication apprehension may exhibit contextually based communication apprehension. That is, some people are communication apprehensive only in certain contexts or situations. The anxiety one experiences varies across contexts. For example, some individuals experience anxiety or fear about communication only with a small group, in public speaking, in interpersonal dyads, or in intercultural interactions. Assume Mr. Ruiz is generally thought of as an effective businessman with good communication skills. He seems to communicate relatively easily when he is communicating with his boss or conducting a small group meeting, such as a staff meeting. He enjoys giving public speeches about his company to the local community. However, when he is asked to interact with someone he doesn't know well in a dyadic situation, he becomes anxious and demonstrates uneasiness by talking very little and engaging in incongruent patterns of speech. His colleagues are confused by Mr. Ruiz's behavior because they have seen him in the other communication settings, where he appears to be an outgoing, talkative, and competent individual. Mr. Ruiz's behavior may represent his fear or anxiety associated with interaction with people of different cultures. Until the negotiator is placed in an unfamiliar cultural situation, he or she may be unaware of this apprehension. In fact, the business negotiator may assume that he or she is highly effective based on previous host culture business transactions. However, when faced with an intercultural or international negotiation, the anxiety and uncertainty generated from the new experience may cause the typically effective negotiator to exhibit genuine anxiety and an inability to communicate in his or her typical manner. Neuliep and McCroskey (1997) referred to this anxiety as intercultural communication apprehension. They recently developed an instrument (called the Personal Report of Intercultural Communication Apprehension (PRICA), included at the end of this chapter) for assessing an individual's communication apprehension in intercultural or interethnic interactions.

Cultures and Communication Apprehension

Are there cultural differences in communication apprehension? Over the past several decades, intercultural communication scholars have investigated the role that culture plays in individual communication apprehension (Klopf, 1984). Although the findings are culturally based, they may provide us with a better understanding when we combine them with the individually based research on communication apprehension and intercultural communication apprehension. This combination of culturally and individually based research provides a strong foundation for understanding the role of communication apprehension in global business negotiations.

For example, research has been conducted in a wide variety of countries, such as Australia (Hutchinson, Neuliep, & More, 1995; Klopf, 1984), Hong Kong, Korea (Bruneau, Cambra, & Klopf, 1989; Klopf, 1984), New Zealand (Hackman & Barthel-Hackman, 1993), Japan (Klopf & Cambra, 1979), Sweden (Watson, Monroe, & Atterstrom, 1989), Puerto Rico (Fayer, McCroskey, & Richmond, 1984), Taiwan (Swagler & Ellis, 2003), and the United States. Communication apprehension has proved to be a broadly based concept that can be applied across cultures (Allen, O'Mara, & Andriate, 1986). Most studies have focused on the differences in trait communication apprehension between cultures. As a result, we know that the Japanese tend to be among the highest in trait communication apprehension (Klopf & Cambra, 1979; Klopf, Cambra, & Ishii, 1981). And Koreans reported the lowest communication apprehension (Keaten, Kelly, & Pribyl, 1997). Little difference was found among the United States, Australia, Guam, and the Republic of China (Bruneau, Cambra, & Klopf, 1989). It is interesting to note that first-language and second-language apprehension are strongly related. Allen, Long, O'Mara, and Judd (2003) concluded that communication apprehension found in the first language spoken was the best predictor of second-language communication apprehension. That is, it did not seem to matter how many years someone had been speaking a second language or how long they had lived in the second-language country or how competent they felt about speaking the second language. What contributed most to communication apprehension in second-language individuals was how communication apprehensive they were in their first language. This suggests that communication apprehension is a stable trait that cannot be explained simply by context.

However, deciphering between true high communication apprehension and the use of silence as a strategy in negotiation remains an issue. As Keaten, Kelly, and Pribyl (1997) warn, "theorizing about the cause of silence without empirical data about the internal state of the communicator increases the potential for erroneous conclusions" (p. 324).

To date, it appears that there are some cultural differences in trait communication apprehension, and most agree that intercultural communication apprehension is an important factor in understanding intercultural communication. It is the cultural-level research in combination with the individual-level research on trait and contextual communication apprehension that will provide a more complete understanding of how communication apprehension affects the international business negotiation. This initial research needs further development before any clear conclusions can be reached about the role that general communication apprehension plays in intercultural interaction.

What seems most important in the global market is the influence of intercultural communication apprehension on the negotiation process. For example, we do not know if the United States has more individuals who suffer from intercultural communication apprehension than Egypt. However, we do know, based on the research on intercultural communication apprehension, that someone high in intercultural communication apprehension is not likely to be an effective communicator in global negotiations. Businesses, when selecting candidates for representing them in global business transactions, may want to consider the individual who is low in intercultural communication apprehension (or be willing to provide the necessary training to reduce apprehension for someone who is high in intercultural communication apprehension). This person, given that he or she has the other necessary communication skills, will be less anxious and thus more comfortable in the intercultural situation, allowing him or her to more easily focus on developing a relationship and reaching a successful agreement.

One important factor to consider when examining the influence of communication apprehension on negotiating interculturally is that high communication apprehension may be viewed as a positive rather than as a negative (as it is in the United States). It depends on the cultural perspective. Gudykunst and Ting-Toomey (1988) warn us against thinking negatively about communication apprehension. They advise us to consider how collectivistic cultures that have higher levels of communication apprehension view talk compared to members of individualistic cultures. Kim et al. (2001) concur by warning us that it is dangerous to assume that communication avoidance (communication apprehension) is a deficiency. They propose that in cultures where conformity, humility, and maintaining harmony are highly valued and rewarded, the behaviors of a communication apprehensive individual may be seen as appropriate and competent (p. 384).

Table 5.2   Communication Apprehension Chart

High Trait Communication Apprehension Characteristics

Avoids interaction with others
Withdraws or uses silence
Exhibits disruptive communication patterns
Exhibits obsessive talking

Low Trait Communication Apprehension Characteristics

Initiates conversation with strangers
Experiences low stress or anxiety when communicating with others

Contextually Based Communication Apprehension Characteristics

Experiences anxiety dependent on situation or context (public, group, dyad)
Culture differences may cause communication apprehension

❖ SELF-MONITORING

Some people are better able to adapt their communication behavior to fit many different social situations, whereas others tend to be less flexible or less concerned or less able to meet the social appropriateness cues. Researchers have studied this personality factor and label it as self-monitoring. Snyder (1974) defines self-monitoring as a personality trait-like variable that reflects an individual's ability to adapt, regulate, or control his or her verbal and nonverbal behaviors in social situations. He goes on to differentiate the high and low self-monitors by stating,

> Individuals differ in the extent to which they monitor (observe and control) their expressive behavior and self-presentation. Out of a concern for social appropriateness, the self-monitoring individual is particularly sensitive to the expression and self-presentation of others in social situations and uses these cues as guidelines for monitoring and managing his own self-presentation and expressive behavior. (p. 536)

Snyder (1974) describes the low self-monitor as someone who has "little concern for the appropriateness of his presentation and expression, pays less attention to the expression of others, and monitors and controls his presentation to a lesser extent" (p. 536). He describes the low self-monitor as one who looks within himself for determining behavior rather than (like the high self-monitor) relying on social cues to assess the appropriateness of the message for the situation.

High and Low Self-Monitoring

Over the years, researchers have found several differences between the high and low self-monitor. For example, high self-monitors in the U.S. culture are generally more effective at persuading others (Dabbs, Evans, Hopper, & Purvis, 1980) and are more effective at judging their behavior (Snyder, 1979; Turner, 1980). They have control of their emotional expressions (Ickes & Barnes, 1977), feel a need to talk more and initiate conversations (Ickes & Barnes, 1977), are better at deceiving and detecting deception (Brandt, Miller, & Hocking 1980; Siegman & Reynolds, 1983; Stiff, Corman, Krizek, & Snider, 1994), can control their nonverbal behaviors in deceptive and truthful messages (Stiff et al., 1994), and can use facial and vocal channels of expression to communicate a variety of emotions (Lippa, 1978; Snyder, 1979). Individuals high in self-monitoring attempt to understand the affective or emotional states of others (Geizer, Rarick, & Soldow, 1977), are more accurate in inferring others' intentions of communicating (Mills, 1984), and seek out social comparison information (Snyder, 1974).

Low self-monitors act according to their internal values and beliefs (Snyder, 1979), are guided by their internal cues (Brockner & Eckenrode, 1977; Snyder, 1976), use passive strategies to reduce uncertainty (Berger, 1979; Berger & Douglas, 1981), and seem less able to use deceptive communication (Stiff et al., 1994).

Snyder (1974) developed a measurement for assessing an individual's self-monitoring behavior. Although there have been a considerable number of versions and modifications (Briggs & Cheek, 1986; Briggs, Cheek, & Buss, 1980; Dillard, Hunter, & Burgoon, 1984; Gabrenya & Arkin, 1980; Lennox & Wolfe, 1984; Snyder & Gangestad, 1986) to Snyder's original self-monitoring scale, it is frequently used and considered a valid measure of self-monitoring. This scale is included at the end of this chapter.

Culture and Self-Monitoring

Self-monitoring has an impact on how we communicate interculturally. For example, Gudykunst (1985) discovered that self-monitoring influences an individual's choice of strategies in attempting to reduce the uncertainty in cross-cultural contexts. Not only is strategy selection affected by self-monitoring, but also one's culture may determine whether one is likely to exhibit high or low self-monitoring behaviors. Gudykunst, Yang, and Nishida (1987) found that the United States is significantly higher in self-monitoring than Japan or Korea. They also compared Koreans and Japanese and found no significant difference. This suggests that individualistic and collectivistic cultures may reflect a difference in an individual's self-monitoring ability. Their research supports Hofstede's contention that individualistic cultures engage in more self-monitoring than collectivistic cultures (p. 27).

Recently, self-monitoring has been studied in the negotiation process. Gelfand and Dyer (2000) contend that self-regulation is an important aspect of understanding how the intercultural negotiator attempts to achieve his or her goals. Specifically, they suggest that individuals use primary control, which is an attempt to change others in order to meet their own needs, or secondary control, which refers to changing themselves to fit with the environment. This secondary control of communication behavior is what high self-monitors do well.

We suggest that the culture does not determine whether an individual uses primary or secondary control (as suggested by Schwartz, 1994), but rather the high self-monitor innately is going to respond to the culture and the environment of the intercultural experience. By relying on the cues or stimulus present, the high self-monitor recognizes the most appropriate response manner, given that he or she has the knowledge to evaluate what messages are likely to work. A high self-monitor who is knowledgeable about the other party's culture, organization, and the individual negotiator will likely be a more effective negotiator.

Low self-monitors rely on internal cues that may reflect their culture. Thus, their communication behavior may be successful in cultures that are similar to theirs. Low self-monitors may be viewed as consistent in their behavior and thus seen as honest and trustworthy. This is true only if the other party has similar values; otherwise, the low self-monitor may be viewed as rude and ethnocentric.

❖ CONCLUSION

Successful negotiators develop certain communication characteristics and behaviors that are influenced by their personality; their culture; their experiences, including educational and experiential; and their situations, as well as many other contributors that we have yet to study. The importance for the international business negotiator is not to be bogged down in the question, is it our personality trait or is it the situation that determines behavior? Rather, the goal is to understand ourselves, others, and situations so that we can attempt to negotiate with others who are individually and culturally different from us in a respectful and efficient manner. To do this, individuals need to know how they characteristically communicate in negotiating and how others may use messages differently, especially in an intercultural interaction.

To move forward into the new paradigm of the global economy, international business negotiators and managers must reconsider the role that argumentativeness, verbal aggressiveness, self-monitoring, and communication apprehension may play in one's ability to be a competent and successful negotiator in the international marketplace.

❖ GUIDELINES FOR GLOBAL NEGOTIATION SUCCESS

1. Educate yourself on the communication styles and characteristics of the other negotiating party.

2. Know your communication style by examining your argumentativeness, verbal aggression, self-monitoring, and intercultural communication apprehension.

3. Do you know the style of the individual you will be primarily working with?

4. Educate yourself on behaviors that may represent communication traits and characteristics (here are some possible questions for you to think about):

   a. Do you enjoy debating issues with people who are different from you?

   b. Are swearing, threats, and attacking competency part of your communication and/or the other party's communication?

   c. Are you or the other party able to notice subtle cues from each other's nonverbal facial expressions? Do you adjust quickly to a change in topic, style, or mood?

   d. Do you engage in obsessive talk or disruptive communication patterns that are not due to language barriers?

5. Examine your communication expectations about intercultural interactions.

❖ DISCUSSION QUESTIONS

1. What are the benefits of being a high argumentative negotiator?

2. What countries/cultures would most likely value a low verbally aggressive negotiator? What cultures would be least likely to be offended by verbal aggression, if any?

3. High self-monitors might find difficulty negotiating with what level of argumentative? Verbal aggressive? Communication apprehension?

4. What communication characteristics would the most effective global negotiator in the marketplace have today?

5. What characteristics do you view as destructive to the negotiation process? Are there any exceptions to this?

❖ SHORT-FORM VERSION OF THE INFANTE AND RANCER (1982) ARGUMENTATIVENESS SCALE

Instructions: This questionnaire contains statements about arguing controversial issues. Indicate how often each statement is true for you personally by placing the appropriate number in the blank to the left of the statement. Use the following scale:

1 = almost never true
2 = rarely true
3 = occasionally true
4 = often true
5 = almost always true

_____ 1. While in an argument, I worry that the person I am arguing with will form a negative impression of me.

_____ 2. I am energetic and enthusiastic when I argue.

_____ 3. I enjoy a good argument over a controversial issue.

_____ 4. I prefer being with people who rarely disagree with me.

_____ 5. I enjoy defending my point of view on an issue.

_____ 6. When I finish arguing with someone, I feel nervous and upset.

_____ 7. I consider an argument an exciting intellectual challenge.

_____ 8. I find myself unable to think of effective points during an argument.

_____ 9. I have the ability to do well in an argument.

_____10. I try to avoid getting into arguments.

SOURCE: From Infante, D. A., Anderson' C. M., Martin, M. M., Herington, A. D., & Kim, J. Subordinates' satisfaction and perceptions of superiors' compliance-gaining tactics, argumentativeness, verbal aggressiveness, and style, in *Management Communication Quarterly, 6*, 307–326, copyright © 1993. Reprinted with permission of Sage Publications, Inc.

❖ SHORT-FORM VERSION OF THE INFANTE AND
    WIGLEY (1986) VERBAL AGGRESSIVENESS SCALE

Instructions: This survey is concerned with how we try to get people
to comply with our wishes. Indicate how often each statement is true
for you personally when you try to influence other persons. Use the
following scale:

1 = almost never true
2 = rarely true
3 = occasionally true
4 = often true
5 = almost always true

_____ 1. I am extremely careful to avoid attacking individuals'
            intelligence when I attack their ideas.
_____ 2. When individuals are very stubborn, I use insults to
            soften their stubbornness.
_____ 3. I try very hard to avoid having other people feel bad
            about themselves when I try to influence them.
_____ 4. If individuals I am trying to influence really deserve
            it, I attack their character.
_____ 5. I try to make people feel good about themselves even
            when their ideas are stupid.
_____ 6. When people simply will not budge on a matter of
            importance, I lose my temper and say rather strong
            things to them.
_____ 7. When individuals insult me, I get a lot of pleasure
            out of really telling them off.
_____ 8. When I attack others' ideas, I try not to damage
            their self-concepts.
_____ 9. When I try to influence people, I make a great effort
            not to offend them.
_____10. When nothing seems to work in trying to influence
            others, I yell and scream in order to get some movement
            from them.

SOURCE: From Infante, D. A., Anderson' C. M., Martin, M. M., Herington, A. D., & Kim,
J. Subordinates' satisfaction and perceptions of superiors' compliance-gaining tactics,
argumentativeness, verbal aggressiveness, and style, in *Management Communication Quarterly*,
6, 307–326, copyright © 1993. Reprinted with permission of Sage Publications, Inc.

❖ SELF-MONITORING SCALE

Instructions: The statements below concern your personal reactions to a number of different situations. No two statements are exactly alike, so consider each statement carefully before answering. If a statement is a TRUE or MOSTLY TRUE as applied to you, mark T. If it is FALSE or MOSTLY FALSE as applied to you, mark F. It is important to answer as frankly and honestly as you can.

_____ 1. I find it hard to imitate the behavior of other people.

_____ 2. My behavior is usually an expression of my true inner feelings, attitudes, and beliefs.

_____ 3. At parties and social gatherings, I do not attempt to do or say things that others will like.

_____ 4. I can only argue for ideas that I already believe.

_____ 5. I can make impromptu speeches even on topics about which I have almost no information.

_____ 6. I guess I put on a show to impress or entertain people.

_____ 7. When I am uncertain how to act in a social situation, I look to the behavior of others for clues.

_____ 8. I would probably make a good actor.

_____ 9. I rarely need the advice of my friends to choose movies, books, or music.

_____10. I sometimes appear to others to be experiencing deeper emotions than I actually am.

_____11. I laugh more when I watch a comedy with others than when alone.

_____12. In a group of people, I am rarely the center of attention.

_____13. In different situations and with different people, I often act like very different people.

_____14. I am not particularly good at making other people like me.

_____15. Even if I am not enjoying myself, I often pretend to be having a good time.

_____16. I'm not always the person I appear to be.

_____17. I would not change my opinions (or the way I do things) in order to please someone else or win someone's favor.

_____18. I have considered being an entertainer.

_____19. In order to get along and be liked, I tend to be what people expect me to be rather than anything else.

_____20. I have never been good at games like charades or improvisational acting.

_____21. I have trouble changing my behavior to suit different people and different situations.

_____22. At a party, I let others keep the jokes and stories going.

_____23. I feel a bit awkward in company and do not show up quite as well as I should.

_____24. I can look anyone in the eye and tell a lie with a straight face (if for a right end).

_____25. I may deceive people by being friendly when I really dislike them.

Scoring the Self-Monitoring Scale

The following is the scoring key as if answered by a pure high self-monitor. Compare these answers with your own and give yourself 1 point for every answer that matches this key.

Give yourself one point each if you answered F to questions 1,2,3,4,9,12,14,17,20,21,22,23.

Give yourself one point each if you answered T to questions 5,6,7,8,10,11,13,15,16,18,19,24,25.

If your score was between 18–25, you are a HIGH self-monitor.

If your score was between 11–17, you are in the MIDrange, having characteristics of both HIGH and LOW self-monitors. Your position in the midrange indicates toward which end you may lean.

If your score is between 0–10, you are a LOW self-monitor.

SOURCE: From Snyder, M. Self-monitoring of expressive behavior, in _Journal of Personality and Social Psychology, 30_, copyright © 1974. Used with permission by Center for the Study of the Individual and Society.

❖ PERSONAL REPORT OF INTERCULTURAL
COMMUNICATION APPREHENSION

Use the following scale:

1 = strongly agree, 2 = agree, 3 = are undecided, 4 = disagree,
5 = strongly disagree

_____ 1. Generally, I am comfortable interacting with a group of people from different cultures.

_____ 2. I am tense and nervous while interacting in group discussions with people form different cultures.

_____ 3. I like to get involved in group discussions with others who are from different cultures.

_____ 4. Engaging in a group discussion with people from different cultures makes me tense and nervous.

_____ 5. I am calm and relaxed when interacting with a group of people who are from different cultures.

_____ 6. While participating in a conversation with a person from a different culture I feel very nervous.

_____ 7. I have no fear of speaking up in a conversation with a person from a different culture.

_____ 8. Ordinarily I am very tense and nervous in conversations with a person from a different culture.

_____ 9. Ordinarily I am very calm and relaxed in conversations with a person from a different culture.

_____10. While conversing with a person from a different culture, I feel very relaxed.

_____11. I'm afraid to speak up in conversations with a person from a different culture.

_____12. I face the prospect of interacting with people from different cultures with confidence.

_____13. My thoughts become confused and jumbled when interacting with people from different cultures.

_____14. Communicating with people from different cultures makes me feel uncomfortable.

To score the instrument, reverse your original response for items 2, 4, 6, 8, 11, 13, and 14. For example, for each of these items 1 = 5, 2 = 4, 3 = 3, 4 = 2, 5 = 1. If your original score for Item #2 was 1, change it to a 5. If your original score for Item #4 was 2, change it to a 4, etc. After reversing the score for these seven items, then sum all 14 items. Scores cannot be higher than 70 or lower than 14. Higher scores (e.g., 50–70) indicate high intercultural communication apprehension. Low scores (e.g., 14–28) indicated low intercultural communication apprehension.

SOURCE: From Neuliep, J. W., & McCroskey, J. C. The development of intercultural and interethnic communication apprehension scales, in *Communication* Research Reports (14)2, copyright © 1997. Reproduced by permission of Taylor & Francis Group, LLC., http://www.taylorandfrancis.com

❖ REFERENCES

Allen, J. L., Long, K. M., O'Mara, J., & Judd B. B. (2003). Verbal and nonverbal orientations toward communication and the development of intracultural and intercultural relationships. *Journal of Intercultural Communication Research, 32*(3), 129–160.

Allen, J. L., O'Mara, J., & Andriate, G. (1986). Communication apprehension in bilingual non-native U.S. residents part II: Gender, second language experience and communication apprehension in functional contexts. *World Communication, 15*(1), 39–48.

Avtgis, T. A., & Rancer, A. S. (2002). Aggressive communication across cultures: A comparison of aggressive communication among United States, New Zealand, and Australia. *Journal of Intercultural Communication Research, 31*(3), 191–200.

Barnlund, D. C. (1989). *Communicative styles of Japanese and Americans: Images and realities.* Belmont, CA: Wadsworth.

Beatty, M. J., & McCroskey, J. C. (1998). Interpersonal communication as temperamental expression: A communibiological paradigm. In J. C. McCroskey, J. Daly, M. M. Martin, & M. J. Beatty (Eds.), *Communication and personality: Trait perspectives* (pp. 41–68). Cresskill, NJ: Hampton.

Beatty, M. J., & McCroskey, J. C., & Heisel, A. D. (1998). Communication apprehension as temperamental expression: A communibiological paradigm. *Communication Monographs, 65,* 197–217.

Beatty, M. J., McCroskey, J. C., & Valencic, K. M. (2001). *The biology of communication: A communibiological perspective.* Cresskill, NJ: Hampton.

Berger, C. R. (1979). Beyond initial interaction: Uncertainty, understanding, and the development of interpersonal relationships. In H. Giles & R. St. Clair (Eds.), *Language and social psychology* (pp. 122–144). Baltimore, MD: University Park Press.

Berger, C. R., & Douglas, W. (1981). Studies in interpersonal epistemology III: Anticipated interaction, self-monitoring, and observational context selection. *Communication Monographs, 48,* 183–196.

Brandt, D. R., Miller, G. R., & Hocking, J. E. (1980). Effects of self-monitoring and familiarity on deception detection. *Communication Quarterly, 28,* 3–10.

Briggs, S. R., & Cheek, J. M. (1986). The role of factor analysis in the development of an evaluation of personality scales. *Journal of Personality, 54,* 106–148.

Briggs, S. R., Cheek, J. M., & Buss, A. H. (1980). An analysis of the self-monitoring scale. *Journal of Personality and Social Psychology, 38,* 679–686.

Brockner, J., & Eckenrode, J. (1977). *Self-monitoring and the actor-observer bias.* Unpublished manuscript, Department of Psychology, State University of New York at Brockport.

Bruneau, T., Cambra, R., & Klopf, D. (1989). Communication apprehension: Its incidence in Guam and elsewhere. *Communication, 9,* 46–52.

Dabbs, J. M., Evans, M. S., Hopper, C. H., & Purvis, J. A. (1980). Self-monitors in conversation: What do they monitor? *Journal of Personality and Social Psychology, 39,* 278–284.

Dillard, J. P., Hunter, J. E., & Burgoon, M. (1984). *Question about the construct validity of the emotional empathy scale, the self-consciousness scale, and the self-monitoring scale.* Paper presented at the meeting of the International Communication Association, San Francisco.

Fayer, J. M., McCroskey, J. C., & Richmond, V. P. (1984). Communication apprehension in Puerto Rico and the United States: Initial comparisons. *Communication, 13,* 49–66.

Fisher, R., Ury, W., & Patton, B. (Ed.). (1991). *Getting to yes, negotiating agreement without giving in* (2nd ed.). New York: Penguin Books.

Gabrenya, W. K., & Arkin, R. M. (1980). Self-monitoring scale: Factor structure and correlates. *Personality and Social Psychology Bulletin, 6,* 13–22.

Geizer, R. S., Rarick, D. L., & Soldow, G. F. (1977). Deception and judgment accuracy: A study in person perception. *Personality and Social Psychology Bulletin, 3,* 446–449.

Gelfand, M. J., & Dyer, N. (2000). A cultural perspective on negotiation: Progress, pitfalls, and prospects. *Applied Psychology: An International Review, 49*(1), 62–99.

Gudykunst, W. B. (1985). The influence of cultural similarity, type of relationship, and self-monitoring on uncertainty reduction processes. *Communication Monographs, 52,* 203–217.

Gudykunst, W. B. (1997). Cultural variability in communication. *Communication Research, 24*(4), 327–349.

Gudykunst, W. B. (Ed.). (2005). *Theorizing about intercultural communication.* Thousand Oaks, CA: Sage.

Gudykunst, W. B., & Ting-Toomey, S. (with Chua, E.). (1988). *Culture and interpersonal communication.* Newbury Park, CA: Sage.

Gudykunst, W. B., Yang, S., & Nishida, T. (1987). Cultural differences in self-monitoring and self-consciousness. *Communication Research, 14,* 7–34.

Hackman, M. Z., & Barthel-Hackman, T. A. (1993). Communication apprehension, willingness to communicate, and sense of humor: United States and New Zealand perspectives. *Communication Quarterly, 41,* 282–291.

Hofstede, G. (1980). *Culture's consequences: International differences in work-related values.* Beverly Hills, CA: Sage.

Hutchinson, K., Neuliep, J., & More, E. (1995). Communication apprehension across cultures: A test of the PRCA-24 and comparisons between Australia and the United States. *Australia Journal of Communication, 25,* 267–293.

Ickes, W., & Barnes, R. D. (1977). The role of sex and self-monitoring in unstructured dyadic interaction. *Journal of Personality and Social Psychology, 35,* 315–330.

Infante, D. A. (1982). The argumentative student in the speech communication classroom: An investigation and implications. *Communication Education, 31,* 141–148.

Infante, D. A. (1987). Aggressiveness. In J. C. McCroskey & J. A. Daly (Eds.), *Personality and interpersonal communication* (pp. 157–192). Newbury Park, CA: Sage.

Infante, D. A., Anderson, C. M., Martin, M. M., Herington, A. D., & Kim, J. (1993). Subordinates' satisfaction and perceptions of superiors' compliance-gaining tactics, argumentativeness, verbal aggressiveness, and style. *Management Communication Quarterly, 6,* 307–326.

Infante, D. A., Chandler, T. A., & Rudd, J. E. (1989). Test of an argumentative skill deficiency model of interspousal violence. *Communication Monographs, 56,* 163–177.

Infante, D. A., Hartley, K. C., Martin, M. M., Higgins, M. A., Bruning, S. D., & Hur. G. (1992). Initiating and reciprocating verbal aggression: Effects on credibility and credited valid arguments. *Communication Studies, 43,* 182–190.

Infante, D. A., Myers, S. A., & Buerkel, R. A. (1994). Argument and verbal aggression in constructive and destructive family and organizational disagreements. *Western Journal of Communication, 58*(2), 73–83.

Infante, D. A., & Rancer, A. S. (1982). A conceptualization and measure of argumentativeness. *Journal of Personality Assessment, 46*(1), 72–80.

Infante, D. A., & Rancer, A. S. (1996). Argumentativeness and verbal aggressiveness: A review of recent theory and research. In B. R. Burleson, & A. W. Kunkel (Eds.), *Communication yearbook 19* (pp. 319–351). Thousand Oaks, CA: Sage.

Infante, D. A., Trebing, D., Shepherd, P. E., & Seeds, D. E. (1984). The relationship of argumentativeness to verbal aggression. *Southern Speech Communication Journal, 50,* 67–77.

Infante, D. A., & Wigley, C. J. (1986). Verbal aggressiveness: An interpersonal model and measure. *Communication Monographs, 53,* 61–69.

Jenkins, G. D., Klopf, D. W., & Park, M. S. (1991). *Argumentativeness in Korean and American college students: A comparison.* Paper presented at the annual meeting of the World Communication Association, Jyvaskyla, Finland.

Johnson, D. W., & Johnson, R. T. (1974). Conflict in the classroom: Controversy and learning. *Review of Educational Research, 49,* 51–70.

Keaten, J., Kelly, L., & Pribyl, C. B. (1997). Communication apprehension in Japan: Grade school through secondary school. *International Journal of Intercultural Relations, 21*(3), 319–343.

Kim, M., Kim, H., Hunter, J. E., & Kim, J. (2001). The effect of culture and self-construals on predispositions toward verbal communication. *Human Communication Research, 27*(3), 382–408.

Klopf, D. W. (1984). Cross-cultural apprehension research. A summary of Pacific Basin studies. In J. A. Daly & J. C. McCroskey (Eds.), *Avoiding communication: Shyness, reticence, and communication apprehension* (pp. 157–172). Beverly Hills, CA: Sage.

Klopf, D. W., & Cambra, R. (1979). Communication apprehension among college students in America, Australia, Japan, and Korea. *Journal of Psychology, 102,* 27–31.

Klopf, D. W., Cambra, R. E., & Ishii, S. (1981). A comparison of communication styles of Japanese and American college students. *Current English Studies, 20,* 66–71.

Klopf, D. W., Thompson, C. A., & Sallinen-Kuparinen, S. (1991). Argumentativeness among selected Finnish and American college students. *Psychological Reports, 68,* 161–162.

Lennox, R. D., & Wolfe, R. N. (1984). Revision of the self-monitoring scale. *Journal of Personality and Social Psychology, 46,* 1349–1364.

Lippa, R. (1978). Expressive control, expressive consistency, and the correspondence between expressive behavior and personality. *Journal of Personality, 46,* 438–461.

Ma, R. (1990). An exploratory study of discontented responses in American and Chinese relationships. *Southern Communication Journal, 55,* 305–318.

McCroskey, J. C. (1977). Oral communication apprehension: A summary of recent history, theory, and research. *Human Communication Research, 4,* 78–96.

McCroskey, J. C. (1978). Validity of the PRCA as an index of oral communication apprehension. *Communication Monographs, 45,* 192–203.

McCroskey, J. C. (1997). Willingness to communicate, communication apprehension, and self-perceived communication competence: Conceptualizations and perspectives. In J. A. Daly, J. C. McCroskey, J. Ayres, T. Hopf, & D. M. Ayres, *Avoiding communication: Shyness, reticence, and communication apprehension* (pp. 75–108). Cresskill, NJ: Hampton Press.

McCroskey, J. C. (1998). *Communication and personality: Trait perspective.* Cresskill, NJ: Hampton Press.

Mills, J. (1984). High and low self-monitoring individuals: Their decoding skills and empathic expression. *Journal of Personality 52,* 372–388.

Neuliep, J. W., & McCroskey, J. C. (1997). The development of intercultural and interethnic communication apprehension scales. *Communication Research Reports, 14*(2), 145–156.

O'Keefe, B. (1988). The logic of message design: Individual differences in reasoning about communication. *Communication Monographs, 55,* 80–103.

Olaniran, B. A., & Roach, K. D. (1994). Communication apprehension and classroom apprehension in Nigerian classrooms. *Communication Quarterly, 42*(4), 379–389.

Prunty, A. M., Klopf, D. W., & Ishii, S. (1990a). Argumentativeness: Japanese and American tendencies to approach and avoid conflict. *Communication Research Reports, 7,* 75–79.

Prunty, A. M., Klopf, D. W., & Ishii, S. (1990b). Japanese and American tendencies to argue. *Psychological Reports, 66,* 802.

Rahoi, R., Svenkerud, P., & Love, D. (1994). *Searching for subtlety: Investigating argumentativeness across low-context cultural boundaries.* Unpublished manuscript, Ohio University.

Rancer, A. S., Baukus, R. A., & Infante, D. A. (1985). Relations between argumentativeness and belief structures about arguing. *Communication Education, 34,* 37–47.

Rudd, J. E., & Burant, P. A. (1995). A study of women's compliance-gaining behaviors in violent and non-violent relationships. *Communication Research Reports, 12,* 134–144.

Samovar, L. A., & Porter, R. E. (Eds.). (1985). *Intercultural communication: A reader.* Belmont, CA: Wadsworth.

Sanders, J. A., Gass, R. H., Wiseman, R. L., & Bruschke, J. C. (1992). Ethnic comparison and measurement of argumentativeness, verbal aggressiveness, and need for cognition. *Communication Reports, 5,* 50–56.

Schwartz, S. H. (1994). Beyond individualism/collectivism: New cultural dimensions of values. In U. Kim, H. C. Triandis, C. Kagitcibasi, S. C. Choi, & G. Yoon (Eds.), *Individualism and collectivism: Theory, method, and applications* (pp. 85–122). Thousand Oaks, CA: Sage.

Siegman, A. W., & Reynolds, M. A. (1983). Self-monitoring and speech in feigned and unfeigned lying. *Journal of Personality and Social Psychology, 6,* 1325–1333.

Singelis, T., & Brown, W. (1995). Culture, self, and collectivist communication: Linking culture to individual behavior. *Human Communication Research, 21,* 354–389.

Snyder, M. (1974). Self-monitoring of expressive behavior. *Journal of Personality and Social Psychology, 30,* 526–537.

Snyder, M. (1976). Attribution and behavior: Social perception and social causation. In J. W. Harvey, W. J. Ickes, & R. F. Kidd (Eds), *New directions in attribution research* (Vol. 1, pp. 53–72). Hillsdale, NJ: Lawrence Erlbaum.

Snyder, M. (1979). Self-monitoring processes. In L. Berkowitz (Ed.), *Advances in experimental social psychology* (Vol. 12, pp. 85–128). New York: Academic Press.

Snyder, M., & Gangestad, S. (1986). On the nature of self-monitoring: Matters of assessment, matters of validity. *Journal of Personality and Social Psychology, 51,* 125–139.

Stiff, J., Corman, S., Krizek, B., & Snider, E. (1994). Individual differences and changes in nonverbal behavior: Unmasking the changing faces of deception. *Communication Research, 21*(5), 555–581.

Swagler, M. A., & Ellis, M. V. (2003). Crossing the distance: Adjustment of Taiwanese graduate students in the United States. *Journal of Counseling Psychology, 50*(4), 420–437.

Toch, H. (1969). *Violent men.* Chicago: Aldine.

Triandis, H. (1995). *Individualism and collectivism.* Boulder, CO: Westview.

Turner, R. G. (1980). Self-monitoring and humor production. *Journal of Personality, 48*(2), 163–172.

Watson, A. K., Monroe, E. E., & Allerstrom, H. (1989). Comparison of communication apprehension across cultures: American and Swedish children. *Communication Quarterly, 37,* 67–76.

6

The Role of Intercultural Communication Competency in Global Business Negotiations

Global considerations impact everyday business decisions for companies large and small. Should we buy this component part from a U. S. supplier, or consider sourcing outside the United States? Where should we produce, market, and sell our products and services? For most, it is a global market to consider. One only needs to examine the current and projected growth of international trade to clearly see the impact on our future.

Corporations are aware that to be successful in tomorrow's marketplace requires employees to be competent in communicating with those from other cultures. In the past, most international managers relied on general cultural guidelines for conducting intercultural negotiations. However, the increase in global trade transactions has resulted in integrated cultural exchanges, new cultural partnerships, and unique cultural interactions, making old, superficial generalities less accurate. One effect of increasing multicultural interactions is a change in homogenous cultures or, indeed, nations. A new culture of world trade is born. Research offered to explain communication based on cultural generalities is helpful but quickly becoming dated and insufficient for providing guidelines for negotiating with other cultures. As discussed in previous chapters, culture is defined by most as socially transmitted beliefs, values, behavioral patterns, norms, and rituals that are shared by a large group of people or a community (Cai, Wilson, & Drake, 2000; Hofstede, 1980; Salacuse, 1991). Communicating interculturally is the process whereby individuals from different cultures attempt to exchange information and interpret or understand the other person. We propose in this chapter that successful intercultural negotiation is not only influenced by an understanding of general cultural knowledge, but also, and more important, by the *negotiators' competency in intercultural communication.*

This chapter examines intercultural communication competency (ICC) in geocentric business negotiations. We present key components of ICC specific to the success of intercultural business transactions. An examination of how these key components specifically affect global business negotiations is included. We also offer 12 guidelines for enhancing communicative behavior in intercultural business negotiations.

❖ OVERVIEW OF INTERCULTURAL COMMUNICATION COMPETENCY

Intercultural communication competency grew out of the interpersonal communication competency research. The contextual distinctiveness of the intercultural interaction is a unique communication competency issue. It is possible that an individual may be highly competent in communicating with others in his or her own culture but not competent when interacting with others who are culturally different. In the past decade, numerous books, articles, and papers have been published on intercultural competency (Gudykunst, 2005; Hampden-Turner & Trompenaars, 2000; Landis, Bennett, & Bennett, 2004).

To understand ICC, we first take a brief look at communication competency in general. Spitzberg and Cupach (1984) define communication competency as the ability to achieve your goals while you fulfill relational and situational expectations (as cited in Cupach & Canary,

1997). Spitzberg and Cupach contend that communication competency is primarily comprised of two dimensions, appropriateness (meeting social expectations and social rules) and effectiveness (achieving one's goals). Although the previous communication competency research is helpful (Cupach & Canary, 1997; Snavely & Walters, 1983; Wiemann, 1977), it is predominantly restricted to general intracultural settings and is not specific to global negotiation. Thus, a void remained in explaining intercultural negotiation for business transactions.

Understanding the individual's role in ICC has gained the attention of several researchers (Gudykunst, 1998; Ting-Toomey, 1988). The focus of ICC has remained in the forefront for understanding intercultural relationships. Questions concerning how to be effective in our messages with others outside our cultural boundaries led to the development of *intercultural communication competency.* Gudykunst as well as others (Klopf, 2001; Ting-Toomey, 1988) have given us a framework for examining the role that general cultural dimensions play in the communication process. Gudykunst, in his 1998 book titled *Bridging Differences: Effective Intergroup Communication,* concludes that "culture influences our communication and our communication influences our cultures" (p. 44). Therefore, an individual's ICC is important in providing communication guidelines for how specific cultures and nations talk. Neither cultural level of competency nor the individual level of competency is adequate to reflect the new multicultural phenomena occurring in our global market. Therefore, a richer understanding of global negotiation will result from an integrative approach (individual factors and cultural factors). Thus, viewing ICC in business negotiations offers important perspectives for the new global market.

Negotiator communication competency is essential for understanding the role that communication plays in global business negotiations. The benefits of moving from a cultural generality model to a geocentric model that includes the individual negotiators' ICC is greatly beneficial for several reasons.

First, negotiators stand their best chance of reaching an optimal agreement when the parties are able to engage in creative problem solving (Fisher, Ury, & Patton, 1991). This problem-solving process often requires the parties to negotiate face to face (or in a dyadic context) and thus is a relational, context-based process in which sensitivity to the recipient's interpretation of a message is essential for shared meaning. Second, unlike other contextually based communication competency (e.g., classroom), global negotiations are heavily reliant upon the development of the parties' relationship. Therefore, examining global negotiations from a communication competency framework incorporates the development of the relationship through the dynamics of communication interactions. Finally, a communication competency approach offers an excellent foundation for building a more advanced model of how communication competency occurs during conflict episodes in the intercultural negotiation setting.

The nature of constructive conflict interactions requires that parties act in a highly appropriate and effective manner if they are to move beyond the point of conflict. For example, at conflict points in the negotiation process, it is essential to maintain face and provide face-saving gestures so that there are opportunities for parties to continue engaging in the negotiation process. The relationship of the negotiating parties is tested during conflict episodes, and it is often the face-to-face communication that frames the opportunities for further relationship development or the destruction of the relationship.

Thus, examining global negotiation and the role of ICC provides an excellent foundation for investigating the dynamics of success in global negotiation. Spitzberg and Cupach argue that ICC can be explained as appropriateness and effectiveness with more emphasis on contextual factors. We argue that appropriateness and effectiveness operate at the basic level for understanding ICC, but other factors must be included to fully understand ICC in geocentric negotiations.

We now turn to a more in-depth look at what factors influence ICC in global business negotiation. The key components for developing ICC in geocentric business negotiations are appropriateness, effectiveness, anxiety reduction, adaptation, face honoring and protection, sensitivity and empathy, mindfulness and presence, and knowledge. These components are discussed in the next section.

Key Components of Intercultural Communication Competency (ICC)

- Appropriateness
- Effectiveness
- Anxiety Reduction
- Adaptation
- Face Honoring and Protection
- Sensitivity and Empathy
- Mindfulness and Presence
- Knowledge

1. Appropriateness

Appropriateness is the ability to communicate with someone in a socially sensitive manner so as not to offend or break any rules that would result in insult, face threat, or rudeness. Communication appropriateness involves considering a variety of strategies and the communication constraints that exist within a specific communication context. Message selection and strategy for communicating are guided by these constraints, or rules. Embedded in the cultural norms and rules is the appropriateness of certain types of behaviors and the manner in which we communicate. Philipsen's (1992, 1997) speech codes theory posits that in order to understand communication, one must understand the cultural speech codes ("a system of socially-constructed symbols and meanings, premises, and rules, pertaining to communicative conduct") (Philipsen, 1997, p. 126). The socially constructed symbols and meanings are culturally distinctive codes for interpreting and explaining intercultural communication. Therefore, when communicating in the international business negotiation context, one must consider the norms, rules, and expectations and how these are determined by an accumulation of culture and regional or subculture, organizational culture, and individual personality, as well as any previous negotiation experiences.

The international business negotiation context has specific constraints that should be considered in appropriate message selection. For example, global business negotiations typically entail procedural rules or guidelines offered to facilitate agreement. Parks (1985) states,

> Competent communicators have a vested interest in maintaining the rules of social conduct because they realize, however dimly, that their ability to pursue their own goals depends on the freedom of others to pursue their goals. Personal control, then, is more often an ally of social appropriateness than its enemy. (p. 197)

Thus, it is important for the global business negotiator to keep in mind how the negotiation process (e.g., structural and procedural issues) is conducted. Also important are the type of business, the parties' relationship, the organizational culture (bureaucratic, lateral, highly structured, informal, etc.), individual style (argumentative, assertive, or passive), the position or role of the negotiator (buyer or seller), and the specific issues of the negotiation as guidelines for appropriate strategy selection. The appropriateness component of becoming a competent communicator in the global market is interrelated to other ICC factors discussed in the following paragraphs.

2. Effectiveness

How we "effectively" achieve our goals is a vital part of the global business negotiation. Spitzberg and Cupach (1989) defined effectiveness as "successful goal achievement or accomplishment" (p. 7). How we attempt to reach effectiveness is related to our ability to maximize our rewards and minimize our costs. Effectiveness is the ability to achieve your goals through the communication process. Specifically, an individual must be able to maximize his or her potential for achieving his or her goals by selecting strategies that will allow the individual to achieve his or her success through interaction. Effective strategy selection is critical for clear communication in intercultural settings. M. Kim (1994) argues that strategic competency entails a person's ability to select an effective message that allows the other party to derive the intended meaning. However, Kim and Wilson (1994) conclude that "different cultural groups have drastically different ideas about what constitutes an effective strategy" (p. 229). Thus, any discussion of effectiveness must consider that cultural perspectives influence the strategy choice and perception of the effectiveness of that strategy.

Western cultures generally view efficiency, or time required to reach an agreement, as an important consideration in measuring effectiveness. However, this may not hold true for other cultures or individuals who do not share the same value of time.

For example, Schmidt Corporation, a manufacturing company headquartered in Germany, wants to obtain a contractual agreement to buy plastics from Paranhos Incorporated, headquartered in Brazil. Schmidt Corporation's negotiator, Ms. Gausser, is under a deadline to go to Brazil to meet with someone from Paranhos and be back home in time to meet with alternative vendors if she cannot reach an agreement with Paranhos Corporation. Ms. Gausser's time line, or what she considers to be efficient use of her time, is one week (based on how she usually conducts business). However, Paranhos Corporation's negotiator, Mr. de Aveiro, thinks that effective agreement has a time line of around 3 months (based on how he usually conducts negotiations). Mr. de Aveiro's goals for the meeting are to begin a relationship with Schmidt Corporation and Ms. Gausser, spend time getting to know each other and understand the other party's company, as well as show Ms. Gausser some of the culture and history of his country.

Goal attainment is not likely to be achieved for either negotiator because their perception of effective use of time is very different. This situation requires each negotiator to acquire an understanding of the other party's values and sense of business in order for either to be effective in achieving his or her goals. More than likely, each will leave dissatisfied, and a business opportunity may be lost.

There have been several studies that reveal specific cultural differences in interpreting effectiveness. For example, Kim and Wilson's (1994) study of cross-cultural request strategies revealed a difference between Americans' and Koreans' rating of effective strategy. They found that Americans rated direct statement requests as the most effective strategy, whereas Koreans rated it the least effective strategy. Thus, a global business negotiator must be sensitive to others' value of certain strategies as he or she attempts to succeed in reaching agreement.

3. Anxiety and Uncertainty Reduction

Uncertainty reduction theory (Berger & Calabrese, 1975) suggests that we are likely to experience uncertainty about communicating with another individual, especially when we are unable to predict or explain a stranger's behaviors. This uncertainty (both predictive uncertainty and explanatory uncertainty), according to Gudykunst, results when we are interacting with someone different from us. Uncertainty hinders the quantity and quality of communication. The nature of international business transactions creates just this type of situation. When we are not able to predict the other's behaviors or attitudes (predictive uncertainty) and we are uncertain how to explain the other's behaviors (explanatory uncertainty), we experience high uncertainty and anxiety. The less certain we are about another individual's behaviors, the more anxious we are. The fast pace of the international market requires negotiators to tread into unfamiliar environments with little predictive knowledge of another's negotiation behavior. Anxiety and uncertainty are often reported when new markets open and new relationships must be established. However, it is also possible in international trade that the negotiator may become anxious about the other negotiator because he or she is aware of the other party's entrenched position. This anxiety based on known differences may cause the negotiator to become uncertain of how to communicate most effectively to achieve a positive outcome. In both experiences, the anxiety is related to our feelings and uncertainty is related to our cognitive processing ability. Gudykunst posits that we have "thresholds of uncertainty."

If our uncertainty is below our minimum threshold level, we will interact with strangers with a great deal of confidence (Gudykunst, 1998). Typically, when our uncertainty is below the threshold level, we act and believe that we can predict the other person's behavior and are in control of the interaction. When dealing with other cultures, this assumption is likely to result in misinterpretations, or worse, communication mistakes, such as face-threatening or insulting behavior. In the case of intercultural business negotiations, this can be devastating to the negotiation process, possibly resulting in a failure to reach agreement and an adverse effect on the relationship. The awareness or mindfulness of others in the communication process is lost (because we are assuming little attention is needed to communicate with the other), and the negotiator may be perceived as disinterested in the other party or even perhaps as exhibiting dislike or disdain for the other.

If uncertainty is above the maximum threshold level, Gudykunst argues we will not want to communicate with the stranger (or oppositional negotiator). The ideal range of uncertainty for communicating with someone from a different culture falls between the minimum and maximum threshold levels of uncertainty. Communicating in this range allows us to experience enough uncertainty to be motivated and open to new information about the other person with a level of comfort.

The anxiety we experience is related to our level of uncertainty. One way to evaluate our anxiety is to be cognizant of our physiological reactions, such as butterflies in our stomach, headache, sweaty hands, shortness of breath, or general nervousness. The issue for successful negotiation in the global business negotiation is being in the range of minimum to maximum threshold of uncertainty/anxiety. Similar to speech-making and test-taking experiences, having a certain amount of uneasiness and anxiety may increase performance. Determining your own level of uncertainty and anxiety requires you to be aware of your own threshold levels. Perhaps the easiest method for determining threshold is through your physiological state. A few butterflies in your stomach increases your ICC, while none or too many decrease your ICC effectiveness. The trick is getting all the butterflies to go in the same direction.

4. Adaptation Component

Adaptation is often referred to as the adjustment to a new or unfamiliar situation or setting. Cultural adaptation occurs when one is willing to accept another culture's customs or worldview. Bennett and Bennett (2004) argue that "adaptation occurs when we need to think or act outside of our own cultural context" (p. 156). Adaptability is often referred to as behavioral flexibility (Bochner & Kelly, 1974; Spitzberg & Cupach, 1989). Having a diverse behavioral repertoire and knowing when to use it is key to adaptability in new situations. In addition, the authors contend that by taking the perspective of the other person, we can begin to feel and construct our identity from their viewpoint. This newly developed identity is an initial step in the integration process, which Kim discusses in her intercultural communication model.

Y. Kim's work that began in 1991 presents a model of ICC focusing on the immigrant and the acculturation of the immigrant to the new host culture. The idea that one must "adapt, adjust, or integrate" into the new cultural ways is essential for ICC. Although our focus is on a sojourner's approach to the intercultural interaction, within the negotiation context, Kim's principles of adaptation and integration are important in the development of long-term negotiation relationships (Kim, 2001).

The global marketplace requires us to think beyond the short-term outcome to the development of long-term relationships and even partnerships for survival in the global business community. The development of a "third culture" effect is highly likely if negotiating parties adapt and integrate their cultures' identities. This shift in identity happens over a period of successful and not-so-successful interactions in negotiation. As Neuliep (2003) suggests, intercultural competence means adapting verbal and nonverbal messages to the appropriate cultural context. As a result of this mutual adaptation in communication behavior, parties can then move to a discussion that reflects a transactional communication process that creates the third-culture phenomenon. As the business world becomes more sophisticated in adaptation and eventually integration, we would expect to see a transformation of how people conduct business in the global market. Perhaps the blurring of culture will result in a truly geocentric identity.

5. Face Honoring and Protection

Dignity and respect are all too often missing from business negotiations. Yet we know that human beings respond positively to others who demonstrate a positive regard for themselves and an appreciation for differences. Goffman (1959) introduced *face* as the wish to have a positive social impression on others. Face embodies the concept that individuals want to have others view them with respect and dignity. Facework is the behaviors and strategies we engage in to establish a positive face. Face and facework are two distinct concepts. Face is the individual's desire for a favorable impression, whereas facework is the "specific verbal and nonverbal behaviors that we engage in to maintain or restore face loss and to uphold and honor face gain" (Ting-Toomey, 2005, p. 73). The concept of face means different things depending on one's culture. For example, in China there are two types of face. There is *lian* (face), defined by Hu (1944) as "representing the confidence of society in the integrity of ego's moral character, the loss of which makes it impossible for him to function properly within the community" (p. 45). The second type of face in China is referred to as *mian* or *mian zi* (image), which means the status or prestige one receives for success in life (Hu, 1944; Oetzel et al., 2001). In every culture, face is considered an important factor in communicating with others. The degree of importance and the distinctive forms of face vary among cultures. For example, Japan has two types of face, *mentsu* (social status success) and *taimen* (self-presentation to others) (Morisaki & Gudykunst, 1994). Part of face for all cultures is associated with one's honor, respect, and social interactions.

There are generally three orientations of face behavior: self-face (concern for one's own image), other face (concern for another person's image), and mutual face (concern for both self and other's image) (Ting-Toomey & Kurogi, 1998). Cultures vary in the level of importance they place in preserving these concerns. For example, in the United States, communication is typically more from a self-face concern, whereas in Mexico and Japan, communication focus tends to be from an other-face or mutual-face concern. It is important not only to consider what face concern one typically has, but also what one expects others to demonstrate. Clearly, one's orientation toward face, as well as the context in which the communication occurs, affects the strategies for issues relating to face. Let us take a closer examination of face strategies that negotiators may engage in during a global business negotiation.

Types of Face Strategies

Inherent in every interaction is face. We propose that there are three critical face strategies to consider in global business negotiation: *face-protection strategies, face-threatening strategies,* and *face-renovation strategies.*

There are two types of face-protection strategies: protection of one's own face and protection for another's face. Self-protection face is reflected in messages that allow for one to defend or preserve his or her image to avoid any damage to face. Other-face protection strategies are messages that bolster the other's competency or trustworthiness to prevent damage to the other's face. Examples of such messages include deflections of embarrassment or shame from the other, providing rationale or justification in the circumstances, or pretending the incident didn't occur.

Face-threatening strategies entail attacking the other person's image. Often this occurs as an attempt to defend oneself when one perceives another acting aggressively, trying to dominate in order to exert more power, or trying to discredit one (e.g., saying something to make you look incompetent or dishonest). Face-threatening strategies are similar to Wilson and Putnam's (1990) face-attacking need. Face threatening includes not only verbal messages but also the role silence (invalidation) plays in threatening face. Silence as a face-threatening situation occurs quite often in the U.S. culture. For example, Ms. Tompkin, a negotiator for a food distribution company, is meeting with Mr. Jones and his sales team to renegotiate a contract agreement for the upcoming year. Ms. Tompkin is unhappy with the quality of service she has received from Mr. Jones. The meeting begins with Mr. Jones asking, "Haven't I done a great job of providing you with on-time deliveries?" Instead of responding to Mr. Jones's question, Ms. Tompkin remains silent. This silence in the U.S. business culture is viewed as embarrassment, or a way of devaluing Mr. Jones.

Face-renovation strategies are used when damage to one's face has already occurred and credibility and trust must be restored. Face renovation is also self and other oriented. That is, one can engage in self-face renovation by engaging in behaviors that others perceive as honest and competent. It is also possible to restore another's face by providing arguments or information that increases the other's credibility and sincerity or by using humor to deflect an embarrassing moment. Cupach and Imahori (1993) caution that humor is sensitive to one's culture and therefore requires care in its application. Even if a negotiator believes he or she has a sense of what is viewed as humorous in a specific culture, it is necessary to consider the individual differences in acceptable humor. Humor is typically revealed over a period of time as one develops a relationship with another person. We suggest relationship development becomes a key factor in how humorous attempts are interpreted—as face-attacking insults or laughable moments.

Face renovation allows for repair of damaged face to occur so that communication can continue in the intercultural relationship. For example, in self-face renovation, a negotiator may have a person who is highly respected by the other party speak on his behalf. Here is an example of other-face renovation. Assume the other's face has been damaged; perhaps he was caught in a dishonest statement. The other negotiator offers a reasonable explanation for his statement and suggests that it must all be a misunderstanding because the other is above reproach. Another tactic might be to cover his deception with another lie. For example, Negotiator Jim claims that your partner, Ted, has already agreed to buy his bolts for 2 million dollars. Just then, Ted walks in and hears this statement. Both Jim and Ted realize that the claim is untrue. However, Ted offers other-face renovation by stating, "I can't keep that agreement; can we discuss the price further?" Both parties know there was no agreement on price. However, by offering a face renovation, the parties are able to continue the negotiation without long-term damage. In fact, the relationship may be enhanced by the face-renovation gesture made by Ted. In cultures where face is very important and face damage has long-term effects, face renovation is an important strategy to have available.

Face-Negotiation Theory

Ting-Toomey's conflict face-negotiation theory (Ting-Toomey, 1985, 1988, 2004, 2005; Ting-Toomey & Kurogi, 1998) makes an important contribution to understanding face in intercultural interaction. The significance of her contribution to face is important for our understanding of global business negotiations and therefore is briefly described in the following paragraphs.

This theory presents an integrative view of face negotiation, conflict, and culture (conflict face-negotiation theory; see Ting-Toomey, 2005). The seven core propositions follow.

1. People in all cultures try to maintain and negotiate face in all communication situations.

2. The concept of face is especially problematic in emotionally vulnerable situations (such as embarrassment, request, or conflict situations) when the situation identities of the communicators are called into question.

3. The cultural variability dimensions of individualism-collectivism and small/large power distance shape the orientations, movements, contents, and styles of facework.

4. Individualism-collectivism shapes members' preferences for self-oriented facework versus other-oriented facework.

5. Small/large power distance shapes members' preferences for horizontal-based facework versus vertical-based facework.

6. The cultural variability dimensions, in conjunction with individual, relational, and situational factors influence the use of particular facework behaviors in particular cultural scenes.

7. Intercultural facework competence refers to the optimal integration of knowledge, mindfulness, and communication skills in managing vulnerable identity-based conflict situations appropriately, effectively, and adaptively.

SOURCE: From Ting-Toomey, S. (2005).

These general theorems lay the framework for how face and face-work strategies can help those who are intercultural negotiators. Culture and communication are intertwined, and face is always present in the communication process regardless of the issue. Within these propositions advanced by Ting-Toomey lie guidelines for international negotiators, especially when conflict arises.

In conflict situations such as negotiating a contract for *x* number of goods or services between intercultural parties, face may be an integral part of the outcome. Negotiators must examine the role that face plays in their culture, the rules of appropriateness for face and preserving the other's face, the strategies that are likely to be used by one's self and the other party (individualistic versus collectivistic), as well as the conditions surrounding the negotiation episode. In addition, Ting-Toomey presents intercultural facework competence. Inclusive in her presentation of facework competence is the appropriateness, effectiveness, and adaptive (adaptability) behavior in intercultural conflictual situations (such as negotiations).

Following is a brief summary of Ting-Toomey's research comparing individualistic and collectivistic cultures. These have been paraphrased.

Individualistic cultures when compared to collectivistic cultures tend to

- express more self-maintenance concerns;
- use more direct, dominating facework strategies;
- use more dominating/competing conflict styles;
- use more emotionally expressive conflict styles; and
- use more assertive to aggressive conflict styles.

Collectivistic cultures compared to individualistic cultures tend to

- express more other-face concerns;
- express more mutual-face maintenance concerns;
- use more avoidance facework strategies;
- use a greater degree of integrative facework strategies;
- use more avoiding conflict styles;
- use more obliging conflict styles; and
- use more compromising to integrating conflict styles.

SOURCE: From Ting-Toomey, S. (2005). The matrix of face: An updated face-negotiation theory. In W. B. Gudykunst (Ed.), *Theorizing about intercultural communication*. Reprinted with permission of Sage Publications, Inc.

6. Sensitivity and Empathy

What does it mean to be a sensitive, empathetic individual in the intercultural interaction? We all like those who make us feel listened to, validated, and understood, and we dislike those who pretend to understand. Bennett and Bennett (2004) offer in their model of development of intercultural sensitivity that, "as one's experience of cultural difference becomes more sophisticated, one's competence in intercultural relations increases" (p. 152). We develop cognitively as well as behaviorally into a sensitivity of cultures that moves beyond our ethnocentric perspective of viewing others into an integrated view of others and self. This cannot be achieved by acquiring general knowledge about cultural generalities or by personal experience alone. Rather, competency is a result of a new cognitive structure that is authentic and global. The process of reframing one's perspective may lead to a global identity, thus creating a better opportunity for successful communication in the international business negotiation.

Empathy is an affective feeling. You can teach people to act empathetic but not to feel empathy. One way to enhance our ability to feel empathy toward other cultures is developing a physiologically connection. Bennett and Castiglioni (2004) suggest that to be interculturally communication competent, we need to know cognitively about another culture *and* generate the feeling for the other culture. They suggest, "With that feeling, behavior appropriate in the other cultural context can flow naturally from our embodied experience, just as it does in our own culture" (p. 260). By opening ourselves up to our feelings and allowing ourselves to experience what represents the other's cultural experiences, we are likely to gain valuable knowledge on how others different from us experience or feel life. This affective phenomenon provides opportunities in negotiation for enlightenment and recognition (Bush & Folger, 1994), which ultimately lead to transformative agreements.

Sometimes individuals experience a great sense of difference from the other person and their culture. This experience can result in "culture shock." Empathy, as Redmond (2000) reported, increased the individuals' intensity of culture shock because they could recognize the differences between themselves and the other culture. A highly sensitive individual may have a culture shock response, but over time, the empathy may result in a much richer understanding and multilevel identity for the individual.

For example, Ms. Rudolph from England is negotiating with Mr. Yawlan from a small village in Zimbabwe. Ms. Rudolph arrives in the village, where she is to negotiate the mining of diamonds. She notices that around noon, everyone quits working and walks to an area outside the village. She assumes there must be some daily ritual that she is unfamiliar with. Ms. Rudolph mentions that to Mr. Yawlan, and Mr. Yawlan explains that the community members are going to bury their dead. Ms. Rudolph comments, "But I see this every day!" Mr. Yawlan simply responds with, "Yes, people are dying daily here from disease and malnutrition." Ms. Rudolph feels a true sense of the living tragedy that her business associate experiences regularly. Her response to this sense of overwhelming sadness may be a sense of isolation, guilt for her wealthy culture, detachment, or confusion by the way the village continues to function. These may all be signs of culture shock. Her sensitivity and empathy toward the village people may have intensified her view of the differences between her culture and theirs. However, this same sensitivity can make her a more competent communicator because of her heightened sense of awareness and authenticity or genuine connection to their grief.

The relationship that develops between Ms. Rudolph and Mr. Yawlan is in part a result of Ms. Rudolph's sensitivity and ability to empathize with Mr. Yawlan. The business relationship is enriched by her empathetic and sensitive communication about Mr. Yawlan's world that extends beyond the substantive issues. The end result is that a richer, culturally sensitive relationship may have emerged for both parties.

7. Mindfulness or Being Present

Mindfulness is a key factor in becoming interculturally communication competent (Langer, 1989; Ting-Toomey, 1999). Mindfulness, as described by Langer (1989), involves developing new categories, being open to new information, and being more aware of others' perspectives (p. 62). The Chinese word *ting* refers to "listening with your ears, eyes and one heart" (Ting-Toomey & Kurogi, 1998, p. 204); this may best describe what we refer to as being mindful and present. Being able to imagine new solutions and reach creative agreements is essential in global business negotiations. Focusing on opportunities to see someone differently, or a willingness to think beyond the past roadblocks, requires negotiators to be present in the moments of the conversation. The negotiator must rely not on past scripts to get them to resolution but rather moments of creativity that are developed through mindful acts and thoughts. Bush and Folger (1994) describe this as transformative conflict resolution.

Ting-Toomey suggests engaging in "mindful reframing" as a strategy for managing skill in conflict resolution. She suggests that negotiators must be able to translate the other party's verbal and nonverbal messages from their cultural standpoint. Furthermore, acquiring the skill to listen during a conflict to the other party in a mindful and non-evaluative manner is important. This requires an individual to be attentive to underlying assumptions that are occurring during the interaction.

The concept of mindfulness is relatively new to Westerners, but many Eastern cultures embrace mindfulness as part of their cognitive practice in communicating with others. We have used the words *be present* in communicating and negotiating with others. Oftentimes we are thinking ahead to the next point we want to make or what strategy we will use, or we are even evaluating the individual's clothes instead of listening to the words and watching the expressions on the other party's face. Being present requires us to not think about ourselves, nor to be distracted by external psychological or environmental noises, but rather to search for meaning and commonness with the other person. The mindfulness of communication is choosing language that has taken into consideration the other person's culture, interacting with a multicultural identity, and embracing opportunities to act verbally and nonverbally in a reciprocal and thoughtful way. Mindfulness and presence are essential parts of the global business negotiation and are critical for creative and competent global business negotiators.

8. Knowledge

Knowledge about the other person's culture is a critical component of ICC. To truly share in meaningful discourse in intercultural negotiations, we must have knowledge about the other's religion, customs, values, language, and linguistic and politeness strategies. Competency is not simply learning a foreign language. One must have an understanding of how language is used to facilitate meaning appropriately. In addition, languages vary in terms of the amount of variation available to show respect and politeness (Dolinina & Cecchetto, 1998). For example, English has few grammatical mechanisms for differentiating status, whereas Japanese has several grammatical structures for communicating politeness in regards to inequity, status, and power. Hazleton and Cupach (1986) conclude that we need to have knowledge about a variety of areas. For example, they suggest that ICC is more likely to occur if we know (a) what communication strategies will lead to achieving our goals, (b) the rules that govern the appropriateness of messages in the specific context, (c) the possible consequences that might occur if we deviate from the rules, and (d) how to create meaningful messages given the other's cultural perspective.

There are several different but related types of knowledge that aid in the development of ICC in global negotiations. First, Hazelton and Cupach present *linguistic knowledge* (Chen & Starosta, 1996, referred to as linguistic competency), which is concerned with how cultures assemble their messages, how they grammatically construct their sentences, and the degree to which the word provides the meaning. Second, knowing how and when to speak and how to read, and being able to mindfully listen and understand the other culture's language is another important aspect (Redmond, 2000). Research has shown that fluency in speaking the other party's language is important in effective communication (Martin & Hammer, 1989; Ting-Toomey & Korzenny, 1989).

A third important level of knowledge is *ontological knowledge* (Hazelton & Cupach, 1986). They describe ontological knowledge as being "reflected in communicators' ability to describe, predict, and explain human behavior" (p. 120). The way in which we know something is reflected is our view of reality. This level of knowledge has to do with the interpretation level of meaning. For example, cultures vary in their conceptualization of communication competency. In Asian cultures such as China, creating harmony is viewed as a key element in competently communicating. In Korea, communication competency is the ability to express messages indirectly and transcendentally (Chen & Starosta, 1996).

A fourth type of knowledge is knowledge about the business negotiation process. One has to understand the construction of the negotiation within a given culture. Both the structure and the process for interacting in the negotiation are relevant information for successful interactions, especially during international business transactions.

For example, when purchasing a basket in Mexico, it is expected that the negotiation process occurs something like this:

Person A: How much for the basket?

Person B: (*always ask more than you want*) $200.

Person A: (*always counteroffer*) Oh, would you be willing to take $50?

Person A: Oh, I cannot do that. It is a one of a kind. How about $150?

Person B: (*you want to provide some face saving but not give him the price*) I will give you $75.

Person A: I cannot sell it for that.

Person B: (*walks away*)

Person A: (*yells*) Okay! I will give it to you for $100.

Person B: (*comes back to A and buys the basket for $100*)

This same business transaction would follow a very different process were it to happen in a U.S. shopping mall. The negotiation would be like this.

Person A: How much for the basket?

Person B: Let's see, is the price marked? Oh, here it is: $200.

Person A: Will this basket go on sale anytime soon?

Person B: No, but if you open a credit card account, I can give you 15 percent off today.

Person A: Okay. What do I need to do?

The important difference between the two examples is that the first relies heavily on the relationship aspect of negotiating. The price isn't marked and the communication strategy influences the interaction that ultimately leads to the purchase. The second example is based on the substantive issue of price. The price marked ahead of time is the basis for the negotiation. The relationship (e.g., the credit card) only becomes a possible influencing factor if the price is not acceptable. Thus, if one tries to negotiate in the second example by using the strategies employed in the first, it is highly unlikely that the store clerk would call out to the customer who is unwilling to pay the marked price. A negotiator who can successfully negotiate in either cultural setting is more interculturally competent because he or she has the knowledge about the different cultural communication norms and he or she has the repertoire of strategies from which to select. Furthermore, he or she has the ontological knowledge of human behavior. This, coupled with knowledge of the business negotiation process of the cultural context, leads him or her to achieve his or her goal—buying the basket.

Assessing Competency

There has been a great deal of discussion on assessing communication competency. Some scholars have contended that communication competency is a trait (McCroskey, 1984) and can best be assessed by self-report measures. For example, in a study that used a self-assessment measure of competency, Swedes were higher in competency than Americans (McCroskey, Burroughs, Daun, & Richmond, 1990). Others argue that communication competency is situation based and must be judged from the receiver's perspective (Rubin, 1982). Others present an interactional approach suggesting that communication competency is a product of both trait and situation.

We contend that ICC is influenced by individual predispositional factors (e.g., communication apprehension, argumentativeness, etc.). However, more important is the negotiator's specific knowledge, skill, and motivation (Rubin, 1985; Spitzberg, 1983) for communicating internationally. Knowledge, skill, and motivation are necessary criteria for ICC. Communication norms are culture-bound, and therefore competency is a function of culture and it is how we are evaluated in the interaction that ultimately determines ICC. As Phillips comments, "'competence' is not a 'thing.' It is an evaluation" (1983, p. 25). We now turn to how these components lead to communication competent negotiators.

To be a competent intercultural communicator requires knowledge and performance or, put another way, cognitive ability as well as skill. Without knowledge (e.g., linguistic, ontological, cultural, negotiation), skill (e.g., appropriate and effective strategy selection, empathic listening), or motivation (e.g., uncertainty, communication apprehension), communication competency is not likely to be achieved. For example, Mr. Dufour, buyer for ATI Electronique Company based in France, is going to meet with Mr. Lee, a seller from Delphi Corporation, based in South Korea. Mr. Lee has knowledge about the French culture and about ATI Electronique's organizational culture, goals, and management style, and he speaks fluent French. He considers himself well prepared and appears motivated to negotiate with Mr. Dufour. It appears that Mr. Lee is communication competent for this meeting (at least on the cognitive dimension of communication competency).

However, Mr. Lee is very anxious or has a high degree of uncertainty about meeting with someone different from himself. He is feeling more anxious than usual because he has heard that Mr. Dufour does not "fit" the cultural generalities of the French businessperson. This creates a skill deficiency in Mr. Lee's communication competency because his anxiety reduces his motivation and affects his ability to communicate competently. Therefore, although Mr. Lee is knowledgeable and appears motivated to negotiate, his competency in this intercultural business negotiation is compromised because of his high level of anxiety.

We could easily have adjusted this example to reflect knowledge as the deficient factor and the results would be the same. The key to successful ICC is that one must be motivated, knowledgeable, and skilled to be a successful and competent communicator in the global marketplace. These three general factors are interrelated in that a deficiency in one impacts at least one of the other components. The deficiency reduces the likelihood of achieving a high level of ICC. Spitzberg (1991b) points out in his model of interpersonal communication competency that there is an additive effect of these three factors, resulting in "communication satisfaction, perceived confirmation, and conversational appropriateness and effectiveness" (p. 22).

❖ CONCLUSION

We propose that communication competency in the intercultural business negotiation context is influenced by communication abilities, culture of origin, importance of the negotiation relationship, knowledge of other cultures reflected in the global business community, and the motivation and skills to negotiate. In addition, highly competent negotiators will possess a multicultural knowledge base that they embrace as part of their identity. This restructuring of how they view themselves and others results in a multicultural identity. This multicultural identity as described by Bennett and Bennett is a result of cognitive restructuring, which leads to an integration stage in cultural sensitivity.

The "appropriateness" of the communicative message is highly influenced by the cultural rules and norms. It is essential that the international negotiator have the cultural knowledge about the other party as well as knowledge about the other party's individual communication style to communicate in an appropriate manner. Remember, it is the combination of cultural knowledge plus individual knowledge that optimizes the chances for successful communication and ultimately an effective negotiated agreement.

Much of the discussion to this point has focused on each individual element that enhances a negotiator's ICC. Intercultural communication competency is both an individual-based and interaction-based concept. The individual's skills and predispositions may help him or her achieve a higher level of competency, but it is the interaction that occurs between the negotiating parties that ultimately determines ICC. An individual can have all the training, knowledge, and motivation to communicate, yet fail in communicating competently with another. The interactional effect created by the two parties ultimately determines competency. Thus, although this chapter presents key factors in optimizing ICC for the individual, we must always be cognizant of the dynamics of discourse, especially in intercultural problem-solving settings such as global business negotiations. Ultimately, ICC in the business negotiation is heavily reliant on the mutual understanding of the negotiation process and the other person. In addition, we must also recognize that communication competency is conceptualized differently in other cultures. We have addressed the common elements in communicating in intercultural business negotiations. Sensitivity to how different cultures conceptualize communication competency within their own culture is always an important variable.

❖ GUIDELINES FOR GLOBAL NEGOTIATION SUCCESS

There are 12 communication guidelines that should be followed when entering into global business negotiations. Competency is the most important factor for obtaining a successful agreement.

1. Do I have the necessary information about the other party's culture, individual style, and the negotiation process to communicate verbally and nonverbally in a sensitive, mindful, appropriate manner?

2. Do I have the knowledge and the ability to listen for opportunities for common ground to be established and shared interests to emerge?

3. What is my level of competency in the other party's native language and interpretation of meaning?

4. How can I allow for face saving when conflict arises?

5. What face-saving strategies do I know how to use, and do I know when to use them?

6. How do I establish a relationship with the other party, knowing that relationship is interpreted differently in various cultures? For example, formal, hierarchical structure is an important component of developing a working relationship in Japan; whereas informal, equal status is assumed among various levels of authority in the United States.

7. What goals do I want to achieve in the negotiation? Do I have a diverse repertoire of strategies and tactics to facilitate a meaningful discussion with the other party?

8. What role does silence play in the negotiation process?

9. What is my threshold level of uncertainty with negotiating with the other party?

10. Do I have a wide range and number of behaviors and am I comfortable using them?

11. Am I flexible in my behaviors?

12. Am I able to stay focused and present when I am interacting with others without making judgments or evaluations?

❖ DISCUSSION QUESTIONS

1. What key factor is the most important to successful ICC? Explain your answer.

2. How does *face* affect the communication competency of a global negotiator?

3. What projections would you make about the role of ICC for the next generation?

4. What are the critical components of individual success in the international marketplace?

5. How can you best prepare for the evolving global marketplace?

6. What critical communication skills are necessary for international negotiation?

7. What difficulty lies ahead for those who remain focused on cultural differences rather than individual differences?

❖ REFERENCES

Bennett, J. M., & Bennett, M. J. (2004). Developing intercultural sensitivity: An integrative approach to global and domestic diversity. In D. Landis, J. M. Bennett, & M. J. Bennett (Eds.), *Handbook of intercultural training* (3rd ed., pp. 147–165). Thousand Oaks, CA: Sage.

Bennett, M. J., & Castiglioni, I. (2004). Embodied ethnocentrism and the feeling of culture: A key to training for intercultural competence. In D. Landis, J. Bennett, & M. Bennett (Eds.), *Handbook of intercultural training* (3rd ed., pp. 249–265). Thousand Oaks, CA: Sage.

Berger, C. R., & Calabrese, R. (1975). Some explorations in initial interaction and beyond: Toward a developmental theory of interpersonal communication. *Human Communication Research, 1,* 99–112.

Bochner, A., & Kelly, C. (1974). Interpersonal competence: Rationale, philosophy, and implementation of a conceptual framework. *Speech Teacher, 23,* 279–301.

Bush, R. A. B., & Folger, J. P. (1994). *The promise of mediation, responding to conflict through empowerment and recognition.* San Francisco: Jossey-Bass.

Cai, D. A., Wilson, S. R., & Drake, L. E. (2000). Culture in the context of intercultural negotiation: Individualism-collectivism and paths to integrative agreements. *Human Communication Research, 26,* 591–617.

Chen, G., & Starosta, W. J. (1996). Intercultural communication competence: A synthesis. *Communication Yearbook, 19,* 353–383.

Cupach, W. R., & Canary, D. (Eds.). (1997). *Competence in interpersonal conflict.* New York: McGraw-Hill.

Cupach, W. R., & Imahori, T. T. (1993). Managing social predicaments created by others: A comparison of Japanese and American facework. *Western Journal of Communication, 57,* 431–444.

Cupach, W. R., & Spitzberg, B. H. (1981, February). *Relational competence: Measurement and validation.* Paper presented at the Western Speech Communication Association, San Jose, CA.

Cupach, W. R., & Spitzberg, B. H. (1983). Trait versus state: A comparison of dispositional and situational measures of interpersonal communication competence. *Western Journal of Speech Communication, 47,* 364–379.

Dolinina, I. B., & Cecchetto, V. (1998). Facework and rhetorical strategies in intercultural argumentative discourse. *Argumentation, 12*(2), 117–135.

Fisher, R., Ury, W., & Patton, B. (Ed.). (1991). *Getting to yes, negotiating agreement without giving in* (2nd ed.). New York: Penguin Books.

Goffman, E. (1959). *The presentation of self in everyday life.* Garden City, NJ: Doubleday.

Gudykunst, W. B. (1998). *Bridging differences: Effective intergroup communication* (3rd ed.). Thousand Oaks, CA: Sage.

Gudykunst, W. B. (Ed.). (2005). *Theorizing about intercultural communication.* Thousand Oaks, CA: Sage.

Hampden-Turner, C., & Trompenaars, F. (2000). *Building cross-cultural competence: How to create wealth from conflicting values.* New Haven, CT: Yale University Press.

Hazleton, V., Jr., & Cupach, W. R. (1986). An exploration of ontological knowledge: Communication competence as a function of the ability to describe, predict, and explain. *Western Journal of Speech Communication, 50,* 119–132.

Hofstede, G. (1980). *Culture's consequences: International differences in work-related values.* Beverly Hills, CA: Sage.

Hu, H. C. (1944). The Chinese concepts of "face." *American Anthropologist, 46,* 45–64.

Kim, M. (1993). Culture-based conversational constraints in explaining cross-cultural strategic competence. In R. L. Wiseman & J. Koester (Eds.), *Intercultural communication competence* (pp. 132–150). Newbury Park, CA: Sage.

Kim, M. (1994). Cross-cultural comparisons of the perceived importance of conversational constraints. *Human Communication Research, 21,* 128–151.

Kim, M., & Wilson, S. R. (1994). A cross-cultural comparison of implicit theories of requesting. *Communication Monographs, 61,* 210–235.

Kim, Y. Y. (2001). *Becoming intercultural: An integrative theory of communication and cross-cultural adaptation.* Thousand Oaks, CA: Sage.

Klopf, D. W. (2001). *Intercultural encounters: The fundamentals of intercultural communication* (5th ed.). Inglewood, CA: Morton.

Landis, D., Bennett, J. M., & Bennett, M. J. (Eds.). (2004). *Handbook of intercultural training* (3rd ed.). Thousand Oaks, CA: Sage.

Langer, E. (1989). *Mindfulness.* Reading, MA: Addison-Wesley.

Martin, J. N., & Hammer, M. R. (1989). Behavioral categories of intercultural communication competence: Everyday communicators' perceptions. *International Journal of Intercultural Relations, 13,* 303–332.

McCroskey, J. C. (1984). The communication apprehension perspective. In J. A. Daly & J. C. McCroskey (Eds.), *Avoiding communication: Shyness, reticence and communication apprehension* (pp. 13–38). Beverly Hills, CA: Sage.

McCroskey, J. C., Burroughs, N. F., Daun, A., & Richmond, V. P. (1990). Correlates of quietness: Swedish and American perspectives. *Communication Quarterly, 38*(2), 127–137.

Morisaki, S., & Gudykunst, W. B. (1994). Face in Japan and the United States. In S. Ting-Toomey (Ed.), *The challenge of facework: Cross-cultural and interpersonal issues* (pp. 47–94). Albany: State University of New York.

Neuliep, J. W. (2003). *Intercultural communication: A contextual approach* (2nd ed.). Boston: Houghton Mifflin.

Oetzel, J., Ting-Toomey, S., Masumoto, T., Yokochi, Y., Pan, X., Takai, J., & Wilcox, R. (2001). Face and facework in conflict: A cross-cultural comparison of China, Germany, Japan, and the United States. *Communication Monographs, 68*(3), 235–258.

Parks, M. R. (1985). Interpersonal communication and the quest for personal competence. In M. L. Knapp & G. R. Miller (Eds.), *Handbook of interpersonal communication* (pp. 171–201). Beverly Hills, CA: Sage.

Phillips, G. M. (1983). A competent view of "competence." *Communication Education, 32,* 25–36.

Philipsen, G. (1992). *Speaking culturally: Explorations in social communication.* New York: State University of New York at Albany Press.

Philipsen, G. (1997). Speech codes theory. In G. Philipsen & T. Albrecht (Eds.), *Developing theories of communication.* New York: State University of New York at Albany Press.

Redmond, M. V. (2000). Cultural distance as a mediating factor between stress and intercultural communication competence. *International Journal of Intercultural Relations, 24,* 151–159.

Rubin, R. B. (1982). Assessing speaking and listening competence at the college level: The communication competency assessment instrument. *Communication Education, 31,* 9–18.

Rubin, R. B. (1985). The validity of the communication competency assessment instrument. *Communication Monographs, 52,* 173–185.

Salacuse, J. (1991). *Making global deals.* Boston: Houghton Mifflin.

Snavely, W. B., & Walters, E. V. (1983). Differences in communication competence among administrator social styles. *Journal of Applied Communication Research, 11*(2), 120–135.

Spitzberg, B. H. (1983). Communication competence as knowledge, skill, and impression. *Communication Education, 32,* 323–329.

Spitzberg, B. H. (1991a). Intercultural communication competence. In L. A. Samovar & R. E. Porter (Eds.), *Intercultural communication: A reader* (pp. 353–365). Belmont, CA: Wadsworth.

Spitzberg, B. H. (1991b). An examination of trait measures of interpersonal competence. *Communication Reports, 4*(1), 22–30.

Spitzberg, B. H., & Cupach, W. R. (1984). *Interpersonal communication competence.* Beverly Hills, CA: Sage.

Spitzberg, B. H., & Cupach, W. R. (1989). *Handbook of interpersonal competence research.* New York: Springer-Verlag.

Ting-Toomey, S. (1985). Toward a theory of conflict and culture. In W. Gudykunst, L. Stewart, & S. Ting-Toomey (Eds.), *Communication, culture, and organizational processes* (pp. 71–86). Beverly Hills, CA: Sage.

Ting-Toomey, S. (1988). Intercultural conflict styles: A face-negotiation theory. In Y. Y. Kim & W. B. Gudykunst (Eds.), *Theories in intercultural communication* (pp. 213–238). Newbury Park, CA: Sage.

Ting-Toomey, S. (1999). *Communicating across cultures.* New York: Guilford Press.

Ting-Toomey, S. (2004). Translating conflict face-negotiation theory into practice. In J. M. Bennett, M. J. Bennett, & D. Landis (Eds.), *Handbook of intercultural training* (3rd ed., pp. 217–248). Thousand Oaks, CA: Sage.

Ting-Toomey, S. (2005). The matrix of face: An updated face-negotiation theory. In W. B. Gudykunst (Ed.), *Theorizing about intercultural communication.* Thousand Oaks, CA: Sage.

Ting-Toomey, S., & Korzenny, F. (Ed.). (1989). *Language, communication, and culture: Current directions.* Newbury Park, CA: Sage.

Ting-Toomey, S., & Kurogi, A. (1998). Facework, competence in intercultural conflict: An updated face-negotiation theory. *International Journal of Intercultural Relations, 22*(2), 187–225.

Wiemann, J. M. (1977). Explication and test of a model of communication competence. *Human Communications Research, 3,* 195–213.

Wilson, S. R., & Putnam, L. L. (1990). Interaction goals in negotiation. In J. A. Anderson (Ed.), *Communication yearbook 13* (pp. 374–427). Newbury Park, CA: Sage.

7

The International Business Context

The activities of negotiation are much more complicated for international business managers than for domestic business managers. Most of the types of transactions that occur domestically also occur internationally, such as buyer/seller agreements, licensing agreements, contract manufacturing, mergers, acquisitions, and joint ventures. There are some additional types of transactions unique to international business that will be discussed in this chapter along with other elements important to doing business internationally.

International business negotiations are complicated by a number of variables, including the political and legal environment of the foreign country as well as its culture. Business practices follow rules. Understanding those rules is critical to success. When the rules are not known or understood, meeting business goals and expectations becomes more difficult. The rules of business are based on the political environment, the legal environment, and the cultural values and norms of a country. The political environment sets the general scope of business in areas such as ownership issues, how involved government should or should not be in business, with what countries firms are allowed to do business, and the general disposition of government toward business in terms of laws governing business activities. The stability of a political system within a country will affect business in that country. There is greater risk in doing business in countries with unstable governments where changes in government regime occur frequently. With every regime change, there is potential for the laws governing business practices to change. Sometimes the laws can be beneficial to business and other times they may be detrimental.

The legal environment of business is complicated on two levels. First, laws vary from country to country. Therefore, the set of laws by which a business operates will be different from one country to another. Firms doing business internationally must be familiar with the laws of each country in which they do business. For example, in the United States, the legal workweek for hourly employees is 40 hours per week. In France, the legal workweek is 35 hours per week. In the United States, foreign companies are allowed to have 100 percent ownership of a U.S. subsidiary. In many countries, this is not the case; foreign subsidiaries must be partially owned by locals.

Even when all the laws pertaining to business in another country are known, doing business is further complicated by interpretation of the law. Most countries around the world govern businesses by one of two legal systems: common law system or civil law system. While there are many differences between the two systems, a major difference affecting business involves interpretation of the law. In a common law system, interpretation of a law is usually based on past precedent. Thus, interpretation of a law applied to similar situations will result in congruous interpretations. In a civil law system, interpretation of the law applied to a situation is determined independently of other, similar situations. Therefore, it may be possible to have very different outcomes even in the interpretation of the same law in similar situations. Further, the disadvantage of being a foreigner in another country compounds the challenge of maneuvering through the political and legal environment of a foreign country. International business law is a specialty within a legal system and all attorneys and judges may not be trained in the international aspects of their legal system.

Another component of the legal and political systems of a country that affects international business activities is the transparency (or lack of) of these systems. The developed world has well-established systems with relatively high levels of transparency. Transparency in business relates to the ability to follow the business activities of a firm in order to determine that the rules of business for that country are being followed. Systems with high levels of transparency also have strong systems of checks and balances, which help maintain accountability at various levels of the organization.

Countries without high levels of transparency make it difficult for economic development to occur. If an investor firm does not know where its money is going or how it is being accounted for, it is less likely that the firm will invest in that country. This has become a major challenge for developing countries. The lack of stability in governments and tendency toward corruption tend to reduce the level of transparency with the legal, political, and business systems.

Culture (see Chapter 4) transcends all other systems of a country. It is so important that you see it woven through other topics as well. Culture determines our values (what we believe) and our norms (how we should behave). Our values and norms influence our decisions, our actions, and our thoughts. Thus, culture has played a large role in the development of political and legal systems of each country. Understanding cultural differences helps in understanding the political and legal systems and in the interpretation of those systems in which it is necessary to operate when in a foreign country.

❖ ECONOMIC INTEGRATION

As briefly noted in Chapter 2, countries no longer operate in a completely independent manner. Increased global competition has led to a greater level of economic cooperation between countries in order to gain competitive advantages over other countries. The term *economic integration* is used to generally identify these groupings of country cooperation. The depth and breadth of economic cooperation can and does vary greatly from one country grouping to another. Explanation of the specific differences is beyond the scope of this book. However, a brief explanation of economic integration in general will help in understanding today's international business environment. Additionally, a number of the most prominent country groupings are discussed.

The level of economic development varies widely from one country to another and influences the effect on the country's companies' business strategies and practices. Most country governments strive to strengthen their economic position internally as well as globally. Economic strength is a means to political power and influence in the world, and therefore governments create policies to encourage economic growth. As economies grow, cultures become more individualistic (Hofstede, 1983). The collective necessity (for survival) in poor economies is replaced by a desire for more individual identity. Even in highly collective societies such as Japan, this change can be seen. Twenty-five years ago, Japanese businessmen (only men held managerial positions in business other than support positions such as secretarial supervisors) stayed with the same company for their entire careers. They did not consider moving to another company to improve their managerial or economic position. Today this is no longer the case. Japanese business managers (still mostly men, but there are now some women in managerial positions) now move from one company to another in order to advance their careers. This is an indication of the Japanese culture becoming more individualistic. However, this is not to imply that the Japanese culture is rapidly approaching the individualistic orientation of Western cultures.

Along the same line, as countries adopt more market-oriented economic policies such as a reduction of trade barriers and the adoption of a free-market orientation, individuals have an opportunity to innovate and gain individual economic wealth. To improve the potential for and level of economic development, countries have entered into cooperative agreements that provide competitive advantages for firms doing business within those countries.

One of the most dynamic changes in the global environment affecting competitive strategies of firms has been the increase in economic integration at the country level. By definition, economic integration is

> a process and state of affairs. Regarded as a process, it encompasses measures designed to abolish discrimination between economic units belonging to different national states; viewed as a state of affairs, it can be represented by the absence of various forms of discrimination between national economies. (Balassa, 1961, p. 1)

Discrimination between economic units relates to the policies developed by national governments (the economic unit) in order to protect the economic stability and growth of its country and its economic activities. In other words, governments create barriers to protect domestic businesses from foreign competition. Typically, the policies involved relate to trade, foreign direct investment (FDI), and generally the activities of a foreign firm within the country's national boundaries. There are several levels of economic integration, but it is beyond the scope of this book to go into a detailed explanation of them. However, any discussion of economic integration should at a minimum identify the various levels. The levels of economic integration begin with a free trade area (elimination of tariffs between countries) and gradually deepen between country policy agreements to a customs union (a common external tariff schedule among member countries); a common market (free flow of labor and capital across member country borders); an economic union (a common economic policy); and finally a complete economic, political, and social union (a "united states").

All countries hold some level of protectionist policies, but strong discriminatory (protectionist) policies have resulted in weakened domestic economies. Protectionist barriers tend to support inefficient businesses that are unable to compete globally and many times do not have a domestic market able to sustain growth. For example, prior to the revived push for deeper economic integration by the European Economic Community (now the European Union) in the mid-1980s, member countries experienced high unemployment and low economic growth rates resulting in stagnating economies (which over time leads to a reduction in the standard of living). A primary cause of this poor economic performance was the lack of standardization within industries across member countries as well as the establishment of many non-tariff barriers[1] between member nations in order to protect self-interests and national sovereignty. In other words, European countries each required different standards (product specifications) for the same product, making it difficult to gain economies of scale in manufacturing. Companies would have to modify products for each country market, which would increase the cost of production and therefore make them less profitable and unable to grow. Individual countries were too small to provide the volume needed for cost advantages in manufacturing, and varying standards made it difficult to sell a product outside the country's borders. Prior to the deepened integration of the European Union in the late 1980s and early 1990s, each European Union country separately set the standards for over 300 product categories. Thus, company activities occurred on a country-by-country basis because cross-border interaction did not provide a competitive advantage. Countries were faced with aging firms unable to update due to lack of a competitive position.

Economic integration has impacted business in all regions of the world. Countries involved in economic integration agreements give preference to other member countries. There is greater potential for doing business in member countries and fewer barriers to trade.

Economically integrated areas are relevant to understanding the international business environment. When developing strategies for business in other countries, managers must take a wider perspective than just a country-by-country approach.

❖ EUROPEAN UNION

The initial agreement of what today is the European Union was created in the early 1950s. Over the decades since that time, the evolution of the European Union has resulted in a cooperative agreement among 25 countries that cumulatively rivals the economic and competitive strength of the United States. Companies doing business with one or several EU countries no longer approach countries individually. Individual member countries of the European Union are no longer strategically viewed individually. Instead, the European Union is looked at as one large market of 27 member countries with a population of over 485 million people and a GDP of over 11 trillion dollars (USD). This includes the addition of Romania and Bulgaria in 2007 which contributes about 29 million people to the population of the European Union and about 230 million dollars to its GDP. Additionally, Turkey and Croatia are currently under consideration for EU membership and will add about 77 million to the population and increase the European Union's GPD by at least a half-billion dollars (Central Intelligence Agency, n.d.). Table 7.1 provides a size perspective comparing the European Union, the United States, and China. It also illustrates the need for looking at the European Union as a unit as well as individual countries. The European Union is not a united states of Europe. However, from a competitive position in the global environment, many of the benefits of a united states are being realized by EU countries and companies within its borders. Taken together, the EU countries have comparable economic strength to the United States. Further, the creation of a single currency, the Euro, for a large portion of the European Union has simplified international business transactions significantly by reducing exchange rate risk and making performance assessment easier. Table 7.1 also indicates the countries that have adopted the Euro.

Note that the population of the European Union is substantially greater than the U.S. population while the geographic size of the European Union is substantially smaller. One may rightly conclude that the population of the European Union is denser. From a cultural perspective, this is an important point; as people from different cultures interact, cultural assimilation takes place and people begin to

Table 7.1   Population and GDP of European Union Countries

Member Country	Population (millions)	GDP (billion $)	GDP/capita (ppp) ($)
Austria[b]	8.2	255.9	31,300
Belgium[b]	10.4	316.2	30,600
Cyprus	0.8	15.7/4.5[a]	20,300/7,135[a]
Czech Republic	10.2	161.1	15,700
Denmark	5.4	174.4	32,200
Estonia	1.3	19.2	14,300
Finland[b]	5.2	151.2	29,000
France[b]	60.6	1,737.0	28,700
Germany[b]	82.4	2,362.0	28,700
Greece[b]	10.7	226.4	21,300
Hungary	10.0	149.3	14,900
Ireland[b]	4.0	126.4	31,900
Italy[b]	58.1	1,609.0	27,700
Latvia	2.3	23.9	10,200
Lithuania	3.6	40.9	11,400
Luxembourg[b]	0.5	27.3	58,900
Malta	0.4	7.2	18,200
Poland	38.6	38.6	12,000
Portugal[b]	10.5	181.8	18,000
Slovakia	5.4	72.3	13,300
Slovenia	2.0	39.4	19,600
Spain[b]	40.3	885.5	22,000
Sweden	9.0	255.4	28,400
The Netherlands[b]	16.4	481.1	29,500
United Kingdom	60.4	1,782.0	29,600
EU Total	458.7	11,568.1	25,200
New EU Members			
Bulgaria	7.5	61.6	8,200
Romania	22.3	171.5	7,700
Applicant Countries			
Croatia	4.5	50.3	11,200
Turkey	69.7	508.7	7,400
Applicant Total	74.2	559	7,534
Comparison Countries			
China	1,306.3	7,262.0	5,600
United States	295.8	11,750.0	40,100

SOURCE: Central Intelligence Agency, n.d.

[a]Cyprus statistics are shown for Republic of Cyprus/Northern Cyprus.

[b]Countries that have adopted the Euro

adapt behaviors to fit the new multicultural environments. An anecdotal example will help illustrate these changes. One of the authors of this book has been teaching master's-level classes in France since the mid-1990s. Every year she has asked her students a simple question, "Do you consider yourselves French or European?" In the early years, the response from students was an emphatic "Of course, we are French!" implying that it was an insult to be considered European. As the years continued and European integration deepened, the response changed. To the same question, less than 10 years after it was first asked, the response was, "We are European and we are French." Although the students still identify with their country, their perspective is much broader; they have embraced the integration of Europe into their attitudes and perspectives.

From a macro, or European Union perspective, policies and behaviors are also influenced by a multicountry, multicultural governing body. The result is an agglomeration, or hybrid, of all countries/ cultures involved. This shift from an individual-country perspective to a regional or multicountry perspective also leads to a shift in competitive strategy for firms. Firms must take a more geocentric approach to their planning. In other words, planning becomes more complicated because it needs to involve elements from a variety of countries and cultures when determining its direction. Likewise, the related business transactions involve regional teams that consist of individuals representing a variety of countries. Firms must take a geocentric approach internally in order to communicate and come to agreement on strategic priorities and direction. Especially in the cases of larger, more experienced multinational firms, regional teams will also be multinational; employees from a variety of countries will serve together on a regional team. Therefore, internal communication and negotiation will require cultural adaptation.

The second layer of complication occurs when a multinational regional team interacts with a foreign company. The individuals from the foreign company involved in the international business transaction may come from similar or different cultures, may include one or several individuals, and may include businesspeople as well as government officials. Thus, the potential for complicated negotiation interactions increases. For example, an American expatriate living in France headed a project management team for a major French computer company. One of his projects involved a strategic alliance with a large American computer firm and a large Italian computer firm. Meeting locations for the team would rotate among the three countries. The language spoken at each meeting also rotated, making it necessary to use interpreters when in Italy, even though the Italians could each speak at least one of the other languages.

❖ THE AMERICAS

North, Central, and South America make up the area of the world referred to as the Americas. The historical political divide between the north and the other regions has been dissolved, with the exception of recent political developments in Venezuela and Bolivia. Central and South American governments have been restructuring over the past 20 years to create a more democratically oriented framework and to open "the Americas'" doors to the global marketplace. As you may recall from the discussion of FDI (foreign direct investment) in Chapter 2, developing economies such as those in Central and South America struggle to develop economically without FDI. For most developing countries, the need for FDI has necessitated political reforms. Basically, without political reform, foreign companies will not invest in those countries whose political and economic policies are too risky to the investing company.

Although the countries of Central and South America are categorized as developing economies, many of the countries have made substantial progress toward improving their economies through their involvement in economic integration. Existing agreements such as NAFTA, Mercosur, and the Andean Community have helped member countries improve regional and global competitiveness. Cooperative agreements under discussion such as CAFTA and FTAA aim to unite more countries economically in order to improve the potential for economic development for all involved.

The Andean Community and Mercosur

The Andean Community originated in 1969 as the Andean Pact. The goal was to establish common policies for trade, including the elimination of tariffs between member countries, establishment of a common external tariff policy, and free movement of labor and capital across borders. Member countries include Bolivia, Colombia, Ecuador, Peru, and Venezuela.

Mercosur was formed in 1991 with the signing of a treaty to establish a common market. The countries involved were Argentina, Brazil, Paraguay, and Uruguay. Mercosur has a total population of 235.4 million and a cumulative GDP of 2054.7 billion. More recently, representatives of Mercosur and the Andean Community have been negotiating an agreement to establish a free trade area between the two groups. A free trade area means products can move from one member country to another without tariffs. This typically makes products from within the member countries more price competitive than products coming from outside the trade bloc. As you can see in Table 7.2, Mercosur and the Andean Community combined have a population of over 320 million. Although the cumulative GDP is relatively low compared to a developed country with a similar population, there is great potential for economic growth as these trading blocks increase their levels of cooperation. The potential for economic growth can already be seen. The 2005 Financial Times Top 100 firms in Latin America indicates that half of the firms come from countries that are members of either Mercosur or the Andean Community.

Table 7.2   Mercosur and the Andean Community

		Population (millions)	GDP (purchasing power in billion $)	GDP/ Capita ($)
Mercosur	Argentina	39.5	483.5	12,240
	Brazil	186.1	1492.0	8,017
	Paraguay	6.4	29.9	4,672
	Uruguay	3.4	49.3	1,450
	Total	235.4	2054.7	8,729
Andean Community	Bolivia	8.9	22.3	2,506
	Colombia	43.0	281.1	6,537
	Ecuador	13.4	49.5	3,694
	Peru	27.9	155.3	5,566
	Venezuela	25.4	84.8	3,339
	Total	118.6	593.0	5,000

SOURCE: Central Intelligence Agency, n.d.

NAFTA

One of the fastest-growing economies of Central and South America is Mexico. Much of Mexico's success can be attributed to the competitive advantage held by Mexico due to its membership in the North American Free Trade Area (NAFTA). Established in 1994 between Canada, the United States, and Mexico, the NAFTA agreement created a free trade area between member countries. Most products originating from one of the member countries can be distributed to other member countries without tariff charges. The benefit for Mexico has been substantial. Mexico has the second-largest population in Latin America, of 102.2 million people. Brazil is 45 percent larger with a population of 186.1 million people. However, Brazil's GDP, 1,492.0 trillion (USD), is only 33 percent larger than Mexico's 1,006 trillion (World Bank Group, 2005). Thus Mexico has a larger per capita GDP than Brazil ($9,843.40 compared to $8,017.00, respectively), indicative that Mexico arguably has a stronger economy than Brazil.

Table 7.3   NAFTA Members

	Population (2005 est. in millions)	GDP (2005 est. in billion $)	GDP/capita ($)
Canada	32.8	1,023.0	31,189
Mexico	102.2	1,006.0	9,843
United States	295.7	11,750.0	39,736
Total	430.7	13,779.0	31,992

SOURCE: Central Intelligence Agency, n.d.

CAFTA-DR and FTAA

Two other initiatives to further integrate the Americas are noteworthy. As the number of countries involved is large and the negotiations occur between representatives of the country governments, the process has been slow. However, the vision behind the initiatives has strong political support from many countries.

CAFTA-DR, the Central American-Dominican Republic Free Trade Agreement, is an agreement that has been negotiated among Costa Rica, El Salvador, Honduras, Guatemala, Nicaragua, the Dominican Republic, and the United States. Before the agreement can be implemented, it must be ratified by each of the member countries. The agreement is intended to promote economic growth throughout Central America and the Dominican Republic through the elimination of trade barriers between member countries. In other words, products going from one country to another within the free trade area will be tariff- or duty-free. The expectation is that more firms will be attracted to doing business within the area and the rate of economic growth will increase for member countries.

In 1994, discussion began for the creation of a free trade area of the Americas. Thirty-four countries agreed to construct a cooperative agreement outlining the progressive elimination of trade barriers between member countries. The impact of this agreement is significant. Economic integration of the Americas could help the developing regions of Central and South America to become developed at a much faster rate than countries could develop independently.

Table 7.4   CAFTA-DR Members

	Population (2005 est. in millions)	GDP (2004 est. in billion $)
Costa Rica	4.0	37.97
El Salvador	6.7	32.35
Honduras	7.0	18.79
Guatemala	14.7	59.47
Nicaragua	5.5	12.34
Dominican Republic	9.0	55.68
United States	295.7	11,750.00

SOURCE: Central Intelligence Agency, n.d.

Table 7.5   Proposed FTAA Members

Antigua & Barbados	Dominica	Nicaragua
Argentina	Dominican Republic	Panama
Bahamas	Ecuador	Paraguay
Barbados	El Salvador	Peru
Belize	Grenada	Saint Kitts & Nevis
Bolivia	Guatemala	Saint Lucia
Brazil	Guyana	Saint Vincent &
Canada	Haiti	The Grenadines
Chile	Honduras	Suriname
Colombia	Jamaica	Trinidad & Tobago
Costa Rica	Mexico	United States
		Uruguay
		Venezuela

SOURCE: Central Intelligence Agency, n.d.

FDI from the United States, Canada, and some of the more developed southern economies such as Brazil and Mexico, to the lesser-developed economies would increase substantially, creating more jobs and stimulating the economies. As the economies grow, demand for consumer goods and services increases, which benefits the developed countries within the cooperative agreement.

❖ IMPACT OF ECONOMIC INTEGRATION ON BUSINESS

Economically integrated countries provide greater economic opportunities for business. A firm choosing to do business in one country of an economically integrated group can improve its competitive position within the entire area. This means that entry decisions (how, when, and where to enter a foreign market) have wider ramifications than the immediate decision. Individual decisions affect the firm's international strategy. For example, many U.S. companies have used Mexico as their first entry into Latin America, because of its membership in NAFTA. Companies could produce products in Mexico for export to the U.S. and Canadian markets tariff-free. Eventually, those plants would also serve other Latin American countries. A long-term benefit of such a strategy is that the Mexican subsidiaries of U.S. companies can be used to integrate Latin American culture (at a general level) with U.S. business practices and create effective international business managers and negotiators.

However, when doing business in an economically integrated area, there may be an additional level of legal and political systems to deal with. Some laws regarding international business transactions occur at the country level while other applicable laws may be at the regional level, with the region being the governing system of the economically integrated area. And, there is not always agreement between the governing system of the region and the member-country government. The international business negotiator must be familiar with both levels of governance as well as home-country requirements.

Negotiating a specific transaction must also take into account the bigger picture of the firm's international strategy. To understand the bigger picture potential, negotiators must understand the importance of economic cooperation between countries.

Types of FDI Activities

There are various types of business transactions that involve FDI. In this section, we will discuss some of the most common. By understanding these activities, you will better be able to assess the types of communication activities needed for successful transactions as well as gain an idea of the dynamics involved in these activities.

There are two major categories of FDI activities: *wholly owned investments* and *joint venture investments*. Wholly owned investments involve only the investing firm. In this case, a firm chooses to set up an operation (a subunit of the parent firm) in another country of which the investing firm maintains 100 percent control. In order to do this, the investing firm must obtain permission from the host government. Additionally, all the negotiations involved in setting up a new operation (construction contracts, land sales/leasing, supplier contracts, etc.) are usually handled by the investing firm. If a firm has little experience in the foreign market, these interactions can be difficult. The investing firm must be able to navigate the legal system, political system, and cultural system of the foreign country. All of these systems complicate the related negotiations and in many cases extend the time from start to completion of the investment project.

Wholly owned subsidiaries can take the form of new ventures as discussed in the previous paragraph. These are typically called greenfield investments, the name being derived from the fact that investing firms find a piece of land (i.e., a greenfield) and build a building (e.g., a manufacturing plant or building for company personnel). In 2003, there were over 9,000 greenfield investments in developing countries alone, with China as the receiving country of the largest number of these investments (UNCTAD, 2004). Greenfield investments typically take substantial investment and time, but allow for a great deal of control over the design and operation of the facility.

Other forms of wholly owned investments can occur through *cross-border mergers and acquisitions*. A *merger* involves two companies combining to become one entity, typically under one of the original company names or a hybrid name derived from the two original names. For example, when Daimler AG of Germany and Chrysler Corporation of the United States merged, they changed their name to Daimler Chrysler. In an international merger, two firms from different cultures combine to become one firm. As you might expect, merging country cultures as well as organizational cultures magnifies the normal challenges of doing business. Daimler Chrysler's merger has been faced with the challenge of convincing German managers to go to the United States for extended periods of time (2–3 years) and American managers to go to Germany. This exchange of management is an important strategy for a newly merged company because it facilitates the transfer of management know-how and technology between the two formerly independent organizations. It also helps to integrate organizational cultures, although this is a difficult task. In the Daimler Chrysler example, Americans did not want to give up their expansive lifestyle for a relatively small apartment flat, away from friends, family, country clubs, and so on. The Germans did not want to live in the American culture. Interestingly, another issue in this example was the disparity between compensation levels for expatriates from each country (firms pay premiums to entice employees to live and work in a foreign country for an extended period of time). From a communication perspective, every day becomes more of a communication challenge (with mergers, management of the company is shared by executives from both of the original firms) in both formal and informal business transactions/interactions.

Acquisitions present a different type of challenge. In an acquisition, one firm acquires another firm. The acquiring firm maintains ownership and management control over the acquired firm. The communication challenges occur as the acquiring firm makes changes (e.g., strategic changes, operational changes) within the acquired firm in order to bring the acquired firm in line with the business practices and strategies of the acquiring firms. As with mergers, this involves changing the organizational cultures of the acquired firm (keep in mind, the acquired firm in this context is a foreign firm).

The mechanics of a *joint venture* are different from mergers and acquisitions, but many of the international business challenges are similar. In a joint venture investment, there are typically two firms each from a different country (joint ventures do occur between firms from the same country, but that doesn't involve FDI). Each firm contributes certain agreed-upon assets to form a third, independent company that is typically located in one of the partners' home country. The assets brought by each company to the joint venture are determined through the initial negotiations between the partner companies, and typically the newly created company is managed by both partners. The balance of power within the management structure will vary according to the negotiated outcome. Since the 1980s, joint ventures have been a very attractive way for firms to expand into the international business environment. In terms of assets contributed to the joint venture, the foreign firm contributes capital, technological know-how, and management know-how. The partner firm that is located in the same country as the new joint venture firm usually contributes local market knowledge such as understanding the customer, the channels of distribution, laws related to business, and how the political system within the country works. These elements would take time for a foreign firm to acquire on its own.

Thinking about the structure of the organization resulting from a joint venture, the management challenge should become clear. Two firms from different countries and therefore different cultures, as well as different organizational cultures, agree to work together in the management of a company. Unfortunately, in many cases, this seems easier than it is. Research has shown that a main reason joint ventures fail is management conflict. This conflict can be linked back to differences in management styles (organizational culture) as well as differences in strategic perspectives (Anderson & Jap, 2005; Harrigan, 1985). Even with well-negotiated contracts, the management challenges can hurt the relationship.

The joint venture can take the form of an acquisition, where two companies agree to buy an already-existing firm. This form further complicates communication, as discussed earlier. A joint venture can also be formed as a greenfield project, which adds the challenges of this type of strategy. In summary, with joint ventures, you have the same communication challenges of wholly owned subsidiaries relative to the type of investment made (acquisition or greenfield). In addition, you also have the challenges of internal communication between managers and employees from different countries and cultures. It is not only the formal negotiations that require cross-cultural understanding but also the day-to-day informal negotiations (communication).

As previously noted in Chapter 4, the acquisition of Firestone, a U.S. company, by Bridgestone, a Japanese company, in 1987 serves as a good illustration of how organizational and cultural differences can cause difficulties. When Bridgestone acquired Firestone, they sent a number of personnel from Japan to work in the United States. The integration of Japanese and American employees expected to work together created conflict and disharmony; the Japanese viewed Americans as being lazy. Of course, this was not well received by Americans. If you compare the number of hours worked by U.S. managers to the number of hours worked by Japanese managers, it is easy to see a discrepancy. In general, American managers work Monday through Friday until early evening and, in many cases, a partial day on Saturday. In contrast, Japanese managers typically work every night of the week, many times until 11:00 or 12:00 at night, and full days on Saturday. Much of their evening work may be in a social setting (e.g., dinner), but it is considered work because, in a collective country like Japan, building strong relationships with business associates is critical to doing business. For American culture, the U.S. managers were meeting cultural expectations. Applying Japanese cultural expectations to American managers, however, caused a conflict. As an aside, from an American individualist perspective, the Japanese could have been viewed as being inefficient because they focused so much of their time on the company. Perspective is critical, and understanding the perspective of others improves the likelihood of successful international business negotiation.

Non-FDI Activities

There are several options, other than FDI, for companies to become involved in the international business environment. Each mode requires agreements with other companies, most of which are foreign firms.

Exporting

Exporting involves the manufacture of a product in the home country that is shipped and sold in a foreign country. Exports can be sold directly through the home-country company or indirectly through a home-country intermediary such as a foreign freight forwarder, an export trading company, or other types of intermediary organizations (intermediaries take care of the numerous tasks involved in physically exporting a product). When exporting, an agreement with the buyer is needed to outline the terms of the transfer of goods and subsequent distribution of those products. This can involve several intermediaries with whom a negotiated contract is needed. In addition to the sales contracts, agreements must also be reached with the domestic transporter and the foreign-country transporter, as well as the financial services company that finances the production and distribution of and payment for the product sold. The company responsible for each negotiation depends on the initial sales agreement, which specifies which party in the buyer/seller agreement is responsible for each step in the export process.

Exporting requires that the exporting company follow home-country regulations (e.g., customs requirements) as well as host-country regulations. Regulations regarding exporting vary from country to country. Exporting, and much of other international trade, is governed by the World Trade Organization (WTO). The WTO is a multilateral, non-governmental international organization that works to promote free and fair trade between member countries; the majority of countries worldwide are members of the WTO. Thus, international business managers and negotiators must stay abreast of WTO negotiations and discussions.

Contractual Agreements

A variety of contractual agreements exist in international business. In all types, there is some type of contractual agreement between two parties, each typically from a different country. Because of differences in political and legal systems, cultures, and business practices, it is difficult to standardize the approaches and expectations across countries.

Licensing and Franchising

In a licensing agreement, a firm (the licensor) agrees to allow another firm (the licensee) to use some part of its business process, such as its brand name or the manufacture of a specific product. The license agreement typically stipulates a time period for the license, a specific territory in which the licensee can use the licensed product or service, and a fee structure under which a certain percentage of revenues from the licensee (pertaining to the licensed product or service) go to the licensor. Licensing can benefit the licensor by increasing revenues, typically through expansion into markets where the licensor was not expanding. This type of agreement is beneficial for aging technologies and processes that are not considered intellectual property (intellectual property should always be protected in contractual agreements). A potential problem with licensing agreements is the payment of fees to the licensor. As the licensee operates in a different country, oversight of how a contract is carried out, as well as monitoring revenues from the licensed product/service, becomes very difficult. Additionally, as in all forms of contractual agreements, resolving contract issues or disputes can be costly and difficult due to differences in legal systems between countries. The elements of a licensing agreement typically include the product/service specifications, the length of the license, the license territory, the licensing fee, and a royalty payment.

Franchise agreements are a specific type of licensing agreement in which specific assets and know-how are expected from each party. The franchisor usually provides the company/brand name and the product or service associated with it. It also provides technological and management know-how. The franchisee usually provides the capital necessary for the construction and operation of the franchise, the personnel to operate the franchise, and the local market knowledge. Income to the franchisor is primarily in the form of franchise and royalty fees. Because brand name, and therefore brand/company image, are involved in franchising, it is important that the contractual agreement is very detailed and specific in order to maintain consistency in the brand worldwide. Probably the best example of a well-conceived franchise system is McDonald's Worldwide. McDonald's has been able to maintain consistency of its operations and brand throughout the world. The headquarters of McDonald's (the franchisor) must approve all suppliers, systems, and ingredients used in a McDonald's franchise. Contractually, the franchisor has a great deal of control. Of course, in this case, franchisees benefit from the efficiencies of the McDonald's systems as well as its widely recognized and valuable brand name.

Contract Manufacturing

When you look at the label on a piece of apparel, a pair of shoes, or a small appliance in the United States, it will indicate where the product was made. By law, this is required. You will also notice that the majority of products in these categories are produced outside the United States. The company that sells these products, such as Sears or the Gap, does not usually own the manufacturing facility that produces the product. Instead, the retailer contracts with a textile manufacturer (in the case of apparel) or other product-specific manufacturer to manufacture a product to the retailer's specifications including input materials, design, quantity, price, and delivery expectations (this is not an all-inclusive list). Over time, negotiating these contracts should become easier because companies tend to stay with the same manufacturers as a relationship develops. Although we have only discussed contract manufacturing in terms of retailers, the same type of agreement is used for third-party production of component parts of many manufactured goods. In most cases, contracts cover multiple production runs and delivery periods.

Turnkey Agreements

Turnkey projects most frequently involve process technologies, such as oil refineries, that do not include intellectual property of the constructing company. In a turnkey agreement, a company with a specific technology contracts with a foreign government to build and bring into operation a plant using the company's technology. Payment from the contracting government typically occurs in lump sum payments at specific negotiated intervals throughout the project. Once all payments have been received by the constructing company, ownership of the new plant is turned over to the government.

The involvement of government in a turnkey agreement implies that turnkeys typically occur in developing countries where governments remain directly in control of commercial activities, especially those involving raw materials such as oil. In situations like this, businesses find themselves negotiating with businesspeople in the foreign country who may be political appointees. Thus, the goals of the foreign partner may be commercially (e.g., profit, market share) as well as politically (e.g., position, employment) motivated.

Another type of agreement that is related to turnkey agreements is a management contract. As will be discussed a little later in this chapter, companies who build turnkey plants many times develop secondary agreements with the foreign entity to purchase some or all of the output from the newly constructed plant. In other words, the turnkey becomes a new supplier for the constructing firm. One of the problems with many turnkey operations is the ongoing management of the new operation. The developing country does not always have the management and technical skill to efficiently operate the new facility. To overcome this problem, the company constructing the turnkey will negotiate a management contract to provide the personnel needed to manage and efficiently operate the new facility. The turnkey contract and the management contract are usually negotiated at the same time because the output from the turnkey operation is as important (maybe more important) to the constructing company as the income from the turnkey construction itself. Without a management contract (or control over the operations of the new facility), companies have experienced problems receiving the required quality and quantity of output expected.

Another element frequently included in management contracts is training for local personnel. The goal of this component is to train locals in technology and management skills so they will be able to take over the management of the operation in the future. This is beneficial for two reasons. First, the cost of foreign managers is substantially higher than the cost of using local managers. Second, improving local technology and management skills aids the foreign country in building the assets needed for economic development.

Countertrade

International business transactions affect many aspects of a country's economy. Thus, country governments monitor the flow of goods, services, and capital that move across its borders. The tracking of transactions coming into a country and going out of a country is done through balance-of-payments accounts.[2] The goal of most countries is to have a balanced flow between monetary inflows (what comes into a country) and monetary outflows (what goes out of a country).

To understand the basic concept of balance of payments, it is important to remember that an international business transaction generally involves a two-way flow of goods/services and money. The seller sells a product/service to a buyer in another country and the buyer pays for the product. From the seller's country perspective, the product/service flows out of the country and the payment (traditionally money) flows in, thus a two-way flow. For the buying country, the flows would be in the opposite direction (inflow of product/service and outflow of money). When the amount of money flowing out of a country is greater than the amount of money flowing into a country, this creates a balance-of-payments deficit. At the simplest level, this means there is less money within the country to use in domestic economic development and growth as well as for purchasing foreign products and services.

A complicating element of the international business transaction is the issue of currency. Specifically, countries each have their own currency. Part of the negotiation is determining the currency in which payments will be made. Companies look at the exchange rate volatility (how much change there is in the exchange rate between their own currency and the foreign country currency). The greater the volatility, the more difficult it is to determine the expected profits from a transaction. When negotiating an agreement between two developed countries, the currency negotiation is typically not difficult because both countries have hard currencies,[3] which tend to be relatively stable. The number of currencies from developed countries (hard currencies) was reduced substantially by the creation of the Euro in 1999,[4] thus reducing exchange rate volatility.

Not only is exchange rate volatility an issue in an international business contract, but also the repatriation of profits can be problematic, especially in countries where there is a lack of hard currency. Repatriation of profits relates to the ability to take profits from your foreign operation out of the country to your home country or another country. Developing countries may have restrictions on the amount of money (hard currency) that can be taken out of the country. This is an issue that should be discussed and resolved, if possible, early in the negotiation process.

Determining the monetary currency to be used in a contract when negotiating with a developing country is not quite as simple. Developing-country currencies are usually considered soft currencies (see Note 3) and are more volatile in terms of exchange rate than currencies of developed countries. Most companies, especially those from developed countries, will not accept soft currencies as the currency of payment of a contract. Therefore, developing countries must accumulate reserves of hard currencies in order to pay for goods and services purchased from other countries (in most cases, from developed countries). With the exception of China and the major oil-producing countries, most developing countries tend to buy more goods/services internationally than they sell, creating a balance-of-payments deficit (more outflow of money for the goods/services purchased than inflow of money for goods/services sold), which can hinder internal economic growth.

As a way to overcome some of the balance-of-payments deficits caused by a large outflow of money for the purchase of goods and services in international transactions, countries have long used barter agreements, where goods/services purchased from the selling country (company) are paid for with goods/services from the buying country (company). In addition to barter agreements, a growing area of international business agreements, called countertrade agreements, helps deal with payment and currency issues. *Countertrade* is the general term used for business transactions that are based on negotiated agreements involving some level of reciprocity. Some of the specific types of countertrade are offsets, buyback, counterpurchase, and umbrella countertrade agreements. Tracking the volume of countertrade done worldwide is difficult, but it is estimated that countertrade agreements account for 20 to 40 percent of trade worldwide (Daniels & Radebaugh, 2001). Because countertrade is involved in a substantial portion of world trade, it warrants further discussion.

Barter, the earliest form of exchange, usually involves the trade of goods and services where the seller receives goods/services in payment for the goods/services sold. The obligations of each party in the transaction would be detailed in the same contract. One of the best-known barter agreements was between PepsiCo and the former Soviet Union in the 1970s. PepsiCo wanted to set up bottling plants in the former Soviet Union. PepsiCo agreed to accept vodka in payment for the Pepsi syrup and bottling equipment they sold to the former Soviet Union (Okoroafo, 1993). This relationship between PepsiCo and (now) Russia still exists today, with additional barter agreements being made. The result is that Pepsi has been a successful product in Russia for over 30 years.

Offset agreements are used in large-scale industries such as the defense, aircraft, and energy industries, where the products sold have very high price tags. In an offset agreement, the seller agrees to buy a specific amount (based on value of the original sale) of products/services from the buying country. The offset can be either a direct offset, in which the products/services purchased are directly related to the product being sold by the seller, or an indirect offset, in which the product being purchased is not related to the product being sold (by the seller). An example may help in understanding an offset agreement. In 1994, China agreed to purchase as many as 50 aircraft worth more than five billion dollars from Boeing ("Offsets and Countertrade," 1994). As part of the agreement, Boeing signed a contract with the China Aviation Supply Company to supply the rear fuselage for the aircraft. This would be considered a direct offset agreement. In direct offsets, the parts produced by the buyer country (in this case, China) are exported to the seller country (the United States), where they are integrated into the final product, which is then sent back to the buyer country. Thus, the inflow of money (to China) from the sale of the fuselage parts to the United States helped offset the outflow of money from China to the United States for the aircraft.

In an indirect offset agreement, the products/services purchased by the seller to help offset capital outflows from the buying country are not related to the product/service involved in the primary transaction. In these situations, sellers accumulate what are called offset obligations

(obligations to purchase a certain amount of products or services from the buyer country). The seller company then looks for partner companies to help meet these obligations. McDonnell Douglas Helicopters assumed indirect offset obligations as part of a contract to sell helicopters to the United Arab Emirates. A U.S. law firm, Squire, Sanders, & Dempsey, helped McDonnel Douglas Helicopters fulfill those obligations through the services they were providing to the UAE government relating to environmental regulations ("Offsets and Countertrade," 1994). Trying to clarify the flow of money may help in understanding indirect offset obligations from the sale of helicopters to the UAE. McDonnell Douglas sold helicopters to the UAE. Thus, helicopters (product) flowed to the UAE, and money (payment for the helicopters) flowed to the United States. The indirect offset agreement would stipulate that at some date in the future, McDonnell Douglas, or another company on behalf of McDonnell Douglas, would purchase products or services from UAE, which would cause a flow of money into UAE. In this example, instead of money flowing into UAE, there was an inflow of value in the form of legal services from the law firm cited above. Instead of the UAE government paying directly for the legal services, McDonnell Douglas would have arranged payment to the law firm for the services provided to the UAE in order to fulfill some of its offset obligations.

Another form of countertrade, the *counterpurchase agreement*, typically involves two separate contracts where one contract is contingent on the other. In a counterpurchase agreement, the seller country from the first contract enters into a second contract with the buyer agreeing to purchase a set amount (value) of products/services from the buyer country of the first contract. The monetary values of the two contracts do not have to be equal. As a side note and reminder, it may seem unusual to refer to the buyer or seller as a country. It is important to keep in mind that in developing countries, much of the commercial activity is owned and controlled at least partially by the governments. Therefore, in many situations, companies are negotiating with country governments.

The final type of countertrade agreement to be discussed is the *buyback agreement*. Buyback agreements are typically used with turnkey agreements where the seller company contracts with another country to build a processing or manufacturing facility. The seller company also agrees, in many cases, to buy some or all of the products produced in the new facility (thus the need for the management contract discussed earlier). In some instances, payment for the facility or equipment is made through the buyback arrangement. In other cases, payment for the facility is made with monetary instruments (money), followed by the buyback arrangement. The strategic benefit of buyback agreements is that the company who builds the new facility or sells the processing equipment is essentially creating a new supplier for its other operations. This is where the management contract, in the case of a turnkey facility, becomes important. As the seller company plans to use the output of the new operations, controlling the quality of that output becomes very important.

❖ IMPORTANT ISSUES FOR NEGOTIATORS

Pricing becomes a major factor when negotiating an agreement that includes some form of countertrade. It is difficult to value noncomplementary products and services. In the case of PepsiCo and Russia, exchanging Pepsi for vodka is relatively simple; both are beverages. However, barter and counterpurchase situations where the products are not similar become more difficult. Also associated with pricing is the cost to the seller company of selling the products received as payment for the product it sold. There are businesses that aid companies in marketing products received as part of countertrade agreements. They are known as *switch traders* or *countertrade companies*. They act as brokers for the countertraded products and services and are usually paid on a commission basis. When negotiating a contract using some form of countertrade, the switch trader or countertrade company may need to be involved in the negotiation or at least consulted or retained prior to the negotiation of a countertrade agreement.

In the case of offset agreements, offset obligations can accumulate quickly. In many cases, the company with the offset obligations is unable to fulfill all of those obligations internally. Therefore, other companies need to be identified to help fulfill the offsets (in return for some negotiated benefit from the original seller company). Thus, when negotiating business transactions involving countertrade, it may be necessary to negotiate multiple agreements with multiple parties simultaneously.

❖ CONCLUSION

The context in which international business transactions take place is important to the international negotiator. Economic integration has changed the face of international competition. It requires firms to take at least a regional approach to their negotiation strategy. An agreement in one country could affect an operation in another country. And many negotiation agreements will involve more than one country within an economically integrated area. FDI is a substantial portion of international negotiations in both developed and developing countries. The number of contracts to negotiate may vary from one country to another. The lower the level of economic development, the more likely it will be necessary to negotiate contracts up and down the supply chain. In some cases, the investment may end up being more than expected in the beginning (for an illustration of this, see Chapter 9 for an account of an auto manufacturer investing in India).

Another example of the need for greater investment in developing economies is the experience of McDonald's in Russia. When McDonald's first entered Russia to form a joint venture and open the first McDonald's in Moscow, they not only had to invest in the restaurant itself, but they also had to invest in a processing plant that could make all the products (buns, burgers, French fries, etc.) needed to supply the restaurant. Additionally, they had to contract with agricultural specialists from around the world to come to Russia and train farmers on farming techniques that would produce the quality and quantity of raw materials (potatoes, beef, lettuce, etc.) needed. All of these activities had to have contracts negotiated (primarily with the Russian government).

Countertrade is also a growing component of the international business environment. More and more international business transactions, especially with developing countries, are carrying with them the expectation of reciprocity. The types of countertrade agreements reviewed in this chapter are only a few of the more frequently used agreements. There are many other arrangements, and new ones are continually developed.

As an international business negotiator, it is important to understand the economic framework in which the foreign firm operates. It is also necessary to be familiar with the various types of business transactions that take place internationally and how the legal, political, and cultural environments affect those transactions. The following guidelines should help in understanding the business environment of the foreign partner.

❖ GUIDELINES FOR GLOBAL NEGOTIATION SUCCESS

1. Know the level of FDI in the country and specifically in the industry in which you compete. If possible, identify the primary sources (countries, companies) of that FDI.

2. Determine any ownership restrictions or other obstacles to doing business in that country. Be sure to understand the laws regarding repatriation of profits (taking money out of the country).

3. Have a clear understanding of the partner firm's competitive position within its country. Is it strongly tied to the country's government?

4. Is the country a member of any economically integrated area? If so, what is the partner firm's position in other member countries?

5. Have a good understanding of the use of various entry strategies (licensing, joint ventures, etc.) in the country and region of the world you are entering. Know the legal and political environment related to these strategies.

6. Have a good understanding of countertrade options. For many transactions, the partner firm may expect some level of reciprocity. Know ahead of time what options your firm is willing to consider.

7. Assess the level of transparency in the country. Keep in mind that laws and policies that may seem similar to those in your home country may have very different interpretations.

❖ DISCUSSION QUESTIONS

1. Why is economic integration important to international business? How would economic integration fit into your negotiation strategy?

2. How would the lack of transparency affect your ability to negotiate a good agreement in another country?

3. Define each of the following entry strategies: licensing, franchising, joint venture, greenfield development, turnkey, and contract manufacture. Identify important negotiation points for each of the strategies.

4. What is countertrade and why is it important for an international business negotiator to have knowledge about it? Explain buyback agreements, offset agreements, and counterpurchase agreements.

5. What is meant by repatriation of profits? How would you negotiate this as part of an agreement?

6. As an international business negotiator, how would you go about gathering information on the topics discussed in this chapter?

❖ NOTES

1.   A tariff is a government-imposed tax on a foreign-produced product coming into a country as it crosses the country's border. Nontariff barriers are nontax policies imposed on products entering a country, such as product standards, quotas, administrative policies, and local content requirements.

2.   A balance-of-payments account tracks a country's payments to other countries as well as its receipts of payments from other countries and includes the current account, capital account, and reserve account.

3.   Hard currencies are currencies that are easily exchanged in the world market. Soft currencies are not easy to exchange and tend to have more volatile exchange rates.

4.   The Euro replaced the currencies of France, Germany, Ireland, Greece, Spain, Belgium, Luxembourg, the Netherlands, Italy, Portugal, Finland, and Austria.

❖ REFERENCES

Anderson, E., & Jap, S. (2005). The dark side of close relationships. *MIT Sloan Management Review, 46*(3), 75–82.

Balassa, B. (1961). *The theory of economic integration.* Homewood, IL: R. D. Irwin.

Central Intelligence Agency. (n.d.). Country reports. *World Factbook.* Retrieved May, 2006, from www.cia.gov/

Daniels, J. D., & Radebaugh, L. E. (2001). *International business: Environments and operations.* Upper Saddle River, NJ: Prentice Hall.

Harrigan, K. R. (1985). Joint ventures: Linking for a leap forward. *Planning Review, 14*(4), 10–15.

Hofstede, G. (1983). National cultures in four dimensions: A research-based theory of cultural differences among nations. *International Studies of Management and Organization, 12*(1–2), 46–74.

Offsets and countertrade. (1994). *Project & Trade Finance, 140,* 26–27.

Okoroafo, S. (1993). An integration of countertrade research and practice. *Journal of Global Marketing, 6*(4), 113–127.

UNCTAD. (2004). *World investment report: 2004: The shift toward services.* Geneva: United Nations.

World Bank Group. (2005). *Data and statistics: Country classification.* Retrieved May, 2006, from http://www.worldbank.org/data/countryclass/countryclass.html

8

Alternative
Dispute Resolution

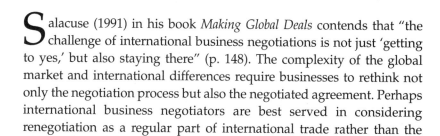

Salacuse (1991) in his book *Making Global Deals* contends that "the challenge of international business negotiations is not just 'getting to yes,' but also staying there" (p. 148). The complexity of the global market and international differences require businesses to rethink not only the negotiation process but also the negotiated agreement. Perhaps international business negotiators are best served in considering renegotiation as a regular part of international trade rather than the exception. There are several factors that contribute to the need for international agreements to be renegotiated. Three major contributors to failed agreements are substantive issues, differences in general perspectives or communication styles, and an unstable world environment.

Substantive issues are factors that relate directly to the function of trade or operations, such as management control, pricing, equity ownership, and general business practices issues (Mattli, 2001). For example, some governments, such as China, request that outside businesses that want to open a new plant facility in their country should be willing to give majority ownership (e.g., 51%) to the host country as part of the agreement. Thus, the substantive issue of majority ownership is an important factor that affects governmental regulations, stock issues, and in general the effectiveness of how everyday business and profit will occur.

There are also issues that focus on *perspective*, or the "way" in which we perform our business tasks. Influences such as national culture, organizational culture, or individual communication style may create perceptual differences that cause a breakdown in the business relationship. These perceptual factors often appear as language misunderstandings or miscommunication, differences in appropriate behaviors for handling conflicts, and bias for preferred resolution processes. Perspective factors that occur are often simple issues such as whether subordinates are free to question upper-management's orders (in China, this questioning would be inappropriate, whereas in the U.S. it would be acceptable), or what is meant by "prompt delivery" of a good or service. (Promptness in Germany may be considered "tomorrow," whereas in Brazil it may be "in two weeks.") The important point in perceptual differences is that we often don't recognize the need to discuss different views until a conflict has occurred because of these differences. Renegotiation becomes an important factor in working through perceptual or communication breakdowns.

Finally, *external factors* outside the specific agreement can cause a failure in honoring an agreement. Negotiations, especially those in the global market, are susceptible to unstable times. Political (natural sovereignty), economic (i.e., inflation), and social changes (i.e., wars) within a country where companies are housed can often disrupt and sometimes prevent the negotiated agreement from follow-through or being upheld. Thus, it is not surprising that many commercial disputes break down. Failures in completing the agreement may be influenced by one or a combination of factors. Ultimately, the result in failed agreements is that parties must contend with the next step. Parties may choose from several options when breakdowns occur. Parties can litigate in court, walk away, attempt to resolve the conflict on their own through renegotiation, or seek assistance from a third party through alternative dispute resolution processes (ADR).

Let us look at a simple example of how this might occur in an international trade agreement. A U.S. company, Unionaid, agrees to buy screws from Arione Company in France. Unionaid could buy them cheaper from a company in China, but because of the longtime government policy of no trade with China, the only viable option is to purchase screws from Company Arione. So a deal is made between

Unionaid and Arione. However, the dynamics of political relations change between the United States and China, and trade opens between the two countries. Unionaid can now buy screws from Zho-Chin in China for much less. The U.S. company Unionaid breaks the negotiated agreement or retracks their end of the agreement to purchase one billon screws and is negotiating with Zho-Chin from China. At this point, Arione may select to do one of the following:

1. Let the break in contract stand and walk away

2. Enter into a renegotiation

3. Use legal action in the international courts or U.S. or French domestic courts

4. Seek alternative dispute resolution

Which option is best? Serious consideration should be given to each of the options. The alternatives for Company Arione (from France) are influenced by cost, future relationships, efficiency in resolution, and the likelihood of a favorable outcome.

The first and most important source of information when things go awry during the performance phase of a contract is the contract terms and conditions. The contract takes priority over general rules of law in the vast majority of situations.

The major question is whether the contract has been breached, and if so, by whom? The question may also be, will the action contemplated by us or them amount to a breach of the contract?

Assuming a breach, the next questions involve what the contract or the law says about the rights or remedies of the victim of the breach. Our focus is on how the victim can assert the rights or remedies.

Every international contract should contain choice of law and choice of forum/venue clauses. The choice of law clause identifies applicable law governing the agreement. There may be three or more possible laws from which to select: U.S. law; French law, assuming the buyer is located in the U.S. and the seller is located in France; and the international law, embodied in one of the treaties that have been signed by both the U.S. and France as well as many other countries of the world to facilitate international transactions.

The choice of venue clause identifies the geographic location for court litigation or ADR in any form. If the companies agreed to any form of ADR in the contract, the specific form and procedures for implementing the ADR processes should be spelled out in the agreement.

Many international and domestic contracts contain detailed requirements necessary to enforce rights. Prior to litigating in court, or submitting claims for arbitration, mediation, or conciliation, the parties may be required to submit detailed written complaints from specific management-level employees to specific management-level employees. If that does not resolve the dispute, face-to-face meetings between corporate officers may be the next required step. If that fails, the third step may be mediation, to be conducted by a third party. Finally, if mediation fails to resolve the dispute, arbitration may be the final step (Hughes, 2006).

The arbitration clause in the agreement, in addition to identifying applicable law and location, should be very detailed on other points, including (a) who will conduct the arbitration points (the AAA, the ICC, or other); (b) the language to be used in the arbitration hearing; (c) the rules of evidence, if any, for the arbitration hearing; (d) rules for discovery and review of documents prior to the arbitration hearing; (e) how many arbitrators there will be and how the arbitrators will be selected; and (f) the power or authority limits of the arbitrators.

The contract should also clearly state whether the arbitrator's decision is binding or nonbinding. The vast majority of international arbitration agreements are legally binding, meaning the arbitrator's decision will be enforced in a court of law if need be, with no rights of appeal or new trial or hearing. Some arbitration agreements are nonbinding, meaning the loser of the arbitration may commence a litigation in court and have a trial, during which the arbitrator's decision would be of no force and effect (Hughes, 2006).

If the contract contains no ADR clause at all, the options are to commence litigation in court, negotiate with the other company regarding a possible agreement to engage in some ADR process voluntarily to avoid court, or negotiate for resolution of the issues (renegotiate).

One way for Arione to weigh its options for the next step is to consider the following questions. These questions are helpful guidelines for negotiators to consider when one of the parties has defaulted on their agreement.

1. How will I cover losses of product revenues and positioning in the market if I refuse to fulfill the negotiated agreement?

2. How much time is left on the agreement? (The less time left on the agreed contract, the less likely renegotiation will succeed.)

3. How will I communicate my actions to the negotiated party, the country, the law, the industry, and other business associates?

4. Does my government offer a program for companies who lose revenues due to unstable international conditions?

5. How can the established relationship help or hurt in the renegotiation process? For example, if negotiators established an effective intercultural communication environment in the original contract negotiation, that experience may provide the communication rules for the renegotiation. Relationships generally evolve workable communication patterns. These patterns can facilitate renegotiating issues because the social maintenance issues are in place. The established relationship, provided it is effective for both parties, provides certain conversational rules for exchanging information and decision-making conversations (Salacuse, 1991).

6. What is my BATRA, or best alternative to a renegotiated agreement?

7. What is my WATRA, or the worst alternative to a renegotiated agreement? (In the example of the United States and China, Unionaid may consider legal costs and ramifications to breaking the negotiated agreement with France.)

8. What are the applicable laws and what does the law say in this situation? (The applicable laws may include international law, the law of either country in which the contracting parties are located, or some other local laws.)

9. Are there any extraordinary circumstances that should be considered, such as future losses?

10. Will the failed agreement destroy entry into other markets?

11. What face-saving strategies will I employ to protect me and the other party? If I can provide face for the other party (especially in cultures where face is very important), I may lessen the resistance or reaction to my behavior. (See Chapter 6 for further discussion of face.)

12. If I choose ADR, what institution is best able to handle the type of conflict and the parties represented (such as the ICC, ILCA, or IAA, discussed in this chapter)?

This chapter discusses the options of parties who seek the latter two options, renegotiation on their own or third-party help through ADR.

❖ RENEGOTIATING

Negotiation breakdown rates are at distressingly high levels (Reynolds, Simintiras, & Vlachou, 2003; Tung, 1988). Given the investment in global business negotiation, most companies initially try to work out their differences themselves by renegotiating. Parties come to the negotiation table again in hopes of salvaging the business deal. The cost of failure is high in most global business agreements. Parties have invested a significant amount of money and time in reaching a deal and do not want to lose their investment, especially if the conflict occurs at the beginning of the original agreement. The least costly method is to enter into renegotiations to work out the problems in the original agreement. In addition to cost and life stage of the contract, issues such as the party's renegotiation power, their alternatives to reach their goal, the long-term relationship damage to the other party, and the potential reputation in the global market must be considered. If the contract is reaching the end of its life, the party (in this case, Arione) has little bargaining power. Renegotiation works best when both parties have a significant amount to lose with a failed agreement. Negotiators want to reassess their BATRA (best alternative to the renegotiation agreement) and WATRA (worst alternative to renegotiation agreement).

The stronger one's BATRA, the stronger one's position will be in the renegotiation attempt. The wider the range between BATRA and WATRA, the greater is the flexibility and openness in the renegotiation process. This is because parties can see a wide range of possibilities, thus giving them room for creative solutions. Finally, parties may want to consider the possible damage to their reputation from failed agreements. If possible, it is better to find a way to settle the conflict between the disputing parties. It is discrete, less time consuming and costly, and ultimately can strengthen the relationship if the parties are able to work through their conflict successfully, leading the way to future endeavors.

❖ ALTERNATIVE DISPUTE RESOLUTION OPTION

International business trade agreements often result in conflict that requires third-party intervention. The sheer numbers of possible issues that international business negotiators face increase the chances of needing third-party help. The plethora of possible differences coupled with the increase in trade and new trade alliances, such as GATT, EU, NAFTA, and CAFTA, have resulted in a significant rise in cases seeking ADR, particularly arbitration. For example, the International Chamber of Commerce (ICC) headquartered in Paris, France, reports receiving over 500 cases per year (www.iccwbo.org).

What Is ADR?

Alternative dispute resolution refers to any alternative to litigation in a court of law. There are two ways parties may find themselves involved in ADR. The first and most common is that there is a legally binding ADR clause in the original contract between the parties. Historically, major corporations resisted ADR, choosing instead to have their day in court if needed. This has changed, first in international transactions and more recently in domestic contracts. Most major corporations now favor some form of ADR agreement to be included in the original international contract. When such a clause is included and agreed to by the parties, the terms and conditions of the ADR clause are legally binding on the parties. The second method of availing oneself of ADR is to mutually agree, after a dispute has arisen, to voluntarily submit the dispute to ADR.

ADR comprises three major options: *arbitration, mediation*, and *conciliation* (other options, such as mini-trials with private judges, are not discussed here). These methods of resolving disputes vary by the formality of the process, the role of the third party, and the legality of the agreement. The procedural guidelines for conducting ADR may vary by the ADR institutions and by the original ADR contract terms and conditions. Each major ADR institution provides clear process guidelines for parties seeking arbitration or mediation.

The role of the third party varies. In the case of arbitration, parties may select one arbitrator to hear their case or a panel of arbitrators, usually comprising three arbitrators. Traditionally, the number of mediators used in mediation is limited to one and sometimes two, if co-mediation is desired. The third-party role and number needed in conciliation is similar to mediation.

The amount of power in decision making (if any) the third party has in the final award or agreement varies with ADR process. In arbitration, the arbitrator has the authority and power to grant the final award. In fact, arbitrators act as judges. Arbitrators arguably have even more power than judges because of the extremely limited right to appeal an arbitrator's decision, compared to appeal rights in courts. Mediators and conciliators, on the other hand, have no decision-making authority. In mediation and conciliation, the third party has no power or authority in determining the outcome, and the role is limited to facilitating or providing a structure for the parties to reach mutual agreement. The decision-making authority in these methods remains with the parties. Furthermore, typical mediation and conciliation agreements are nonbinding by their terms, meaning other dispute resolution methods are available.

The primary difference between mediation and conciliation is the goal of the resolution. The goals of the ADR methods vary as well. The conciliation process is best served when the parties desire to resolve relationship issues. Often, parties have entered into a long-term agreement and require assistance in working out issues related to cultural behaviors, respect, and trust that may have been damaged. Typically, a long-term arrangement is in place that requires parties to work together in a mutually beneficial way. Mediation, on the other hand, is especially useful for resolving problems that are content or specific task related. Arbitration's focus is similar to mediation's in that it works to resolve task-related conflicts, not rejuvenate relationships. Although the primary focus may be task versus relationship or vice versa, there are times when the ADR method results in both relationship- and task-related resolution.

Although there are many possible ADR processes when an international business agreement is challenged, arbitration is the preferred method. Approximately 80 to 90 percent of the cases seeking assistance request arbitration. Mediation is a distant second. Although conciliation is the third predominant method in ADR, little research exists on its application to the international market. Therefore, this chapter focuses its discussion on arbitration and mediation in resolving failed negotiated agreements.

Arbitration

Arbitration is the preferred process for resolving disputes in the international market. Arbitration is defined as "a binding, nonjudicial, and private means of settling disputes based on an explicit agreement by the parties involved in a transaction" (Mattli, 2001, p. 920). Arbitration agreements, by their written terms agreed to by the parties, may be nonbinding, meaning resort to the courts may be reserved by any party dissatisfied with an arbitration decision. However, the number of nonbinding arbitration agreements is low compared to the number of binding arbitration agreements. Binding arbitration eliminates virtually all appeal rights in the vast majority of cases.

The need for arbitration arises typically when attempts at renegotiating fail. The terms of arbitration are often written into the original agreement. Companies usually prefer arbitration to national public courts for a variety of reasons. First, it is private and confidential. Therefore, the companies can avoid bad publicity. Second, it is generally less costly compared to public courts. Third, the venue or location for the arbitration, subject to contract terms, may be in a neutral location, rather than in either home country. The laws of the host country may be very different in their interpretation of the contract, thus the nonhost party may become vulnerable to the bias of the homeland country. Fourth, arbitration is a much quicker process for reaching a decision than judicial courts. Public courts generally move at a much slower pace than international arbitration tribunals. The courts' slow movement in commercial disputes is financially costly to both parties, and therefore parties prefer to use other methods besides public courts.

There are several major international arbitration institutions for commercial business disputes:

1. International Chamber of Commerce (ICC)

2. London Court of International Arbitration (LCIA)

3. American Arbitration Association (AAA)

4. Arbitration by other local and regional arbitration courts and institutions (see the following discussion)

International Chamber of Commerce

The International Chamber of Commerce (ICC) is a widely known and credible source for arbitrating international business disputes. It receives numerous requests to handle commercial disagreements between parties from across the world. Established in 1923 as the International Court of Arbitration, it was the leader in arbitration being accepted worldwide (International Court of Arbitration, n.d.). The ICC has heard over 13,000 cases representing over 170 countries (www .iccwbo.org). More than 50 percent of the parties are from non-Western countries (Blageff, 2004). The ICC has over 60 regional offices around the globe. The benefits of ICC arbitration are plentiful. Parties choosing arbitration through the ICC may choose their arbitrators, the place of arbitration, the language of the proceedings, and the applicable rules of law. Other ADR options are also available from the ICC. These options include the International Centre for Technical Expertise, which can help supply parties with technical information if they desire during their arbitration process. For example, the Centre for Technical Expertise has provided services in a variety of technical areas, such as chemical plant operations and quality of powdered milk, as well as a bakery factory processes (Blageff, 2004).

In addition to offering arbitration and ADR services, the ICC also provides pre-arbitral refereeing to give parties an option when they are faced with an urgent need for relief in the international commercial context. Also, the ICC provides rules and guidelines for practices in ADR.

The ICC has also developed a service called "amicable dispute resolution," not to be confused with alternative dispute resolution. This process is different from arbitration in that the third party does not make decisions and the decision is not enforceable by law. Parties who seek an amicable solution, wish to maintain optimum control, and desire an expedient low-cost process would likely seek the ICC's amicable dispute resolution proceedings. The disputing parties under these circumstances need assistance from a neutral third party. One of the important distinctions of ICC ADR is that it allows the parties to choose the method of proceedings. However, if they are unable to agree, mediation is used. Also, ICC ADR allows for the circumstances where the parties are unable to reach a resolution. They may then be referred to ICC's arbitration. Although there is a great amount of freedom in establishing the proceedings, parties are required to follow the terms of the rules established by the ICC. They include such issues as submitting prior agreements or contracts, filing a Request for ADR, and submitting preferences for characteristics or specific qualifications for their desired mediator. Costs of ADR are shared equally unless otherwise agreed. Specific discussion of the ICC ADR rules can be found by contacting the ICC at www.iccwbo.org.

London Court of International Arbitration

The London Court of International Arbitration originated in 1883 as the Court of Common Council of the City of London (London Court of International Arbitration, n.d.). It was created to arbitrate domestic and transnational commercial disputes. Since its inception, the LCIA has remained a key player in global commercial disputes. The LCIA accepts the United Nations Commission on International Trade Law (UNCITRAL) rules for arbitration processes. LCIA is considered a favorable option for international businesses seeking arbitration. It has the advantage of a central location, capable communications, and a long-standing record of outstanding commercial tradition (Blageff, 2004). London has had a history of providing reputable arbitrators and neutral positioning on international commercial disputes. Fee structures for arbitrations are different from those of the ICC. LCIA charges fees on a daily rate comparable to business-related professions. Blageff argued that those seeking arbitration through LCIA will pay less than with ICC and AAA. In addition to its arbitration services, LCIA has developed five Users Councils for its membership worldwide. The Users Councils offer members conferences and events on arbitration and ADR. The councils are the European Council, the North American Council, the Asia-Pacific Council, the Pan-African Council, and the Latin-American Council. Membership is open to anyone seeking information on LCIA. There is a strong commitment to the enforcement of the arbitrated award. LCIA states that the award will be "final and binding and will be complied with without delay." The award given by the LCIA or any arbitration tribunal has a greater likelihood of enforcement because over 140 states have ratified the Recognition and Enforcement of Foreign Arbitral Awards (www.lcia.org). The LCIA rules are summarized as follows:

1. There is no specific time limit for reaching a decision. However, arbitrators are encouraged to make a decision as soon as possible. (This is the same guideline set by the UNCITRAL.)

2. The consideration of custom and usage of trade may or may not be considered by the arbitrators in making the award. The AAA and ICC do consider custom and usage of trade. This is unlike the UNCITRAL rules.

3. Arbitrators have the discretionary privilege to determine the use of witnesses. (This is similar to the UNCITRAL rules.) Similar to the AAA and the ICC, the LCIA allows for decisions to be made solely on the documents, without a hearing. (See Blageff, 2004, for further explanation).

American Arbitration Association

The American Arbitration Association (AAA) has played a significant role in international arbitration and legal practices around the world. More than 72 countries have participated in AAA services and its International Centre for Dispute Resolution (ICDR) (www.adr.org). Recently, the ICDR developed an alliance with the Inter-American Commercial Arbitration Commission (IACAC) to widen the use of ADR throughout the western hemisphere. One of the many benefits of the AAA Centre for Dispute Resolution is that it offers not only arbitration but also mediation services. The efficiency of the ICDR allows parties to receive an appointed arbitrator within weeks of their request, and usually awards are given within a year. This quick yet enforceable arbitration allows parties to save time and money. Similar to the London Commercial International Arbitration (LCIA), AAA awards have the approval of more than 132 nations in the enforcement award because of the ratification of the New York Convention on the Recognition and Enforcement of Foreign Arbitral Awards. The AAA has a list of over 60,000 U.S. and non-U.S. arbitrators (Blageff, 2004). Although its headquarters are in New York, the AAA is viewed as a highly sought after arbitration institution worldwide.

The AAA's ICDR operates under similar arbitration procedural rules of the UNCITRAL. Blageff (2004) summarizes the AAA rules on international arbitration in the following way:

1. Arbitrators may apply the laws designated by the parties. They may consider the custom and usage of the trade in their decision. Usually punitive damages are waived unless otherwise specified.

2. Witness testimony can be presented in oral or written form.

3. Arbitrator awards are in writing and are final and binding.

4. Arbitration is confidential.

5. Although a specific time is not stated, awards will be given promptly.

The AAA recommends including a section in the original agreement that allows for arbitration in the event of a dispute. They suggest that the parties include a clause such as "*Any controversy or claim arising out of or relating to this contract shall be determined by arbitration in accordance with the International Arbitration Rules of the American Arbitration Association.*" (See www.adr.org for more information.) In addition, the agreement should include issues such as the number of arbitrators, the location of the arbitration, and the language of the arbitration. The AAA offers example clauses that may be helpful to those who are engaging in international commerce. In addition, the fees are determined relative to the amount of the claim or counterclaim. For example, a claim of $10,000 to $75,000 results in a fee of $1,050.

The AAA offers a variety of services including: room arrangements; bilingual arbitrators; handling of fees and collections; guidelines for writing contractual agreements to include arbitration or mediation method if conflict should arise; publications on international alternative dispute resolution; comprehensive information on arbitration laws, rules, and regulations; and reference cases.

Regional and Localized Courts or Institutions

There are many alternatives to the major arbitral institutions. In the past decade, many more arbitration institutions have emerged in countries and within regions. For example, the Ukrainian Chamber of Commerce and Industry created in 1992 the first Ukrainian international arbitration institution. The International Commercial Arbitration Court at the Ukrainian Chamber of Commerce and Industry received 518 new cases in 2002 alone (Slipachuk, 2003). The emergence of local arbitration courts is seen as a way to enter the international marketplace. Foreign investors are less fearful of entering into a negotiation with another country if there are other means of resolving disputes outside the host's national court system. The flexibility that arbitration process generally allows is a significant benefit to dealing with contract breakdowns.

The United Nations Commission on International Trade Law (UNCITRAL) rules specify that the unsuccessful party will incur the costs of arbitration. This is different from ICC, LCIA, or AAA ruling, which leaves the costs to the discretion of the parties. Despite any of the general rules, the contract terms and conditions govern and take top priority with regard to the terms and condition of ADR.

What are the important factors in preparing for breakdowns in the agreement? The most significant factor that can prevent costly and time-consuming court proceedings is including an ADR. Whether parties decide on an arbitration clause or a mediation clause, parties should consider the following issues.

1. What method of ADR will be used if a dispute should arise?

2. What ADR or arbitration institution will be used?

3. How many arbitrators are desired?

4. What language will be used in the ADR proceedings, in the written agreement, and for the native tongue of the arbitrator?

5. Where will the ADR meeting be held?

6. What procedural rules will the ADR follow (for example, rules for proceeding stated by LCIA or ICC or UNICTRAL)?

7. If allowed under the selected institute's rules, what role should witnesses, documents, and the traditional usage and trade play in the decision making of the award?

8. Who will be responsible for the ADR costs incurred?

9. How will the award be implemented and enforced?

10. What role does national trade law play in reaching an award?

Many contracts contain ADR clauses that form various steps. The first step may encompass management interaction by both sides to attempt to resolve disputes. If that proves unsuccessful, mediation may be the next step. If that proves unsuccessful, binding arbitration may be the final step.

❖ MEDIATION IN INTERNATIONAL COMMERCE DISPUTES

Mediation is a conflict resolution process involving at least two inter-dependent parties who, with the help of a third, neutral party, attempt to reach a mutually acceptable agreement of the issues in the dispute. The mediator is typically one person who is a neutral, impartial third party and who facilitates the negotiation or problem-solving discussion of the parties in conflict (Moore, 2003). The mediation process allows for the parties to explain their side of the story, exchange new information related to the dispute, look for integrative solutions, and redefine the initial agreement so that it reflects the interests of the disputing parties. Most international mediation embraces a problem-solving approach to resolving international disputes. However, the transformative approach developed by Bush and Folger (1994) is gaining recognition as a worldview approach to conflict, which has much potential for international business disputes. Let us first examine the problem-solving mediation.

Mediation from a problem-solving approach is the most widely used approach to resolve disputes. Mediation from this perspective is oriented toward reaching a settlement. Cultures that embrace a more individualistic and logically thinking orientation may prefer to use this method. Keeping the problem separate from the person is often viewed as one of the key principles in this approach. Fisher, Ury, and Patton (1991) provide a simple structure of mediation by offering four key principles: (a) separate the people from the problem; (b) focus on interests, not positions; (c) generate a variety of options before deciding what to do; and (d) insist that results be based on objective standards. Problem-solving mediation works best for individuals who are solution focused in reaching a workable agreement.

In international mediations, parties seek mediation services (that are primarily of a problem-solving orientation) through institutions such as the ICC, AAA, or other ADR organizations. Mediation is used considerably less often in international commercial disputes than arbitration. However, new interest is growing for mediation as a viable option for global disputes. For example, Westfield in 2002 reported in her article titled "Resolving Conflict in the 21st Century Global Workplace: The Role for Alternative Dispute Resolution" that "mediation has become a more widely practiced method of dispute resolution" (p. 4). In fact, countries such as Japan use mediation process as an important component of dispute resolution. Japan's Ministry of Labor offices often refer employment disputes to their Equal Opportunity Mediation Commission for mediation (Westfield, 2002). We can expect to see a continuation in the increase in international commercial mediation as we continue to move toward a global economy. However, with the increase in the intercultural business trade will be the concomitant need to develop ADR methods that reach out to the complexity of cultural diversity. One such attempt is the development of mediation through a transformative perspective.

Transformative Mediation

Bush and Folger (2005) present in their book titled *The Promise of Mediation* a transformative mediation approach. They argue that parties who are able to give *recognition* to the other party and feel that they are *empowered* to make decisions that are good for them will be more successful in resolving future conflicts than those whose goal is a simple search for a solution. Transformative mediation is based on the premise that conflict between people is an opportunity for moral growth to occur. The authors contend that personal strength and compassion for others permits disputing parties to benefit. It is the "capacity to transform the character of both individual disputants and society as a whole" that is unique to the transformative perspective (p. 20). In the process of conversing and discovering the issues, a new sense of identity and connectedness will emerge.

Bush and Folger's work in mediation from a transformative approach is easily applicable to global business disputes. Culture, organizational culture, and individual skills are often the underlying factors that keep parties from finding a workable solution. Because transformative mediation approach is focused on parties achieving a better understanding of the other party and not on the content issues, intercultural barriers are at the forefront of this type of ADR. Transformative mediation purports that when parties are able to understand each other and accept their role in the choices they make, solutions are often reached that are richer in quality and stronger in commitment.

Transformative mediation allows opportunities for parties to relate to others and find a sense of empathy for the other party's circumstances. In addition, giving recognition to another may help the negotiator reinterpret the past behaviors in a new light, ultimately reframing the other's acts and intentions in a more favorable light. Specifically, Bush and Folger argue that through mediation, parties can often find the ability to see one another as human beings despite their differences.

The second key component of transformative mediation is empowerment. Empowerment is created when a party has a sense of "self-respect, self-reliance, and self-confidence" (p. 20). This feeling of what we would call "face with power" creates an awareness of decision making and responsibility for the outcome or resolution. A benefit of using transformative mediation is that it addresses differences that often are an integral part of any global business transaction. The basic premises of compassion to others (recognition) and viewing one's decisions as choices of empowerment rather than defeat are critical to the development of a successful geocentric negotiated outcome. Negotiators who view the world from a collectivist perspective may find the transformative approach similar to their orientation. Ultimately, a gain in understanding oneself and the other party, as well as the problem that brought the parties to the table, provides a much richer worldview of the business transaction.

Regardless of which approach to mediation is selected, it is important that mediators are highly skilled in intercultural communication in order to facilitate the conversation. Not only do mediators need to be competent communicators, they must also have a sensitivity to cultural dynamics and the importance of face in the international arena. The mediator has no power in the decision-making process, thus allowing the mediator to enjoy the freedom to avoid judgment and concentrate on helping the parties reach an amicable decision that is beneficial to everyone.

❖ CONCLUSION

In conclusion, we leave this chapter with four pieces of advice. First, international business negotiators should plan for the contingency that the initial agreement reached will indeed need to be renegotiated at some point. How you plan for this is an important consideration in the original contract. It is best to include a section or clause defining breach of contract. The ICC, AAA, and others provide helpful language to include in the contract. We strongly urge negotiators to become familiar with this information.

Second, consider all your options before selecting a course of action. Refer to the assessment questions for guidelines to consider when faced with a contract dispute.

Third, becoming a global negotiator requires a worldview of conflict and dispute resolution processes. The way in which disputes are resolved is often a product of one's culture. If we are able to view contractual breakdowns as part of the business, we are better equipped to function in a global economy.

Last, planning for the "what ifs" is a difficult task for any negotiator, even when he or she is negotiating an intracultural agreement. International negotiations are compounded by issues such as international laws, governments, culture, politics, organization structure, and the individual personalities of the negotiating team. ADR methods provide the way for us to continue in the international trade market as well as mature and prosper as global negotiators.

❖ GUIDELINES FOR GLOBAL NEGOTIATION SUCCESS

1. Consider substantive, perspective, and external factors in developing an effective agreement.

2. Become well acquainted with the international commerce organizations for resolving disputes.

3. Realize that renegotiated agreements are often better than the original agreements and can help in the development of long-term partnerships, which is money well spent.

4. Assessing the breakdown in the agreement is critical for selecting the appropriate ADR method. For example, if it is a perception issue, transformative mediation approach may be the best option.

5. The competent global negotiator is one who is influenced by other cultures and embraces a geocentric view of agreements and problem-solving approaches.

❖ DISCUSSION QUESTIONS

1. What are some examples of the three major factors that contribute to breakdowns in agreements?

2. What are international commerce organizations and how do they differ in resolving trade disputes?

3. What are the most critical factors for global business negotiators to consider when entering into a trade negotiation?

4. Explain when you would use transformative mediation instead of problem-solving mediation for international trade?

5. Do you think that future international trade dispute resolution methods will change? If so, how and why? If not, why not?

❖ REFERENCES

American Arbitration Association. (n.d.). *When deals go bad!* Retrieved July 25, 2005, from http://www.adr.org/sp.asp?id=25164&printable=true

Blageff, L. V. (2004). International arbitration. In W. A. Hancock (Ed.), *Legal aspects of international sourcing* (pp. 501.001–501.020). Chesterland, OH: Business Laws, Inc.

Bush, R. A., & Folger, J. P. (1994). *The promise of mediation: Responding to conflict through empowerment and recognition.* San Francisco: Jossey-Bass.

Bush, R. A., & Folger, J. P. (2005). *The promise of mediation: The transformative approach to conflict.* San Francisco: Jossey-Bass.

Fisher, R., Ury, W., & Patton, B. (Ed.). (1991). *Getting to yes, negotiating agreement without giving in* (2nd ed.). New York: Penguin Books.

Hughes, D. T. (2006, June 10). Interview with D. T. Hughes. *Hughes Enterprises.*

International Court of Arbitration. (n.d.). *Introducing ICC dispute resolution services.* Retrieved July 25, 2005, from http://www.iccwbo.org/court/english/intro_court/introduction.asp

The London Court of International Arbitration. (n.d.). *About the LCIA.* Retrieved July 25, 2005, from http://www.lcia.org/PRINT/LCIA_main_print.html

Mattli, W. (2001). Private justice in a global economy: From litigation to arbitration. *International Organization, 55*(4), 919–947.

Moore, C. W. (2003). *The Mediation Process.* San Francisco: Jossey-Bass.

Reynolds, N., Simintiras, A., & Vlachou, E. (2003). International business negotiations. *International Marketing Review, 20*(3), 236–262.

Salacuse, J. W. (1991). *Making global deals: Negotiating in the international marketplace.* Boston: Houghton Mifflin.

Slipachuk, T. (2003). International commercial arbitration in the Ukraine: Legislation and practice. *Journal of International Arbitration, 20*(5), 515–521.

Tung, R. L. (1988). Toward a conceptual paradigm of international business negotiations. *Advances in International Comparative Management, 3,* 203–219.

Westfield, E. (2002). Resolving conflict in the 21st century global workplace: The role for alternative dispute resolution. *Rutgers Law Review, 54,* 1221–1250.

9

A Practitioner Perspective

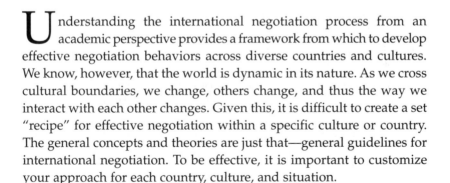

U nderstanding the international negotiation process from an academic perspective provides a framework from which to develop effective negotiation behaviors across diverse countries and cultures. We know, however, that the world is dynamic in its nature. As we cross cultural boundaries, we change, others change, and thus the way we interact with each other changes. Given this, it is difficult to create a set "recipe" for effective negotiation within a specific culture or country. The general concepts and theories are just that—general guidelines for international negotiation. To be effective, it is important to customize your approach for each country, culture, and situation.

To aid in understanding the subtle differences between and within cultures and regions of the world, we went to the people who practice international negotiation. In this chapter, we share the experiences and expertise of several professionals who have significant international negotiation experience. Their insights and advice help us to understand

the application of negotiation practices in the international environment. Hopefully, you will come away with a better understanding of
the importance of each of the elements touched upon in this book.

❖ THE INTERVIEW FRAMEWORK

A standard set of questions was used to structure the interviews. This
allows some comparison to take place. The professionals interviewed
represent a variety of industries as well as international negotiation
experiences in most regions of the world. Figure 9.1 shows the interview questions.

Figure 9.1   Interview Questions

Q1. Please provide your name, company name and industry, your position, and your
home country.

Q2. In what type of international negotiations have you been involved and with what
countries?

Q3. Based on your experiences, please talk about some of the differences you
found in negotiation behaviors between countries/world regions in which you do
business. If you have any specific "war stories," please feel free to include them.

Q4. What role did culture and cultural differences play in the negotiation differences
between countries/regions?

Q5. How was it necessary for you to adapt your negotiation behavior from one
country/region to another?

Q6. What characteristics about yourself do you think helped you to be successful in
international negotiations?

Q7. For students interested in a career that involves international negotiation, what
advice would you give them to help them gain the knowledge and experience
to be successful?

Q8. Please feel free to add any other information you think would be beneficial to
students reading this text.

The Practitioners

Following are summaries of the interviews conducted with professional managers involved in international business negotiations. Their
experiences and perspectives will illustrate many of the concepts presented throughout this text.

Al Zaremba, Senior Vice President for Licensing

Al is retired from a technology manufacturer, where he spent the majority of his career. He began negotiating in 1978 and retired in 1999. When he began his career, his company was a world leader in technology development. The technology owned by this company was patented, but was used by many firms worldwide in manufacturing without the appropriate licensing agreements that would give them legal permission to use the technology. The company saw this as an opportunity to gain licensing revenue from the firms using their technology. The company went on the offensive and set up a patent business. Four negotiators, each with a regional focus, set out to get licensing agreements from the firms that were using their technology without permission. The licensing agreements basically gave firms, already using the technology, permission to use the patented technology. Because Al's firm was a world leader, foreign firms were eager to cooperate with him in developing licensing agreements. These agreements helped assure that the foreign firm would have access to future technologies as they became available. As time went on, however, the technology manufacturing firm was acquired by another multinational and then another due to the consolidation of the technology industry. As a result, patent negotiations became more challenging.

Al's territory was Asia. He was responsible for all Asian countries that manufactured products that used the company's patented technology. The majority of his time was spent dealing with companies from Japan, China, Taiwan, South Korea, Malaysia, and Thailand. He was involved in negotiations for licensing, technology training, and technology transfer. In all countries for which Al had responsibility, he was clear in stating that developing a relationship was critical to long-term success in the region. For many of the countries, Al indicated that it took 2 to 3 years of visiting firms before even getting to an agreement. During this relationship development period, Al would visit with companies individually as well as collectively. This time frame is very different from most Western standards. However, the development of the relationships enabled Al to be accepted by the Asian firms.

Although we tend to look at Asia as a region and try to generalize about the cultural norms, Al indicated that there were some definite differences in negotiation behaviors that required him to adapt his negotiation style from one country to another. In Taiwan, there were 13 firms in an association that used the patented technology. Al would meet with the firms individually. However, he was aware that these firms would meet with each other before and after Al's visit and they would share information. This made it necessary for Al to treat them all equally and offer them all the same terms of the licensing agreements. In China, Al found that the Chinese also shared information. Because these cultures are collective, treating people equally was very important. When negotiating in Japan, it was necessary to have a translator. The people in Japan would meet with the Japanese company and develop a script.

In all negotiation situations, Al did not take notes. Taking notes would hinder the flow of information. Smooth communication would help to develop the relationship with the company. Once in a taxi or on a plane, he would make notes about the meeting.

Al identified several elements that helped to make him successful in international negotiation in Asia. He sincerely likes people and is interested in people from other cultures. He enjoys learning about other cultures. He said he likes to "pick their brains" about their way of life, business, family, and so forth. He also spent a great deal of time reading about the countries he would travel to. Additionally Al enjoys travel and finds it exciting to go to new places. He was away from home about 24 weeks of each year. Usually, on a trip to Asia, he would be gone for 3 weeks. He describes himself as patient, low-key, and internationally oriented.

In today's international environment, Al sees more difficulty in finding Americans who are willing to commit the time needed for success in the international negotiation environment. Most people do not want to spend as much time away from home as he did. More and more, companies are looking for foreigners who have been educated in the United States to help fill some of the positions involving international travel and negotiation. From his experience, Al also advises that Asian firms still prefer to negotiate with men.

When asked about advice for students considering careers in international negotiation, Al reinforced several elements. The person must have an international orientation. People can perceive when someone is not being sincere. They must have a long-term orientation (the person as well as the firm) and be willing to travel. Enjoying adventure is important; going to new places, meeting new people, and learning about new environments is an important part of being successful in the international environment. Finally, the international negotiator must be flexible and be able to adapt to each situation that presents itself. It is important to be able to listen to the other party and adapt your approach to meet both your needs and their needs.

David Turner: Attorney for a U.S. firm with an office in Poland

A corporate and tax attorney for a law firm in the Midwest of the United States, David accepted an assignment to work in their Warsaw, Poland, office in 1993, 2 years after the office was opened. Prior to David going to Poland, many attorneys went over for 2 weeks at a time, but none wanted to go back. However, on David's first trip to Poland, he made a connection and ended up spending a substantial amount of time in the Poland office.

David did not move to Poland, but traveled to the Warsaw office, staying 2 to 3 weeks at a time. An early project in which he was involved required that he stay in Poland for 6 weeks. According to David, this "captured" him from a cultural perspective as well as from a transitional perspective. In 1993, Poland was still in the relatively early stages of development; they were instituting Western-style practices for banking systems (investment, loans, etc.), and participating in this evolution was "heady." David compared it to babies taking their early steps in life.

Most of the work done out of the Warsaw office was for the Polish Development Bank and the European Bank for Reconstruction and Development. The law firm represented the banks on credit negotiations for investment loans from foreign and local companies. One of the functions of banks such as the PDB and the EBRD is to provide loans to investors who are interested in investing in another country. In this case, the PDB would provide loans to foreign and local investors for infrastructure development such as office buildings and apartment buildings.

Countries involved in the negotiations included the United States, the UK, Sweden, and France. He noted that there was very little difference in negotiation styles between countries involved in the negotiations. Because the transactions being negotiated were very structured and consistent, there was little flexibility. Although the negotiations were similar, the legal processes took longer than expected. Patience was an important attribute to have.

For all the legal documents being negotiated, two versions were required, one in English and one in Polish. The Polish document was considered the official document. David recalled that there were many nights when they worked long into the night translating credit agreements. It was not enough to just translate from English to Polish. It was necessary to translate back into English to make sure the meanings translated as expected.

When asked about the characteristics that helped him to be successful in Poland, he identified the emotional connection he was able to make with the Polish people working in the office. He took the time to build a relationship with them through social activities. He had a sincere interest in learning about the Polish culture and Polish legal system; it was more than an assignment from the home office. Adaptability helped him adjust to the Polish culture and way of doing things.

David's advice for students interested in international negotiation is to build skills to become a good listener. Having a sincere interest in learning about other cultures and people is important for success in the international environment. It is also important not to impose your culture on another culture; the ability to adapt is critical. David believed that he learned as much as he taught. Finally, he suggested that learning a second language is important. And, when doing business in another country where you do not know the language, making an effort to speak their language (e.g., learning basic phrases) shows a great deal of respect for that culture, and the people are very appreciative.

Noel Penrose, Global Chief Operating Officer, Interbrand

Noel has had extensive experience in mergers and acquisitions in the advertising and marketing services industry. He has taken the lead in acquiring businesses and setting up joint ventures and other partnerships. Noel has also been involved in negotiating compensation agreements and structures, and negotiating agency remuneration with clients. Most of his negotiation activities have taken place in Europe, the United States, Australia, and New Zealand.

When asked about differences in negotiation behaviors, Noel responded, "The key observation I would make is the difference between those who 'start with the deal' and those who 'start with the relationship.'" Countries that focus on the "deal" include the United States, the UK, Germany, Belgium, Australia, and the Netherlands. These cultures "value control of the process and clarity of purpose, with the value of the deal paramount." Countries that focus on "relationship" first include Latin markets, France, New Zealand, and Portugal. These cultures "value the need for progress but it is progression toward cooperation, trust, and harmony while their expectations for the outcome of the deal itself, and their own value derived from it, can fluctuate."

Regarding culture and cultural differences, Noel noted that "a strong cultural undertone [is] present in ALL [sic] negotiations, even those where the style is like-for-like (German and American). It is different (perhaps less pronounced) but it must not be underestimated and the fact that there are and will be cultural impediments must always be respected."

When negotiating across cultures, Noel recognizes the importance of adapting behavior: how you deal with people and the problem. From his experience, it is also necessary to adapt your negotiation style, including how you act, what you say, and how you say it. According to Noel, "Negotiation behavior is about them and what you do differently as a consequence; the second [negotiation style] is about you and what/how you change yourself as a consequence. Negotiation is about influence and . . . the need to change . . . style, behavior and approach to achieve this influence." Characteristics important for success in international negotiation include recognition of and willingness to change, patience, listening, creativity, empathy, trustworthiness, confidence, and authority.

When asked about advice for students interested in international negotiation, Noel recommended that students read about other cultures and peoples, live in other countries, and observe how people behave. He stressed that it is important to be willing to change your own behaviors in order to be successful. Finally, Noel advises, "Make sure you are both trustworthy and trusted. As a negotiator, particularly in a relationship-style negotiation, trust is key . . . if people don't trust you, it doesn't matter how smart you are."

Gary Giallanardo, Product Manager, European Office, PPG Industries

Gary accepted an assignment to manage the adhesives sales office for PPG in Paris, France. The sales office had a territory covering seven European countries. The main types of negotiations in which Gary was involved were sales negotiations. As part of the PPG organization, a U.S. business perspective had to be used in managing the European sales office. Most PPG expatriates were put in place to jump-start an operation, then were replaced with local managers. The European sales office for adhesives was not meeting expectations, so Gary was sent over to improve sales. The total sales for this office were relatively small compared to other divisions of PPG. Following his assignment in Europe, Gary had opportunities to do business with companies in Latin America.

Gary found a number of differences between American-style negotiation and that of some of the European countries. One difference between the United States and Germany was the level of formality used. Americans move to a first-name basis rather quickly. The Germans, however, remain formal, using Mr. or Mrs. even after years of interacting. In Spain, people were more fun-loving and not as formal.

The technical manager with whom Gary dealt was very nice, more relaxed, and "would do anything for you." Much business in Spain and Italy would occur over food. At the same time, the more relaxed atmosphere is not the same as what we would find in the United States. In the United States, it is not unusual to have social activities involving spouses such as a barbeque or dinner at a restaurant. In Spain, Gary did not meet the technical director's wife (for a social activity) until the end of his 3-year assignment.

Language is a strong element of culture. Most meetings (sales proposals) and negotiations occurred in English. However, in France, this was not always the case. Gary recounted an incident where he and one of the French employees from his office were in a meeting with 15 other people. The meeting was a technical review and a PPG employee was giving the presentation in English. About halfway through the presentation, the head of engineering said, "In France, we speak French." The remainder of the meeting was conducted in French. Gary did not speak French, so the French employee from Gary's office later debriefed him on what took place.

When asked about culture and cultural differences between countries, Gary noted that relationships played an important role in negotiation. He noted that when dealing with Europeans and South Americans, "it is really about getting to know the people first." If there is compatibility between the people, you can theoretically sell a product that is not the best possible product, or your price may not be the lowest price available. From Gary's experience, "The value of the whole package is what you bring . . . the relationship . . . it makes the whole package of greater value." He emphasized, however, that with this type of relationship, you would not try to sell an inferior product or sell at a price that is unreasonably high, because "it becomes your reputation instead of your company's reputation."

When talking about relationships, Gary recalled a conversation with a French customer. According to Gary, the French customer's perspective was that the difference between the French and the Americans is that Americans have many friends, but the relationships are shallow. The French have fewer friends, but the relationships are much deeper. This perspective, that the French have closer relationships than Americans, may have some bearing on some of the business behaviors used by the French. When asked about differences in negotiation behaviors, Gary recounted two situations that illustrate subtle (or not-so-subtle) differences between the United States and France in terms of business and negotiation behaviors.

The first situation relates to competitor relationships. The French competitors of PPG collectively called Gary to tell him that they were not happy with PPG's marketing and pricing practices in France. The spokesperson for the group told Gary that the group agreed that Gary had to change these practices and specified the areas in which the changes needed to occur. Gary responded by thanking the spokesperson for bringing these issues to his attention. Gary also told him that he respected the group's position, but that it was not the normal practice of American firms to follow directives given by competitors and that he would not be changing the marketing and pricing practices being used. Needless to say, the spokesperson, on behalf of the group, was furious. Reflecting on this situation, Gary noted that this would never happen in the United States: "We don't talk to competitors at the same level as in other countries [regarding prices]." It is illegal for U.S. competitors to work together on pricing issues. This deeper level of interaction between competitors can have an effect on negotiation.

The second situation recounted by Gary illustrates how one negotiation can affect or be affected by other negotiations or operations within a firm. As stated earlier, Gary's sales office for PPG was a relatively small operation compared to other PPG divisions and offices in Europe. One of the products sold out of Gary's division was a sealer called PVC Plastisols and used in automotive manufacturing. The prices for the input materials used to make this product were rising, so they were losing money at the currently negotiated price. Gary had to go to PPG's customers (in this particular situation, Renault) and tell them he had to increase the selling price for PVC Plastisols. In the presentation to explain the reason for the price increases, there were four people: two from PPG (Gary and one of his French employees) and two from Renault. Although the Renault buyer was already aware of the need for price increases, Gary had prepared charts and graphs to show the increased costs of inputs and the need for a price increase.

Gary told the customer that he would have to raise the price for the PVC Plastisols by 12 percent. The meeting was being conducted in English, but at this point the Renault buyer began "ranting and raving" in French. He would speak, in French, to Gary's employee, then to his own employee (note: this type of sidebar illustrates a disadvantage to not knowing the language of the country in which you are negotiating). He turned to Gary and, in English, said, "If you demand this price increase, then we are going to take an electrical tank away from you."

Electrical tanks are the "bread and butter" of PPG. They are used for electric coating of steel bodies of automobiles. What the negotiator for

Renault was telling Gary was that one of the Renault plants in northern France would not take one of the electrical tanks they had planned to buy. This added to the complexity of the negotiation, because the electrical tanks were not part of Gary's division and were worth much more to PPG that the products Gary sold. The Renault negotiator repeated to Gary that if he continued to push for a price increase, PPG would lose the sale of a big electrical tank. The Renault negotiator knew very well that the electrical tanks were not part of Gary's division.

Gary described himself as "sweating bullets" because he did not know what to do. In the very short period of time he had before he responded, he had several thoughts. He thought that this could be just a normal part of a negotiation with the French. He also thought that "he [the Renault negotiator] needs PPG with their technology. . . ." After a pause, Gary replied, "I'm sorry, but I need this price increase or I'm going to have to stop selling my product to you." The Renault negotiator again "ranted and raved," and Gary thought that he would be in danger of losing his job if he lost the Renault account because of the stand he took (e.g., risking that PPG could lose the sale of an electrical tank). Finally, the customer responded to Gary's position and said, "I am going to give you a 4 percent increase."

Back at the office, Gary spoke with the people in his office and, although it was not the increase they had wanted, they considered it a moral victory in the sense that Renault agreed to some price increase. Their assessment was confirmed in a later conversation Gary had with a joint venture partner that also sold products to Renault. The joint venture partner told Gary that he had spoken to other Renault suppliers that were also facing the same pricing constraints, and that Gary was the only seller who had been able to get any price increase agreement out of Renault (this situation also illustrates the power a firm—Renault—can have in a supply chain).

As Gary reflected back on this situation, he noted, "This ties in with the ability to manage the U.S. way of managing, but knowing really what these other people want and what you think you can get away with . . . what are their needs and what do you have to offer . . . but also to understand that people talk and it is relationship based."

When asked what characteristics Gary thought helped him to be successful in foreign markets, he noted that he tends to be more of a risk taker than risk averse. He also identified a strong interest in learning new things; he never wants to stop learning, "Markets are dynamic; if you stop learning, someone will find a better way to do what you do." His advice to students is to learn a second language. From this, you will gain respect and appreciation by at least trying to bridge the cultural gap. He also advises learning about the culture of the countries of the people with whom you will be working and negotiating. Know about their art history and important cultural products, such as wine for France and beer for Germany, and learn about the country. In many social situations, you will be faced with conversations regarding many cultural aspects of the country. It is important to have the knowledge to participate in these conversations. Finally, business is people, so it is necessary to have an interest in learning about other people.

Odail Thorns, Global Director, GM/Delphi

Odail Thorns, trained as an organic chemist, held several positions in the GM network prior to taking a position as a global director. As a global director, he was involved in developing new facilities (greenfield and acquisition), expanding existing facilities, developing partnerships, and facilitating new market entry. Each activity could involve a number of different negotiations (land negotiations, construction negotiations, ownership negotiations, etc.). For example, when going into Eastern Europe, it was necessary to negotiate with the government in terms of land and ownership issues. The definition of *ownership* would vary from country to country. Odail's experiences covered most regions of the world. He negotiated agreements in China, Japan, India, Eastern European countries, Western European countries, and Latin America. For each country or region, it was necessary to adapt negotiating behaviors.

Eastern Europe. In Eastern Europe, much of the negotiation occurred with governments over issues such as land ownership, road access, tax considerations, and abatements. Although these countries were no longer considered communist countries, the governments still maintained strong control over commercial activities. From his perspective, Odail observed, "The one thing you have to recognize is that there is no such thing as an empowered person. That person has to go to someone else to get approval." He also noted that from a bureaucratic standpoint, time to make decisions was long. However, the Eastern European countries wanted the foreign direct investment, so it was not a matter of whether or not you would get a deal; you were negotiating the best agreement you could. Beyond the investment agreement, attention had to be given to the process for transferring money (profits) out of the country.

Asia. In China, Odail's company primarily negotiated joint ventures (with Chinese partners). Typically, the Chinese partner would bring to the table a business that was inefficient in terms of operations, structure, management, and human resources. Odail's firm would bring the majority of the investment, yet the Chinese firm would be a partner sharing the products and profits, even though the U.S. firm's investment was larger. Even with the imbalance in investment, the Chinese partner was needed.

When negotiating in China, there would typically be government representation at the table. Additionally, according to Odail, the Chinese are hard bargainers and can be perceived as being ruthless. It is easy to be intimidated by their tactics. Odail recalled from his experience negotiating in China that "there are a lot of hands in the deal and decision . . . and you struggled in terms of determining when a deal was a deal." According to Odail, "It can be frustrating when you have been negotiating and you think an agreement has been reached and that you are going to start the next day. [You wake up] and it's like that never happened."

Also in China, some of the ultimate goals of the partnership differed. The U.S. partner focuses on operational effectiveness and on managing and utilizing people effectively and efficiently. The goal of the Chinese partner, however, focuses more on full employment, "so if you have two people on a job that you really need only one to do, you keep two people. Those are the compromises you have to make." In many cases, these types of compromises will be made because of the attractiveness of getting into the Chinese market.

Another variation when negotiating in China is the difference between the provinces. In the cities, negotiators are more experienced and understand Western negotiating styles. In provinces, it is a different environment. Party bosses in each province have very strong control and there are differences from province to province. Therefore, it is necessary to adapt the negotiation to these differences. In rural areas, interpreters were usually needed.

As also stated by others interviewed, it would take many trips with the Chinese to develop relationships. In the auto industry, the Chinese "cut their teeth" with the Japanese and the Koreans. For these countries, the relationship is most important. For Americans, this (relationship development) is a challenge.

In Japan, the relationship is important, too. You spend a lot of time traveling (for meetings), going to dinner, and talking about jazz or golf, in order to build the relationship and trust. Americans want to "get on with business and it takes patience to wait." Once a relationship and trust has been developed, you then start moving forward on doing business. Odail noted that having this relationship does not mean that Asians will be any softer in the negotiations.

The Japanese tend to use what could be called the pilot approach. They will start with a small piece of a larger vision. They assess the progress and each party's contribution as the agreement is carried out. The relationship and level of business involvement then grows from there if the "pilot" agreement was successful. The bottom line to working with the Japanese is patience. Americans tend to have a shorter-term orientation, about 5 years. The Japanese, on the other hand, look 20 years out, which provides more time for patience.

India. In India, Odail found negotiation behavior to be different from that in Japan and China. He warned that it is important not to be misled into thinking that you have a deal. He found that Indians would promise you things that they could not deliver; they tended to be overly optimistic. When they made presentations, it appeared that everything was running smoothly and efficiently. However, that was seldom the case.

For example, he negotiated the supply of power for a factory being built directly from the power source. He found out later that the power source did not have the capacity to deliver what they promised. Odail's company then had to build a diesel-fueled power plant that had not been included in their cost model, but was necessary because the Indian power source was not able to deliver the power they had agreed to.

Another element of negotiating in India relates to the "above-board" and "below-board" activities. The below-board activities typically involve under-the-radar payouts of some sort. Before going to India, he was not aware of this activity (no one told him about it). This type of below-board activity is not practiced in the United States or other Western countries. In fact, it is illegal in many countries. However, in countries like India, ignoring the below-board activities can delay business processes. Odail cited two examples where below-board activities affected business. At one point, Odail had machines for the manufacturing facility sitting on the docks and he was having trouble getting them delivered to the factory. It took him months of effort until he learned that he had to include below-board activities. Once that happened, his machines were delivered.

In the situation involving the diesel-fueled power plant, below-board activities were required in order for the facility to pass inspection. Once the plant was completed, it had to be inspected. It was inspected on several occasions and each time it failed. The reasons given for failing the inspection were always vague. Finally, Odail asked what it would take to be certified (pass inspection). The inspector simply said, "I want one of those," and pointed to a generator. The company got him a generator and the power plant was certified.

It is important to note that below-board activities are a normal part of business practices in India. Many workers in India make very low wages and below-board activities are expected to supplement their income. In the United States, large-size payoffs are illegal under the Foreign Corrupt Practices Act. However, relatively small-size payoffs are acceptable. The line between small- and large-size payoffs is not always clear. And, in countries where payoffs are part of the business culture, it is a challenge to try to change that behavior.

South/Central America. Negotiations in Latin American countries varied from one country to another. In many countries, business still has strong government involvement, so you end up negotiating with government as well as business. In Brazil, Odail negotiated joint ventures. He found the negotiations to be cooperative and professionally done. A deal was a deal. The biggest problem in Brazil was the currency. He noted that an important part of international negotiations was the currency issue. It is important to protect yourself (e.g., your company) from currency fluctuations. It could mean the difference from making a profit and losing money.

In Mexico, negotiations are becoming more American-style, especially in areas along the U.S./Mexican border. Further inland, negotiations would vary more. Also, in Mexico, below-board activities were frequently part of the negotiation and business process. One aspect of business transactions in Mexico (and other Latin American countries) involved deadlines. Projects were typically not completed on time from an American perspective. However, from a Mexican time perspective, completing a project after the negotiated deadline was considered acceptable.

When asked about what was important for being a successful international negotiator, Odail listed several characteristics. The most important characteristics are listening skills and respect for people. Additionally, it is important to have academic credentials as well as a wide variety of knowledge so you can talk about many topics, such as wine, music, sports, and the arts. A good international negotiator is well read. Many of these topics are discussed as part of the relationship building process.

For advice to students, Odail recommended that students should have a well-rounded education. Knowing at least two languages beyond your native language would be very helpful; it would give you an added advantage. Knowing another language also helps you gain respect from your foreign counterpart. It helps to illustrate your interest in and respect of other cultures. Finally, cultural awareness is critical. Learn about other cultures—not just the general differences, but also the more detailed differences. For example, know the differences between wines produced in Spain and those produced in Italy or France.

Donna Bard, Product Manager, Technical Consumer Products

As product manager for Technical Consumer Products and with past companies, Donna Bard has been involved in international negotiations in China, Australia, New Zealand, the UK, the United Arab Emirates, Canada, South Africa, and Hungary. In China, she negotiated purchase agreements that included letters of credit, and labeling agreements.

Donna agreed that culture plays a role in how the negotiation is communicated. For example, many Chinese are not creative thinkers because they have been dictated to for so long. They are very polite and very friendly. They like everything to be laid out exactly how one wants it. Hungary is an emerging Eastern European market. They tend to have the attitude that they survived communism, so they can survive a company purchase or a company takeover negotiation. They are a warm, hospitable people. South Africa and the UK are very formal. Australia is very Western and laid-back.

Modifying negotiation behavior required a more creative approach to conflict. Instead of getting angry as a result of conflict, it was necessary to look for alternative solutions. When asked about characteristics that help her to be successful in international negotiation, Donna noted that being flexible and laid-back was helpful. "I am helpful and competent and try to deliver information and offer technical resources. A smile goes a long way. Remain upbeat and willing to be helpful."

For students interested in a career that involves international negotiation, Donna suggested that students study a foreign language and participate in study abroad. Learn to be flexible and learn about different cultures and intercultural communication. It is important to be flexible and realize that the other person is not going to think like you or have the same values. From her perspective, Donna notes that the "biggest mistake Americans make is failure to be open to others. Do not assume they are the same . . . people think differently."

Cynthia Y. P. Lee, General Manager, Swiftek Corporation

Swiftek Corporation is an international trading business in Taiwan. As general manager of the company, Cynthia has been involved in the purchase and sale of products from other countries. The company does business with firms/customers in the United States, Canada, Germany, the Netherlands, France, Japan, South Korea, Hong Kong, China, Singapore, and Malaysia.

They have frequent contact with their foreign customers and suppliers, which involve both oral and written communication. As part of the business transactions, they negotiate the price, quality, delivery of products, trade terms, payment terms, and type of cooperation between the involved parties. As part of their international transactions, her company negotiates the contract, follows the logistics of the agreement (shipments) and takes care of any claims that arise as a result of shipments not being received at the expected time. Initial contact with potential customers is made at trade fairs (trade fairs are typically cost-effective ways to meet a relatively large number of potential customers/partners).

When asked to talk about differences in negotiation behavior, Cynthia identified differences in the level of loyalty. In North America, Canadian customers have a higher level of loyalty than those in the United States, and the Western European customer is more loyal than the North American customer. The most loyal customers in the world, according to Cynthia, are the Japanese.

A second factor where there are differences is in terms of keeping promises (doing what is agreed upon in the negotiation). According to Cynthia, "Most of North American, Eastern European, and Japanese contacts keep their promises for what had been negotiated." However, she noted that mainland Chinese broke promises frequently and changed certain parts of a negotiated package.

Another difference identified had to do with entertaining (the social aspects of doing business with customers from other countries). For business contacts from Japan, South Korea, Singapore, and the Philippines, social activities usually involved dinner followed by karaoke or nightclub entertainment. For high-level executives, golf was a frequent activity.

When socializing, drinking and toasting is a popular activity in many countries. From Cynthia's perspective, North American and Eastern European business contacts typically have one or two toasts prior to the beginning of a meal and drink primarily beer or wine. However, with Japanese, Korean, and Chinese business contacts, it is typical to drink a larger volume of alcohol.

Cynthia views the Chinese and Koreans as heavy drinkers. With Koreans, you make a toast with your contact first. Then, after you drink, you pour a drink for the person to whom you made the toast. No one is supposed to pour a drink for oneself; it would be considered unpopular. Koreans also do their best to toast their guest to show their respectfulness. In China it is similar. The host mostly toasts the guest frequently (each time he or she takes a drink) to let the guest feel that he or she is very popular. Also, the Chinese like to force the guest to drink, because Chinese always assume everyone can drink a lot; whenever you say you can't drink, it is interpreted that you are only trying to show your courtesy.

Also, as part of the social interaction, Cynthia noted a difference in attitudes toward religion. Most Westerners believe in one God only, but most Asians believe in many different Gods, and whenever this topic arises, the Westerners feel uncomfortable, but Asians don't feel the same way. The popularity of talking about politics also differs among countries. While Taiwanese like to talk about politics in their country, especially scandals, Cynthia found that talking about politics was not as popular for European and American businesspeople.

When asked about having to adapt her behavior for different countries, she said it was important to adapt her behavior to better fit the culture of her customer/partner in order for the negotiation to go more smoothly. Cynthia identified characteristics about herself that help her to be successful in the international environment. She is respectful of every culture and is interested in doing business with people from various cultures. Cynthia will typically learn some greetings and phrases of her customer's language in order to make him or her more comfortable.

Cynthia also noted, "I think I'm good at detecting slight mood changes of my opponents and at grabbing the main point of the argument given by my contacts, and can immediately respond accurately, which mostly makes my negotiation efficient." Another aspect of successful negotiation is to learn things quickly and have an open mind for accepting new things. When she first hears something new, she does not immediately react. Instead, she finds more information and analyzes the issue before making a decision.

For students interested in a career that involves international negotiation, Cynthia advises that a student should work with or for someone from a different culture. This could even occur in the student's hometown because many countries have large foreign populations. If possible, going to another country is very beneficial. Additionally, mastering another language would help, because when learning another language, you learn more than the language itself; you learn about the country's literature, sense of values, and other aspects of the culture.

❖ SUCCESS FACTORS: SUMMARY OF
THE PRACTITIONERS' PERSPECTIVES

The perspectives presented by the various practitioners in this chapter provide us with a wide range of experiences in international business negotiation. Clearly, there are a number of factors important in the international context. The various experiences appear to fall into three main success factors important to successful negotiation. They are knowledge of others, adaptability and flexibility, and communication skill.

All practitioners identified knowledge of others as an important component. This factor has a broad array of elements, including learning a second language, having knowledge of world history, and having an appreciation for the aesthetic environment of a culture and an understanding of the culture. International negotiators must be well rounded in their education and show a sincere interest in the lives and culture of their foreign counterpart. Much of the knowledge needed for this success component can be attained through formal education. University educations typically provide the broad liberal arts education for most students through their general curricula. However, as several practitioners noted, it is important to continue learning throughout your career in order to be up-to-date on these topics and to continue to add to your body of knowledge.

The second success factor revolves around the ability to adapt to the foreign environment and negotiation styles as well as the ability to be flexible in your expectations. Having a genuine curiosity and interest about other cultures and countries helps you become more than just a representative of your company. Instead, you develop a relationship and become a partner with your foreign counterpart. In his interview, Al, from the technology manufacturing firm, stated that over time, his Asian counterparts started to consider him more as Asian than American. His ability to adapt to the cultures in which he was doing business showed that he truly respected and honored their culture.

Success also depends on your ability to be flexible regarding business practices and procedures. All cultures view time differently. If we cannot adjust our time expectations—a relatively easy cultural difference to identify once you are aware of its existence—adjusting to other, more subtle cultural differences will be even more difficult. The lack of flexibility in practices and procedures tends to send a message of having an ethnocentric attitude and a lack of regard for others. In assimilating the comments made by the practitioners, flexibility and adaptability appeared to have played a major role in their success.

The third success factor relates to communication ability. Specifically, the area of communication that is critical to success is the ability to listen. Listening can have a very narrow or a very broad definition. When dealing with a relatively low-context culture, listening could be defined as listening to the words spoken by your counterpart. However, listening takes on a much bigger role in high-context countries and in the international environment in general. Not only is it necessary to listen to the words being spoken, but also it is important to "listen" to the context in which the conversation occurs as well as the nonverbal communication occurring. Further, good listening skills enable the listener to identify the processes and practices where adaptation is needed. Listening occurs with our ears as well as with our eyes. It requires attention, concentration, and the ability to interpret what you are "hearing."

In reflecting on the framework presented in Chapter 1 (and repeated below), it is clear that practitioners integrate the elements of both the individual and the environment in order to be successful in international negotiation. The three success factors discussed here encompass all the elements of this model. Thus, it should be clear that a geocentric mindset is critical to success in the international business environment.

Figure 1.1   A Geocentric Approach to Successful Negotiation

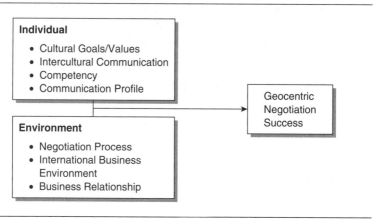

❖ CONCLUSION

The three categories of success factors are all important when building your skills and abilities for international business negotiations. Although some of the elements included in the various factors can be acquired, there is some discussion as to whether others are as easily attainable. The question remains as to whether a person who is relatively inflexible and not adaptable can change. The following guidelines should help you build the knowledge and skills important for successful international business negotiations.

❖ GUIDELINES FOR GLOBAL NEGOTIATION SUCCESS

1. Learn a second language. In most cases, the language you choose is not important unless you are certain about the area of the world in which you want to work. Learning a second language is a difficult task. It is important that you choose a language in which you have interest. Knowing a second language, even if it is not the language of countries where you will do business, shows others that you have an interest in and respect for other cultures.

2. Pay attention to what is going on in the world. Be aware of current events; know about current political, legal, and cultural events in the world. As a cautionary note, do not depend on only the major news network sound bites for information. Magazines like the *Economist* and newspapers like the *Financial Times* provide news and information about world events and activities. For example, the *Financial Times* typically has weekend editions that focus on cultural events and topics around the world.

3. For university students, pay attention in the required liberal arts courses. For electives, choose courses that focus on world history, geography, literature, art, music, and so on. Learn about other countries, cultures, and regions of the world.

4. Consider studying in another country for a semester or a year. Studying and living in another country and culture will help you determine if you have the ability and desire to adapt to other cultures.

5. Learn the skills needed to be a good listener in a global environment. Then practice those skills. Interact with people from other cultures whenever possible. The more experience you have interacting with people from other cultures, the stronger your listening and adaptability skills should become.

❖ DISCUSSION QUESTIONS

1. For each element in the geocentric negotiation success model (Figure 1.1), identify experiences from the practitioners that fit each factor.

2. If you had to advise a person new to the international business negotiation environment, what would you tell him or her were the three most important issues critical to success?

3. In Odail's experiences, there was a need for below-board payments. If you were from a country where this type of behavior is not readily accepted, what would you do?

4. Can an individual learn to become flexible and adaptable? How?

5. What experiences of the practitioners did you find to be the most surprising relative to your preconceived ideas about international business negotiations?

1 0

Conclusion

The advancement of technology and the race for success and prosperity are upon us. No longer do corporations have the luxury of conducting business "my way." Rather, the respect and flexibility of understanding "many ways" is now part of the international business negotiation. As we accept the geocentric approach, we are given a great opportunity to advance ourselves in many ways. Our organizations are required to be flexible to the new markets, advance in new methods of conducting business, acquire new styles of negotiating, and develop relationships that can and will have a significant impact on future economic and organizational growth. In addition, the dynamic process of international negotiation will promote the merger of cultural differences into a geocentric negotiation perspective. Companies can no longer identify themselves with a particular culture and expect to be successful in the international business environment. In the long run, it is essential that they embrace a geocentric negotiation approach.

The geocentric orientation approach sees the world as a whole, and this view is represented in the organization's practices and procedures for conducting business. The interdependency of international subsidiaries and headquarters is maximized. Strength from each country's subsidiary provides a competitive edge and helps create a strong global position for the corporation. The forethought of viewing cultural differences from a geocentric view can provide global corporations an opportunity to grow in the marketplace. As several practitioners commented, being knowledgeable about other cultures and flexible about how to negotiate provides perhaps the strongest evidence for the geocentric model.

The geocentric approach allows us to integrate and emerge as negotiators who are described by the influence of other cultures combined with ours and thus are developing a new identity—the geocentric identity.

As more businesses, organizations, and individuals evolve into a global culture, the way in which we negotiate will reflect this new style. That is, the idea of culture-specific negotiation style will fade and become obsolete.

The individual negotiator style will require an individual who is interculturally communication competent. This may or may not be the same individual of the last decade who did well domestically. Communication skills such as argumentativeness, aggressiveness, self-monitoring behavior, empathy, and reflective listening will determine whether one has the basic tools necessary for success.

The negotiation process from a geocentric perspective will require less attention on systematic process and more attention on shared perspective taking and relationship building in hopes of gaining a long-term relationship based on trust and mutual understanding. Negotiators must be full of curiosity and genuine appreciation for other countries, other cultures, and others' history.

Negotiators must learn a second language, know world history, and develop communication skills from an interactional perspective. That is, communication is the process of developing shared meaning resulting from conversations created by the parties involved. It is not just "what I said" or "what you said"; rather, it is a shared framework. The "we" becomes critical for developing an understanding beneficial for successful and lasting agreements.

The role of establishing relationships in the international setting is critical for creating "enduring" agreements. The written agreement tends to work well in intracultural settings because parties are more likely to share a sense of interpretation about what the agreement means as well as the enforcement and consequences if the agreement or contract is broken. In international negotiated agreements, the written documents, even well-detailed documents, are more susceptible to misinterpretation and more likely to fail. However, if a strong relationship has been established, the negotiated agreement (even with its misinterpretations) is likely to become a working document that at certain points may be easily renegotiated.

Global business negotiators must embrace the idea that differences in cultural values and goals are an integrative component of governments, organizations, and individuals. International negotiators must contemplate not only other cultural values but also their own. Cultural values are very slow to change. It often takes generations before new cultural values emerge. The slow pace of change may be frustrating to the international negotiator; however, it is this slow change that allows stability and productivity to be maintained. The international negotiator who embraces the geocentric perspective sees the cultural values as part of his or her adaptability.

The role of the organization and the industry is an important component in the amount of flexibility and support that goes into reaching an agreement. The organization entering new markets must be adaptable to new cultures and allow for flexibility in the operation of its subsidiaries in foreign markets.

Communication will be at the forefront of getting and staying at the international negotiation table. In the past, ethnocentric or even polycentric approaches allowed negotiators to rely on their own culture and their knowledge of the other party's culture for strategy development. However, as the marketplace has advanced and the cultural boundaries have blurred, the reliance on cultural norms to provide the guideposts for behavior is less effective, even, perhaps, completely ineffective.

The geocentric approach broadens the view of others and brings us closer to understanding our differences and similarities. The international negotiator of tomorrow not only must be knowledgeable about culture and cultural differences but also must go beyond the mere cultural rules for success. The manner in which the international negotiator is able to establish a relationship based on trust and mutual reward is built on communication.

Individual negotiators will become the primary source for success. Thus, businesses need to consider the communication competency of the negotiator in international contexts. This competency in international negotiation is based partly on one's willingness to embrace a geocentric paradigm of the world.

This book has presented the geocentric negotiation success model by specifically examining the individual and the environmental factors of international business transactions. Each factor was examined closely by presenting key elements that influence the international negotiation.

We are on the cusp of a paradigm shift in how we conduct international business negotiations. Those who have been negotiators feel it. Researchers realizing the limitation of individual disciplines are calling for an interdisciplinary approach to studying the global market. The business negotiator in the global market has the challenge of acquiring cultural, governmental, organizational, and political knowledge; acquiring communication skills that facilitate intercultural communication competency; and obtaining the necessary skills to develop relationships that promote international trade agreements that produce profitable and amicable agreements. The integration of theory, research, and experience gives us a foundation to reach beyond our own view of negotiating business deals. The potential for solid agreements, mutual gains, lasting relationships, and individual growth is greater now than at perhaps any other time in history.

Index

AAA (American Arbitration Association), 217–218
Above-board activities, 237
Achievement culture, 105–106
Acquisitions, 193
Adaptation:
  cultural, 186, 242, 249
  ICC component, 160–161
  of negotiation behavior, 231
  polycentricity and, 12
  practitioner perspective on, 230, 236
  as success factor, 242
Adler, N.:
  on cross-cultural negotiation, 113
  on cultural differences, 98
  on culture-related problems, 86
  on negotiator similarity, 69
  on regionalism, 56
ADR. See Alternative dispute resolution
Aesthetic component, 97–98
Affective component, 85
Africa:
  economic integration of, 5
  issues discussion in, 70
  population/economies of, 40
Age, 105–106
Aggressiveness, verbal, 127–132, 143
Agreement:
  cultural differences regarding, 94–95
  multilateral, 4–5

in negotiation process stage, 76–77
  See also Alternative dispute resolution; Contract; Written agreements
Ahmed, Z. U., 72, 109
Aid, 28, 29
Alcohol, 240–241
Alcox International Manufacturing, 1–3
Allen, J. L., 136
Allerstrom, H., 135
Alternative dispute resolution (ADR):
  American Arbitration Association, 217–218
  arbitration, 214–215
  clauses in contract and, 209–210
  default on agreement, questions for, 210–211
  description of, 213–214
  guidelines for GNS success, 223
  International Chamber of Commerce, 215–216
  London Court of International Arbitration, 216–217
  mediation in disputes, 220–222
  regional/local courts/ institutions for, 219–220
  renegotiation, 207–209, 212
  rise in use of, 212–213
American Arbitration Association (AAA), 217–218

Americans:
  argumentativeness of,
    124–125, 126
  communication competency of, 170
  concessions and, 75
  effective strategy rating, 159
  information sharing manner, 72
  Japanese and, 194
  spatial relationships of, 93
  specific-oriented, 105
  verbal aggressiveness of, 132
  See also United States
Americas, economic integration
    in, 187–190
Amicable dispute resolution, 216
Andean Community, 187–188
Andean Pact, 4, 187
Andersson, S., 43
Andriate, G., 136
Antal, A. B., 61–62
Anxiety, 159–160
Apple, Katayama, 99–100
Apprehension. *See* Communication
  apprehension
Appropriateness, 157, 172
Arbitration:
  alternative dispute
    resolution, 213–214
  American Arbitration
    Association, 217–218
  contract and, 210
  description of, 214–215
  International Chamber of
    Commerce, 215–216
  London Court of International
    Arbitration, 216–217
  regional/local courts/institutions,
    219–220
Arbitration clause, 210
Argumentativeness:
  in global business negotiations,
    122–124, 126–127
  GNS and, 124–125
  of negotiator, 121–122
  verbal aggressiveness and, 130
Argumentativeness Scale, 126, 142
Arkin, R. M., 139

Ascriptive culture, 105–106
ASEAN (Association of
    Southeast Asian Nations), 5
Asia:
  argumentativeness and, 124–125
  concessions and, 75
  foreign direct investment, 31
  masculinity/femininity
    of culture, 101–102
  population/economies of,
    36–37, 38
  practitioner perspective
    on, 227–228, 235–237
  spatial relationship in, 92–93
  See also specific countries
Assessment, of ICC, 170–172
Association of Southeast Asian
    Nations (ASEAN), 5
Attitude:
  centricity, 9–10
  ethnocentricity, 10–11
  organizational culture, 8–9
Australia, 239
Avtgis, T. A., 122
Awareness, 85, 160

Balance-of-payment accounts,
    198–199
Balassa, B., 182
Bard, D., 239
Barnes, R. D., 138
Barnlund, D. C., 125
Barry, B., 16
Barter:
  agreements, 199
  description of, 200
  pricing of, 202
Barthel-Hackman, T. A., 135
Bartlett, C., 23
BATNA. *See* Best alternative
    to a negotiated agreement
Baukus, R. A., 123
Beamish, P.:
  on centricity, 10
  on ethnocentricity, 11
  on firm orientation, 9
  on geocentric approach of firms, 7

Beatty, M. J.:
  on communication
    characteristics, 121
  on communication
    perspective, 119–120
  on verbal aggressiveness, 129
Behaviors:
  adaptation of, 241
  communication apprehension, 133
  communication behaviors, 120
  cultural dichotomies and, 102–107
  cultural learning of, 83
  facework, 161
  guided by culture, 84
  integrative communication
    approach, 120–121
  nonverbal, 89–90
  ontological knowledge of, 169
  See also Communication profile
Beliefs, 61–62
Below-board activities, 237–238
Bennett, J. M.:
  on adaptation, 160
  on intercultural competency, 154
  on multicultural identity, 172
  on sensitivity, 166
Bennett, M. J.:
  on adaptation, 160
  on intercultural competency, 154
  on multicultural identity, 172
  on sensitivity, 166
Berger, C. R.:
  on self-monitoring, 139
  uncertainty reduction theory, 59, 159
Best alternative to a negotiated
    agreement (BATNA):
  knowledge of, 60–61, 62
  in renegotiation, 211, 212
Beyer, J. M., 8, 9
Biases, 61–62
Birkinshaw, J., 23
Blageff, L. V.:
  on AAA, 218
  on International Chamber of
    Commerce, 215–216
  on London Court of International
    Arbitration, 217

Blunders in International
    Business (Ricks), 86
Bochner, A., 160
Boeing, 200
Born global firm, 43
Brandt, D. R., 138
Brazil, 188–189, 238
Brett, J., 16, 112
Bridgestone Corporation, 93, 194
*Bridging Differences: Effective Intergroup
    Communication* (Gudykunst), 155
Briggs, S. R., 139
British Broadcasting Corporation
    (BBC), 97
Brockner, J., 139
Brown, W., 120
Bruneau, T., 135, 136
Bruschke, J. C., 129
Buentesa, 1
Buerkel, R. A., 128
Bulgaria, 184
Burant, P. A., 128
Burgoon, M., 139
Burroughs, N. F., 170
Bush, R. A.:
  on empathy, 166
  on mindfulness, 167
  on transformation of conflict, 74
  on transformative mediation, 220,
    221–222
Business, 183–184, 190–202
  See also International business
    context; International
    business negotiation
Business cards, 68
Business negotiation, 169–170
  See also Global business
    negotiation; International
    business negotiation
Business negotiation, culture and:
  cross-cultural negotiation, 109–113
  cultural dichotomies, 102–107
  dimensions of culture, 99–102
  in general, 85–87
  GNS guidelines, 114
  intercultural challenges, issues, 108
  language, 87–89

microdifferences in culture, 107–108
nonverbal behaviors, 89–90
silent languages, 90–95
thinking, decision-making
    processes, 98–99
values, 95–98
Business relationships. *See*
    Relationships
Business transactions:
    contract manufacturing, 196–197
    contractual agreements, 195
    countertrade, 198–202
    exporting, 195
    FDI activities, 191–194
    licensing/franchising, 195–196
    turnkey agreements, 197–198
Buss, A. H., 139
Buttery, E. A., 49
Buyback agreement, 201–202

CAFTA-DR (Central
    American-Dominican
    Republic Free Trade
    Agreement), 4, 189–190
Cai, D. A.:
    on buyer/seller roles, 66
    culture definition, 154
    on goals, 74
    on issues discussion, 70
Calabrese, R., 59, 159
Calof, J.:
    on centricity, 10
    on ethnocentricity, 11
    on firm orientation, 9
    on geocentric approach
        of firms, 7
Cambra, R., 135, 136
Canada, 188–189
Canary, D., 154, 155
Caribbean Basin, 39–40
Carini, G., 110
Carter, J., 74
Casmir, F., 77
Castiglioni, I., 166
Catholics, 96
Cavusgil, S. T., 43
Cecchetto, V., 168

Central America:
    economic changes of, 25
    economic integration, 187–190
    Odail Thorns' negotiations in, 238
Central American-Dominican
    Republic Free Trade Agreement
    (CAFTA-DR), 4, 189–190
Central Asia, 38
Central Europe, 38–39
Central Intelligence Agency (CIA), 25, 184
Centricity:
    approach of, 9–10
    ethnocentricity, 10–11
    geocentricity, 13–15
    polycentricity, 11–12
    regiocentricity, 12–13
Chaisrakeo, S., 56, 65
Chandler, T. A., 128, 129
Change, 45
Characteristics, communication:
    argumentativeness, 121–127
    intercultural communication
        apprehension, 132–137
    self-monitoring, 137–140
    verbal aggressiveness, 127–132
Cheek, J. M., 139
Chen, G., 168, 169
China:
    agreement in negotiation in, 77
    ascent of, 25
    buyer/seller roles in, 66
    communication competency in, 169
    dialects of, 56
    face concept in, 161–162
    FDI recipient, 4
    foreign direct investment
        in, 30, 31, 32
    greenfield investments in, 192
    individualism, shift towards,
        99–100
    issues discussion in, 70
    mindfulness in, 167
    negotiation team, size of, 66–67
    offset agreement, 200
    power distance/space in, 101
    practitioner perspective on,
        228, 235–236, 239

relationship development in, 68
U.S. impact on culture of, 55–56
win-lose approach and, 64
China Aviation Supply
    Company, 200
Chinese negotiators:
    concessions and, 75
    drinking by, 241
    promises and, 240
    questions for information
        exchange, 72–73
Choice of forum/venue clause, 209
Choice of law clause, 209
Christakopoulou, S., 111
Chrysler Corporation, 192
CIA (Central Intelligence
    Agency), 25, 184
Civil law system, 180
Classification, of countries, 26–28
Cognitive component, ICC, 85
Cold War, 24
Collaborative approach, 64–65
Collectivist cultures:
    argumentativeness in, 123
    characteristics of, 99–100
    communication apprehension
        and, 137
    cultural dichotomy, 103
    emphasis of, 53
    face in, 165
    friendship in, 94
    internal/external dichotomy, 107
    material things in, 93–94
    power distance in, 100
    self-monitoring and, 139
    time and, 91–92
Color, 98
Common law system, 180
Communication:
    cultural dichotomies in, 104
    in geocentric approach, 249
    geocentric negotiation process,
        50–51
    individual negotiator, 17–18
    information sharing manner, 72
    integrative framework for
        geocentric negotiation, 16–18

intercultural communication
    theories, 6
international negotiations and, 2
knowledge of other party's
    culture for, 52–61
language, 87–89
listening, 243
in negotiation conclusion, 77–78
negotiation process stage, 67–76
negotiator skills, 248
power distance and, 100
regionalization and, 35
technology's role in global
    environment, 44–45
See also Intercultural
    communication; Intercultural
    communication competency
Communication apprehension:
    contextually based, 134–135
    cultures and, 135–137
    description of, 132–133
    high, 133–134
    low, 134
    self-assessment scale, 146
Communication competency,
    154–155
    See also Intercultural
        communication competency
Communication profile:
    argumentativeness, 121–127
    guidelines for GNS success,
        140–141
    integrative communication
        approach, 120–121
    intercultural communication
        apprehension, 132–137
    perspectives of communication,
        119–120
    self-monitoring, 138–140
    verbal aggressiveness, 127–132
Communication style, 17, 63
Competency. See Intercultural
    communication competency
Competitive Advantage of Nations,
    The (Porter), 23
Competitor relationships, 233
Concessions, 75–76

Conciliation, 213–214
Conflict:
　face-negotiation theory, 164–165
　ICC and, 156
　See also Alternative
　　dispute resolution
Conflict face-negotiation
　theory, 164–165
Context:
　argumentativeness and, 123, 125
　communication apprehension,
　　134–135, 137
　communication behaviors
　　as factor of, 120
　listening and, 243
　nonverbal behaviors and, 89–90
　prenegotiation contextual
　　insights, 65–67
　silence and, 104
　verbal aggression and, 131, 132
　See also International
　　business context
Contract:
　alternative dispute resolution
　　and, 213
　contractual agreements, 195–196
　for counterpurchase agreement, 201
　for countertrade, 202
　cultural differences regarding, 94–95
　currency issues in, 199
　for exporting, 195
　relationships and, 248–249
　renegotiation and, 209–210, 212,
　　222–223
　universalist/particularist
　　dichotomy and, 103
　See also Agreement; Written
　　agreements
Contract manufacturing, 196–197
Control, 106–107
Cooperation. *See* Economic
　integration
Corman, S., 138
Corn, R. I., 60
Cost:
　of arbitration, 216–217, 218, 219
　of renegotiation, 212

Counterpurchase agreement, 201
Countertrade, 198–202, 203
Countertrade companies, 202
Country classification, 26–28
Croatia, 184
Cross-border merger, 192
Cross-cultural negotiation, 109–113
　See also International business
　　negotiation
Cultural adaptation:
　European Union and, 186
　ICC component, 160–161
　as success factor, 242
Cultural dichotomies, 102–107
Cultural learning, 83
Cultural values, 179, 181, 249
Culture:
　argumentativeness and, 121–127
　behaviors and, 5, 84
　business negotiations and, 85–87
　communication and, 155
　communication apprehension and,
　　135–137
　cross-cultural negotiation, 109–113
　cultural dichotomies, 102–107
　cultural learning, 83
　definition of, 52, 154
　dimensions of, 99–102
　effectiveness, views of, 158–159
　face concept, 161–162
　geocentric approach and, 5–6,
　　247–250
　global business environment
　　and, 3–4
　GNS guidelines, 114
　importance of, 84–85
　in integrative communication
　　approach, 120–121
　intercultural challenges, issues, 108
　interdisciplinary examination, 15–16
　international business negotiations
　　and, 2
　knowledge as ICC component,
　　168–170
　knowledge of other party's, 52–56
　language, 87–89
　microdifferences in, 107–108

nonverbal behaviors, 89–90
organizational culture, 8–9
practitioner perspective on, 230–231
regionalization and, 35
self-monitoring and, 139–140
silent languages, 90–95
thinking, decision-making
    processes, 98–99
values, 95–98
verbal aggression and, 131–132
See also Intercultural communication
    competency; Organizational
    culture
Culture context, 58
"Culture shock," 166
Cupach, W. R.:
    on adaptation, 160
    on communication competency,
        154–155
    on effectiveness, 158
    on humor, 163
    on ICC, 156, 168
    on ontological knowledge, 169
Currency:
    Euro, 184, 199
    fluctuations, 238
    in international business
        transaction, 198–199
    SME accumulation of hard
        currencies, 43, 44
Current events, 244

Dabbs, J. M., 138
Daimler AG, 192
Daimler Chrysler, 192
Damyanoc, A., 43, 44
Daniels, J. D., 200
Daun, A., 170
Debate, 122, 123, 124
Decision making:
    in alternative dispute
        resolution, 213–214
    authority, status dichotomy and, 106
    cultural differences in, 98–99
    time to reach decision, 91–92
Deshpande, R., 8
Detert, J. R., 8

Developed countries:
    classification of, 26–28
    foreign direct investment
        from, 30–32
    growth of developing
        economies and, 32–35
    impact of developing countries, 29
Developing countries:
    classification of, 26–28
    economic integration
        of Americas, 187–190
    FDI in, 3–4
    foreign direct investment, 30–32
    greenfield investments in, 192
    impact on international
        negotiation, 28–29
    SMEs, entrepreneurship in, 42
    SMEs from, internationalization
        of, 43–44
    transparency in business, 181
    turnkey agreements in, 197–198
Developing economies, growth of:
    regionalization, 35–40
    statistics on, 32–35
Dichotomies, cultural, 102–107
Diffuse-oriented cultures, 104–105
Dignity, 161–165
Dillard, J. P., 139
Dinner interactions, 105
Direct offset agreement, 200
Discussion:
    information sharing
        approaches, 71–73
    of issues in negotiation
        process, 69–71
Dispute resolution. *See* Alternative
    dispute resolution
Distributive negotiation
    (win-lose) approach, 71
Documents. *See* Contract;
    Written agreements
Dolinina, I. B., 168
Donohue, W. A., 65, 66
Douglas, W., 139
Drake, L. E.:
    on buyer/seller roles, 66
    culture definition, 154

on information sharing, 71
on negotiation strategies, 49
Drinking, 240–241
Dyer, N., 139

East African Community (EAC), 5
East Asia, 36–37
Eastern cultures, 167–168
Eastern Europe:
  material things in, 94
  negotiation teams in, 67
  negotiations in, 235
  population/economies of, 38–39
Eckenrode, J., 139
Economic Community of West
    African States (ECOWAS), 5
Economic framework, 24–26
Economic integration:
  the Americas, 187–190
  definition of, 182
  description of, 4–5, 181–184
  European Union, 184–186
  impact on business, 190–202
  international business
      negotiation and, 202–203
Economist (magazine), 244
Economy
  country classification, 26–28
  population/economy of countries
      by region, 36–40
ECOWAS (Economic Community
    of West African States), 5
Education, 242, 244
  See also Knowledge; Learning
Educational institutions, 96
Effectiveness, 158–159
Elahee, M., 109
Electrical tank, 233–234
Ellis, M. V., 135
Emotional cultures, 103–104
Emotions:
  anxiety/uncertainty reduction,
      159– 160
  communication apprehension,
      132–137

cultural dichotomies
    related to, 103–104
  empathy, 166
Empathy, 165–167
Employees, 41
Empowerment, 221, 222
English language, 87
Entertaining, 105, 240–241
Entrepreneurship, 41–42
Entry decisions, 191
Environment:
  control over, 106–107
  dynamic nature of, 3–5
  guidelines for global
      environment, 46
  international business
      context, 179–181
  international business
      negotiation and, 18
  of organizational culture, 58
  technology's role in global
      environment, 44–45
  See also Context; Geocentric
      perspective
Equal Employment Mediation
    Commission, 221
Ethnocentricity:
  description of, 10–11
  limitations of, 14, 24
Euro, 184, 199
Europe:
  population/economies of, 38–39
  practitioner negotiation
      perspective, 231–235
  See also Eastern Europe;
      specific countries
European Bank for Reconstruction
    and Development, 229
European Commission, 42
European Union (EU):
  description of, 4
  economic integration with,
      184–186
  population/GDP of, 185
  SME segmentation parameters, 41

standards/economic
    integration, 183
  strength of, 24
Evans, M. S., 138
Exchange rate volatility, 199
Expatriate, 7
Explanatory uncertainty, 159
Exporting, 195
External factors, of renegotiation, 208
External/internal dichotomy, 106–107
Eye contact, 69

Face:
  concept of, 161–162
  conflict interactions and, 156
  empowerment, 222
  face-negotiation theory, 164–165
  goals, 74
  strategies, 162–164
Face-negotiation theory, 164–165
Face-protection strategies, 162
Face-renovation strategies, 163–164
Face-threatening strategies, 162–163
Facework, 161
Faiola, A., 99–100
Family, 96
Farley, J., 8
Fayer, J. M., 135
FDI. *See* Foreign direct investment
Fear. *See* Communication
    apprehension
Feelings. *See* Emotions
Feminine cultures, 53
Femininity, 101–102
Financial Times Global 500, 32, 33, 34
Financial Times (newspaper), 244
Fins, 126
Firestone Corporation, 93, 194
Firm size, 41
Firms:
  centricity of, 9–15
  developing economies,
    growth of, 30–32
  FDI activities, 191–194
  geocentric mindset of, 7

international attitude of, 7–15
  organizational culture of, 8–9
  SMEs, 40–44
Fischer, E., 43
Fisher, R.:
  knowledge for negotiation, 50
  knowledge of other party's
    options, 60
  on mediation, 220
  negotiation approach, 64
  negotiation as communication
    process, 16
  on problem solving, 155
  separation of people from
    problem, 59, 123
  on verbal aggressiveness, 128
  win-win negotiation strategy, 71
Fixed sum error (FSE), 71
Flexibility:
  for geocentric approach, 247, 248
  openness to others, 239
  as success factor, 242
Flowers, 98
Folger, J. P.:
  on empathy, 166
  on mindfulness, 167
  on transformation of conflict, 74
  transformative mediation,
    220, 221–222
Foreign affiliates, 3
Foreign Corrupt Practices
    Act, 238
Foreign direct investment (FDI):
  advantages of, 27
  definition of, 30
  in global environment
    guidelines, 46
  international business
    growth and, 3–4
  negotiation of, 203
  political reforms for, 187
  trends, 30–32
  types of activities, 191–194
Foreign-born negotiators, 29
Formal language, 88

France:
    emotional culture of, 103
    European Union and, 185–186
    power distance in, 100
    practitioner perspective on, 232–234
    time relationship in, 91
    values in, 96, 97
Franchising, 196
Francis, J., 113
Fraser, C., 110, 111
Free trade area:
    CAFTA-DR, 189–190
    in economic integration, 183
    Mercosur/Andean Community
        and, 187–188
    with NAFTA, 188–189
Free Trade Area of the Americas
    (FTAA), 189–190
Friedman, V. J., 61–62
Friendship:
    cultural dichotomies
        related to, 104–105
    cultural differences regarding, 94
    See also Relationships
Frustration, 129
FSE (fixed sum error), 71
FTAA (Free Trade Area of the
    Americas), 189–190

Gabrenya, W. K., 139
Gabrielsson, J., 43
Gangestad, S., 139
Gass, R. H., 129
Gassenheimer, J., 111
GDP. See Gross domestic product
Geizer, R. S., 139
Gelfand, M.:
    cross-cultural negotiation
        research, 111
    negotiation as communication
        process, 16
    on self-monitoring, 139
General Agreement on
    Tariffs and Trade, 35
Geocentric approach:
    argument for, 14–15
    capabilities for, 6–7

conclusion about, 247–250
European Union and, 186
illustration of, 19
integrative, need for, 5–6
integrative framework for, 16–18
overview of book, 18–20
for success in negotiation, 18, 243
Geocentric identity, 248
Geocentric negotiation process:
    agreements, 76–77
    conclusion, new dynamic, 77–78
    GNS guidelines, 78–79
    negotiation process stage, 67–76
    prenegotiation stage, 51–67
    research on negotiation
        strategies, 49–50
Geocentric perspective:
    country classification, 26–28
    developing economies,
        growth of, 32–44
    economic framework, 24–26
    foreign direct investment, 30–32
    global environment guidelines, 46
    impact on international
        negotiation, 28–29
    knowledge for, 23–24
    technology, role of, 44–45
Geocentricity, 13
Germany, 54, 231
Ghauri, P. N., 66, 67, 68
Ghoshal, S., 23
Giallanardo, G., 231–235
Gift giving, 98
Global 500 rankings, 32, 33, 34, 41
Global business negotiation:
    adaptation, 160–161
    anxiety, uncertainty
        reduction, 159–160
    appropriateness, 157
    effectiveness, 158–159
    face honoring, protection, 161–165
    ICC, need for, 153–154
    ICC and, 155–156
    ICC assessment, 170–172
    ICC overview, 154–156
    knowledge, 168–170
    mindfulness, 167–168

sensitivity, empathy, 165–167
  See also Business negotiation;
    International business
    negotiation
Global environment:
  changes in, 18
  dynamic nature of, 3–5
  guidelines for, 46
  See also Geocentric perspective
Global expansion, of SMEs, 42–44
Global managers, 23–24
Global negotiation success (GNS):
  alternative dispute resolution
    guidelines, 223
  argumentativeness for, 124–125
  communication guidelines, 140–141
  communication style and, 63
  cultural guidelines for, 114
  geocentric negotiation stages, 51
  guidelines for, 78–79, 114
  ICC guidelines, 173–174
  knowledge of individual for, 59
  knowledge of yourself for, 55
  negotiator guidelines for, 244
GM/Delphi, 235–239
Goals, 73–75, 214
Goffman, E., 74, 161
Government:
  economic integration and,
    181–184, 191
  international business context, 180
  negotiation in Latin America, 238
  turnkey agreements and, 197–198
Graham, J.:
  cross-cultural negotiation
    research, 113
  cultural differences in
    thinking/decision making, 98
  on culture-related problems, 86
  knowledge of individual, 59
Graham, J. L.:
  on concessions, 75
  multiparty negotiations, 67
  on order of issues discussion, 70
  on similarity, 69
  on U.S., Japanese negotiators, 68
  on values, 95

Greenfield investments, 192
Gresham, L., 109
Griffith, D. A., 56
Gross domestic product (GDP):
  of CAFTA-DR countries, 190
  of China, 25
  of European Union countries, 185
  of Mercosur/Andean
    Community, 188
  of NAFTA members, 189
  population/economy of
    countries by region, 36–40
Gudykunst, W. B.:
  on communication, 120–121
  on communication
    apprehension, 137
  on face, 162
  on ICC, 155
  on intercultural communication,
    6, 49
  on intercultural competency, 154
  on self-monitoring, 139
  on uncertainty reduction, 159, 160

Hackman, M. Z., 135
Hall, E. T.:
  cultural misunderstandings, 86
  on nonverbal behaviors, 89–90
  silent languages, 90, 91, 93, 94, 103
  time orientations, 106
Hall, M. R.:
  cultural misunderstandings, 86
  on nonverbal behaviors, 89–90
  silent languages, 90, 91, 93
Hampden-Turner, C., 154
Hard currencies:
  in international business
    transaction, 199
  SME accumulation of, 43, 44
Harvey, M. G., 56
Hastie, R., 71
Hazleton, V., Jr., 168, 169
Heenan, D., 10
Hendon, D. W., 72, 109
Herbig, P., 53
Heuristic trial and error
    method (HTE), 71–72

High argumentativeness,
    122–123, 124, 126, 127
High communication apprehension,
    133–134, 136–137
High self-monitors, 138–139, 140
High verbal aggressiveness, 129–131
High-context cultures:
    argumentativeness in, 122, 123
    listening in, 243
    nonverbal behaviors in, 89–90
    silence and, 104
    verbal aggression and, 132
Hill, C., 5
Hirsch, R., 42
Hise, R., 109
Hocker, J. L., 62, 73–74
Hocking, J. E., 138
Hofstede, G.:
    on communication, 124
    on cultural analysis, 120
    on cultural differences, 98
    on culture, 84
    culture categorization, 53
    culture definition, 154
    dimensions of culture, 99–102
    economy/culture, 182
Home country:
    definition of, 7
    ethnocentricity and, 10–11
    exports, 195
    geocentricity and, 13
    polycentricity and, 11–12
Homogeneity, 55
Hoobler, G. D., 65
Hopper, C. H., 138
Host country, 7
Host-country nationals, 7
Host-country subsidiary:
    ethnocentricity and, 10–11
    geocentricity and, 13
    polycentricity and, 11–12
    regiocentricity and, 12–13
HTE (heuristic trial and error
    method), 71–72
Hu, H. C., 162
Hughes, D. T., 210
Human capital, 23–24

Humor, 103, 163
Hungary, 239
Hunter, J. E.:
    on argumentativeness, 125
    on intercultural interaction,
        120, 121
    on self-monitoring, 139
Hutchinson, K., 135

IACAC (Inter-American Commercial
    Arbitration Commission), 217
ICC. *See* Intercultural communication
    competency
ICC (International Chamber of
    Commerce), 212–213, 215–216
ICDR (International Center
    for Dispute Resolution), 217, 218
Ickes, W., 138
Imahori, T. T., 163
Immigrant, 161
Immigration:
    to developed countries, 28
    foreign-born negotiators, 29
    value conflict and, 97
"The Importance of Culture in
    International Business
    Negotiation" (Graham), 59
Income, 26–28
India:
    collectivist culture of, 99
    economic changes of, 25
    negotiations in, 237–238
    regions of, 56
Indirect offset agreement, 200–201
Individual, knowledge of, 58–60
Individual negotiator, 17–18
    See also Negotiator
Individualistic cultures:
    characteristics of, 99
    cultural dichotomy, 103
    economic growth and, 182
    emphasis of, 53
    face in, 165
    friendship in, 94
    internal/external dichotomy, 107
    material things in, 93–94
    power distance in, 100

self-monitoring and, 139
time and, 91–92
Infante, D. A.:
  on argumentativeness, 121–122,
    123, 125
  Argumentativeness Scale, 126, 142
  on verbal aggressiveness, 128, 129
  Verbal Aggressiveness Scale, 143
Information sharing, 71–73
Initial bargaining range, 60–61
Institutions, 96–97
Instrumental goals, 74
Integration:
  integrative communication
    approach, 120–121
  integrative framework for
    geocentric negotiation, 16–18
  integrative information sharing, 71
  See also Economic integration
Inter-American Commercial
    Arbitration Commission
    (IACAC), 217
Interbrand, 230–231
Intercultural communication:
  challenges/issues, 108
  communication apprehension,
    132–137
  culture, importance of, 84–85
  integrative communication
    approach, 120–121
  integrative framework for
    geocentric negotiation, 16–18
  language, 87–89
  in mediation, 222
  organizational culture contexts, 58
  self-monitoring and, 139–140
  verbal aggression and, 131–132
  See also Communication
    profile; Culture
Intercultural communication
  apprehension:
  contextually based, 134–135
  cultures and, 135–137
  description of, 132–133
  high, 133–134
  low, 134
  self-assessment scale, 146

Intercultural communication
  competency (ICC):
  adaptation, 160–161
  anxiety, uncertainty
    reduction, 159–160
  appropriateness, 157
  assessment of, 170–172
  communication competency,
    154–155
  components of, 156
  effectiveness, 158–159
  face honoring, protection, 161–165
  global negotiation and, 155–156
  guidelines for GNS success, 173–174
  knowledge, 168–170
  mindfulness, 167–168
  need for, 153–154
  of negotiator, 17
  sensitivity, empathy, 165–167
  summary about, 172–173
Intercultural relations context, 58
Intercultural training, 54–55
Intermediary, 195
Internal/external dichotomy, 106–107
International business context:
  the Americas, 187–190
  economic integration, 181–184
  economic integration's
    impact, 190–202
  European Union, 184–186
  guidelines for GNS success, 203–204
  negotiator issues, 202
  political, legal, cultural
    variables, 179–181
  summary about, 202–203
International business negotiation:
  argumentativeness in, 122–127
  centricity of firm and, 9–15
  changes in, 1–3
  conclusion about, 247–250
  definitions related to, 7
  economic framework of, 24–26
  economic integration and,
    191, 202–203
  geocentric approach, 5–6
  geocentric perspective's
    impact on, 28–29

geocentric skills for, 6–7
global environment, 3–5
global environment guidelines, 46
integrative communication
    approach for, 120–121
integrative framework for, 16–18
intercultural challenges, issues, 108
interdisciplinary examination
    of, 15–16
organizational culture and, 8–9
overview of book, 18–20
verbal aggressiveness and, 127–132
See also Business negotiation, culture
    and; Communication profile;
    Global business negotiation
International business negotiation,
    practitioner perspective:
Al Zaremba, 227–228
Cynthia Y. P. Lee, 239–241
David Turner, 229–230
Donna Bard, 239
Gary Giallanardo, 231–235
guidelines for GNS success, 244
interview questions, 226
Noel Penrose, 230–231
Odail Thorns, 235–239
reason for, 225–226
success factors, 242–243
International Center for Dispute
    Resolution (ICDR), 217, 218
International Centre for Technical
    Expertise, 215–216
International Chamber of Commerce
    (ICC), 212–213, 215–216
International communication
    apprehension, 132–137
Internationalization, of SMEs, 42–44
Internet, 44, 45
Interpreters, 87–88
Interruptions, 73
Interview questions, 226
Intranational regionalism, 56
Introduction stage, 67–69
Investment. *See* Foreign direct
    investment
Investor, 30
Inward FDI, 30–32

Ishii, S.:
    on argumentativeness,
        124–125, 126
    on communication
        apprehension, 136
    on verbal aggression, 132
Issues discussion, 69–71
Italy:
    emotional culture of, 103
    negotiation in, 232
    time relationship in, 91

Japan:
    affective dichotomy and, 104
    communication style of, 54
    face concept in, 162
    gift giving in, 98
    individualistic culture shift, 182
    introductory method in, 68
    issues discussion in, 70
    masculine culture of, 101
    mediation in, 221
    negotiator perspective on,
        228, 236–237
    neutral culture of, 103
    nonverbal behaviors in, 89–90
    power distance in, 53
    punctuality in, 90–91
    self-monitoring in, 139
    U.S. impact on culture of, 55
Japanese:
    agreements of, 95
    Americans and, 194
    argumentativeness of, 124–125, 126
    communication apprehension
        of, 136
    concessions and, 75
    diffuse-oriented, 105
    information sharing manner, 72
    loyalty of, 240
    questions for information
        exchange, 72
    spatial relationships of, 93
    verbal aggressiveness of, 132
Jenkins, G. D., 126
Johnson, D. W., 123
Johnson, R. T., 123

Joint venture investments:
  description of, 193–194
  McDonald's in Russia, 203
  negotiations of, 235–236, 238
Judd B. B., 136

Kanter, R. M., 60
Katayama apple, 99–100
Keaten, J., 136
Kedia, B. L., 49
Kelly, C., 160
Kelly, L., 136
Kim, H.:
  on argumentativeness, 125
  on intercultural interaction,
    120, 121
Kim, J.:
  on argumentativeness, 125
  on intercultural interaction, 120, 121
Kim, M.:
  on argumentativeness, 125
  on communication
    apprehension, 137
  on effectiveness, 159
  on intercultural interaction,
    120, 121
  on strategic competency, 158
Kim, Y., 161
Kirby, S., 109
Klopf, D. W.:
  on argumentativeness,
    124–125, 126
  on communication
    apprehension, 135, 136
  on ICC, 155
  on verbal aggression, 132
Kluckholn, F., 102
Knight, G. A., 43
Knowledge:
  of cultural differences, 85
  for geocentric approach,
    248, 249, 250
  for geocentric negotiation, 50–51
  for global perspective, 23
  ICC component, 168–170, 171
  of other party, 52–61, 242
  of yourself, 61–65

Korea:
  communication competency
    in, 169
  order of issues discussion in, 70
  self-monitoring in, 139
Koreans:
  argumentativeness of, 126, 127
  communication apprehension
    of, 136
  drinking by, 240–241
  effective strategy rating, 159
Krizek, B., 138
Kumar, R., 112
Kurogi, A., 162, 167

Landis, D., 154
Langer, E., 167
Language:
  argumentativeness, 121–127
  knowledge of language,
    168–169
  learning, 244
  for negotiation, 232
  negotiation and, 87–89
  nonverbal behaviors, 89–90
  practitioner perspective on, 230,
    238–239, 241
  silent languages, 90–95
  verbal aggressiveness, 127–132
Latin America:
  economic changes of, 25
  economic integration of, 187–190
  foreign direct investment, 31
  masculinity/femininity
    of culture, 102
  negotiation in, 238
  population/economies of, 39
  spatial relationship in, 92
  time relationship in, 91
Laws:
  choice of law clause, 209
  economic integration and, 191
  international business context,
    179–181
  uncertainty avoidance, 101
LCIA (London Court of International
    Arbitration), 216–217

Learning:
  cultural learning, 83
  knowledge of others, 242
  practitioner advice about,
    234–235
Lee, C. Y. P., 239–241
Lee, T., 1–3
Legal issues:
  of agreements, 76–77
  alternative dispute
    resolution, 212–220
  clauses for international
    contract, 209–210
  David Turner's work in
    Poland, 229–230
  of economic integration, 191
  international business context,
    179–181
  of international negotiation, 29
Leme Fleury, M. T., 110
Lennox, R. D., 139
Leung, T. K. P., 49
Lewicki, R., 16
Licensing, 195–196, 227–228
Linguistic competency, 168–169
Lippa, R., 138
Listening:
  learning skills of, 244
  practitioner perspective on,
    231, 238
  as success factor, 243
Lituchy, T., 112
Livingstone, L., 110
Lloyd-Reason, L., 43, 44
"Logic of Message Design"
  (O'Keefe), 119
Logrolling, 76
London Court of International
  Arbitration (LCIA), 216–217
Long, K. M., 136
Love, D., 126
Low argumentativeness,
  123–125, 126, 127
Low communication
  apprehension, 134, 137
Low self-monitors, 138–139, 140
Low verbal aggressiveness, 130–131

Low-context cultures:
  argumentativeness and, 122
  listening in, 243
  nonverbal behaviors in, 89–90
  silence and, 104
Loyalty, 240

Ma, R., 132
Making Global Deals (Salacuse), 207
Management conflict:
  in joint venture, 193–194
  in turnkey agreement, 197–198
Management contract:
  buyback agreements and, 202
  description of, 197–198
Managers, 18
Manufacturing, contract, 196–197
Marketing, 31
Martin, D., 53
Masculinity, 101–102
Masculinity cultures, 53
Material things, 93–94
Mattli, W., 207, 214
Mauriel, J. J., 8
Mayfield, J., 53
Mayfield, M., 53
McCroskey, J. C.:
  on communication
    apprehension, 132–133, 135
  on communication
    characteristics, 121
  on communication competency, 170
  communication perspective,
    119–120
  on verbal aggressiveness, 129
McDonald's Worldwide, 196, 203
McDonnell Douglas Helicopters, 201
McGregory, Ed, 1–3
Mediation:
  alternative dispute
    resolution, 213–214
  in international commerce
    disputes, 220–221
  transformative mediation,
    221–222
Medium firms, 41
Men, 101–102

Menger, R., 75
Mental activity, 8
MEO (mutually enhancing
    opportunity), 65, 66
Mercosur, 4, 187–188
Merger, 192
Message selection, 157, 172
Mexico:
    face in, 162
    NAFTA and, 188–189, 191
    negotiations in, 238
    time relationship in, 91
MHS (mutually hurting
    stalemate), 65–66 ·
Microfirms, 41
Middle East:
    business blunder in, 86
    issues discussion in, 70
    masculinity/femininity
        of culture, 102
    spatial relationship in, 92
Miller, G. R., 138
Mills, J., 139
Mindfulness, 160, 167–168
Minton, J., 16
Mintu, A., 67, 113
Mintu-Wimsatt, A., 111
Moderate argumentative
    negotiator, 125, 126, 127
Moderate verbal aggressiveness, 131
Moen, O., 43
Money flow, 198–199
Monitoring, 138–140, 144–145
Monochronic cultures, 90–92, 104
Monroe, E. E., 135
Moore, C. W., 70, 220
More, E., 135
Morisaki, S., 162
Motivation, 171
Multicultural communication.
    See Intercultural communication
Multicultural identity, 69, 172
Multilateral agreements, 4–5
Multinational regional team, 186
Mutual face, 162
Mutually enhancing opportunity
    (MEO), 65, 66

Mutually hurting stalemate
    (MHS), 65–66
Myers, S. A., 128

NAFTA. *See* North American
    Free Trade Agreement
Nasif, E., 109
Negotiation:
    agreements, 76–77
    American/European styles of,
        231–232
    approach to, 63–65
    behavior, adaptation of, 231
    conclusion stage, 77–78
    country-specific cultural
        differences in, 108, 109–113
    definition of, 49
    GNS guidelines, 78–79
    knowledge of process, 169–170
    negotiation process stage,
        67–76
    prenegotiation stage, 51–67
    See also Communication profile;
        Geocentric negotiation
        process; International
        business negotiation
Negotiation process stage:
    concessions, 75–76
    introduction/relationship
        development, 67–69
    issues discussion/information
        exchange, 69–75
Negotiation team, 66–67
Negotiator:
    Al Zaremba, 227–228
    appropriateness, ICC, 157
    argumentativeness of, 121–127
    communication apprehension,
        132–137
    Cynthia Y. P. Lee, 239–241
    David Turner, 229–230
    Donna Bard, 239
    effectiveness, ICC, 158–159
    Gary Giallanardo, 231–235
    geocentric negotiation
        approach, 248–250
    guidelines for GNS success, 244

intercultural communication
competency of, 155–156
knowledge of yourself, 61–65
Noel Penrose, 230–231
Odail Thorns, 235–239
self-monitoring, 138–140
success factors, 242–243
verbal aggressiveness of, 127–132
See also Communication;
Communication profile;
Intercultural communication
competency
Neuliep, J. W.:
on communication
apprehension, 135
on intercultural competence, 161
on organizational culture, 58
Neutral cultures, 103–104
Neutral/emotional dichotomy,
103–104
New York Convention on the
Recognition and Enforcement of
Foreign Arbitral Awards, 218
Nicolescu, O., 43, 44
Nishida, T., 139
Nixon, R., 55
Non-European developed
countries, 36–40
Nonverbal behaviors, 89–90
Norms, 157
North America, 187, 188–189
North American Free Trade
Agreement (NAFTA):
benefit to Mexico, 188–189
description of, 4
entry decisions and, 191
Norwegians, 126, 127
Notes, 228

Obsessive talk, 133
OECD. *See* Organization for Economic
Cooperation and Development
Oetzel, J., 162
Offset agreements, 200–201, 202
Ohmae, K., 5
O'Keefe, B., 119
Okumura, T., 112

Olaniran, B., 16, 134
Olekalns, M., 72
O'Mara, J., 136
Ontological knowledge, 169
Options, knowledge of, 60–63
Order, of issues discussion, 70–71
Organization for Economic
Cooperation and Development
(OECD), 30, 41, 42
Organizational culture:
cultural differences, 84
determination of, 8–9
firm acquisition and, 193
of negotiator, 65
of other party, 56–58
Osman-Gani, A., 110
Other face, 162
Other party, 52–61, 242
Outward FDI, 30–32

Pacific, population/economies of, 38
Packaging, 70
Page, T. J., Jr., 76
Paik, Y., 112
Palich, L., 110
Paranhos Incorporated, 158–159
Paris, France, 97
Park, M. S., 126
Parks, M. R., 157
Parnell, J. A., 49
Particularism, 102–103
Patience, 236, 237
Patton, B.:
knowledge for negotiation, 50
knowledge of other party's
options, 60
on mediation, 220
negotiation as communication
process, 16
on problem solving, 155
separation of people from
problem, 59, 123
on verbal aggressiveness, 128
Payoffs, 237–238
Penrose, N., 230–231
PepsiCo, 200, 202
Perceptual context, 58

Performance, 171
Perlmutter, H., 10
Personal Report of Intercultural
    Communication Apprehension
    (PRICA), 135
Personal space, 92–93, 101
Personality, 9
Perspective, 208
Peters, M., 42
Philipsen, G., 157
Phillips, G. M., 171
Pilot approach, 237
Platt, P., 98
Poland, 229–230
Polish Development Bank, 229
Political structures, 29
Political variables, 179–181
Polycentricity:
    description of, 11–12
    limitations of, 14, 24
Polychronic cultures, 90–92
Population:
    of CAFTA-DR countries, 190
    of countries by region, 36–40
    distribution by country
        classification, 26–27, 28
    of European Union countries,
        184–185
    of Mercosur/Andean
        Community, 188
    of NAFTA members, 189
Population Reference Bureau, 28
Porter, M., 23
Porter, R. E., 125
Possessions, materials, 93–94
Power distance, 53, 100–101
Power positions, 62–63
PPG Industries, 231–235
Practitioner perspective. See
    International business
    negotiation, practitioner
    perspective
Predictive uncertainty, 159
Prenegotiation stage:
    guidelines for GNS, 78–79
    know other party, 52–61
    know yourself, 61–65

prenegotiation contextual
    insights, 65–67
steps of, 51–52
Preparation. See Prenegotiation stage
Presence, 167–168
Pribyl, C. B., 136
PRICA (Personal Report of
    Intercultural Communication
    Apprehension), 135
Pricing:
    in agreement negotiation, 202
    competitor relationships, 233
    negotiation of, 169–170
    practitioner perspective on, 233–234
Problem solving, 155, 220–221
Profits, repatriation of, 199
The Promise of Mediation (Bush and
    Folger), 221
Protection, 161–165
Protectionist policies, 183
Prunty, A. M.:
    on argumentativeness, 124–125, 126
    on verbal aggression, 132
Punctuality, 90–91
Purvis, J. A., 138
Putnam, L. L., 163
PVC Plastisols, 233

Radebaugh, L. E., 200
Rahoi, R., 126
Rancer, A. S.:
    on argumentativeness, 121,
        122, 123, 125
    Argumentativeness Scale, 126, 142
Rarick, D. L., 139
Recognition, 221–222
Recognition and Enforcement of
    Foreign Arbitral Awards, 217
Redmond, M. V., 166, 168–169
Regiocentricity, 12–13, 14
Regionalism, 56
Regionalization, 36–40
Relational goals, 74
Relationships:
    cultural dichotomies
        related to, 102–106
    cultures that focus on, 230

environment for negotiation and, 18
face honoring, protection, 161–165
friendship, 94
in geocentric approach, 248–249
ICC guidelines for GNS, 173–174
importance of, 45
individualism/collectivism
   and, 99–100
knowledge of other party's
   culture, 55
in negotiation process stage, 67–69
negotiator's development of, 227
practitioner perspective on, 230,
   232–233, 236–237
sensitivity, empathy, 165–167
spatial relationship, 92–93
values and, 97
Religion:
cultural differences regarding, 241
influence on values, 96–97
uncertainty avoidance, 101
Renault, 233–234
Renegotiation:
advice for, 222–223
alternative dispute resolution for,
   212–220
clauses in contract and, 209–210
default on agreement, questions for,
   210–211
example of, 208–209
factors in need for, 207–208
in geocentric negotiation stages, 51
mediation in disputes, 220–222
methods of, 212
Rennie, M., 43
Repatriation of profits, 199
"Resolving Conflict in the 21st
   Century Global Workplace: The
   Role for Alternative Dispute
   Resolution" (Westfield), 221
Respect, 161–165, 247
Reuber, R., 43
Reynolds, M. A., 138
Reynolds, N., 212
Richmond, V. P., 135, 170
Ricks, D., 86
Rinehart, L. M., 76

Ripeness, 65–66
Risk, 101
Roach, D., 16, 134
Rodgers, W., 67, 113
Rognes, J., 76
Role, 66
Roloff, M. E., 71
Romania, 184
Roy, M. H., 72, 109
Rubin, R. B., 170
Rudd, J. E., 128, 129
Rules:
of appropriateness, 157
of international business
   negotiations, 179–181
universalist/particularist
   dichotomy, 102–103
Russia, 200, 202, 203

Sadat, A., 74
Salacuse, J. W.:
on culture and negotiation, 52–53
culture definition, 154
on international business
   negotiations, 207
trait categories list of, 53–54
Sallinen-Kuparinen, S., 126
Samovar, L. A., 125
Sanders, J. A., 129, 132
Satellite communication, 44–45
Saunders, D., 16
Schmidt Corporation, 158–159
Schroeder, R. G., 8
Schwartz, S. H., 139
Sebenius, J., 67
Seeds, D. E., 129
Self-face, 162
Self-monitoring, 138–140
Self-Monitoring Scale, 139, 144–145
Self-presentation, 138
Self-presentation goals, 74
Sensitivity, 165–167, 173
Sequential discussion, 70
Sequential time orientation, 106
Servais, P., 43
Services, 31
Sexes, 101–102

Shapiro, D. L., 76
Shepherd, D., 42
Shepherd, P. E., 129
Shi, X., 110
Siegman, A. W., 138
Silence:
  communication apprehension
    and, 133, 136
  cultural dichotomies, 104
  as face-threatening strategy, 163
Silent languages:
  agreements, 94–95
  cultural dichotomies and, 103
  friendship, 94
  material things, 93–94
  space, 92–93
  time, 90–92
Similarity, 69
Simintiras, A., 212
Singelis, T., 120
Small firms, 41
Small-and medium-size firms (SMEs):
  entrepreneurship of, 41–42
  internationalization of, 42–44
  relationship development by, 45
  size/definition of, 40–41
Smith, P. L., 72
Snavely, W. B., 155
Snider, E., 138
Snyder, M., 138, 139
Social aspects:
  appropriateness, 157
  dinner interactions, 105
  entertaining, 240–241
  face honoring, protection, 161–165
  social responsibility
    of companies, 29
  See also Relationships
Sociorelational context, 58
Solano-Mendez, R., 109
Soldow, G. F., 139
South Africa, 239
South America, 187–190, 238
South Asia, 36–37
South Korea, 57
Southeast Asia, 36–37
Southern African Customs Union, 5

Soviet Union, 24, 27, 200
Space, 92–93, 101
Spain, 231–232
Specific-oriented cultures,
  104–105
Speece, M., 56, 65
Speech, 168–169
  See also Language
Speech codes theory, 157
Spitzberg, B. H.:
  on adaptation, 160
  on communication competency,
    154–155, 172
  on effectiveness, 158
  on ICC, 156
Squire, Sanders, & Dempsey, 201
Standard of living, 27
Standardization, 183
Starosta, W. J., 168, 169
Status, 105–106
Stiff, J., 138
Strategy selection, 158
Strodtbeck, F., 102
Substantive issues, of renegotiation,
  207–208
Success factors, 242–243
Susskind, L., 69
Svenkerud, P., 126
Swagler, M. A., 135
Swedes, 170
Swiftek Corporation, 239–241
Switch traders, 202
Synchronic time orientation, 106

Taiwan:
  affective dichotomy and, 104
  educational values in, 96
  negotiation in, 227–228, 239–241
Tan, J. S., 110
Tariffs:
  CAFTA-DR/FTAA and, 189–190
  Mercosur/Andean Community
    and, 187–188
  NAFTA and, 188–189
  reduction for economic
    integration, 182–183
Technical Consumer Products, 239

Technology:
  geocentric perspective and, 44–45
  international business and, 3
  licensing negotiation, 227–228
  role in international business
    environment, 44–45
  uncertainty avoidance, 101
Thinking, 98–99
Third culture:
  adaptation and, 161
  creation of, 77–78
  integration of cultures, 85
Third-country nationals, 7
Third-party intervention.
    See Alternative dispute resolution
Thompson, C. A., 126
Thompson, L., 71
Thorns, O., 235–239
Time:
  cultural differences regarding, 90–92
  effectiveness and, 158
  flexibility regarding, 242
  universalist/particularist
    dichotomy and, 103
Time dichotomy, 106
Timing, 75
Ting-Toomey, S.:
  on communication
    apprehension, 137
  on face, 162
  face-negotiation theory, 6, 164–165
  on facework, 161
  on ICC, 155
  on mindfulness, 167
  on values, 95
Toasting, 240–241
Toch, H., 129
Tone, 104
Trade:
  countertrade, 198–202
  exporting, 195
  regionalization of, 35–36
Trade barriers:
  Mercosur/Andean Community
    and, 187–188
  NAFTA and, 188–189
  reduction of for economic
    integration, 182–183

Trade-offs, 76
Training, 54–55, 198
Traits:
  argumentativeness, 121–127
  communication behaviors
    as factor of, 120
  intercultural communication
    apprehension, 132–137
  self-monitoring, 137–140
  verbal aggressiveness, 127–132
Transactional goals, 74
Transformative mediation,
    220, 221–222
Translation, 229
Translators, 88–89
Transnational corporations, 3
Transparency, 180–181
Transportation, 35
Trebing, D., 129
Triandis, H., 120
Trice, H. M., 8, 9
Trompenaars, F.:
  on cultural dichotomies, 102–107
  on cultural differences, 98
  on friendship, 94
  on intercultural competency, 154
  on interpreters, 88
  on time, 91–92
Trust, 231
Tung, R., 112
Turkey, 184
Turner, D., 229–230
Turner, R. G., 138
Turnkey agreements, 197–198, 201
Tutzauer, F. E., 71

Ukrainian Chamber of Commerce
    Industry, 219
Ulijn, J. M., 72–73, 111
Uncertainty avoidance, 53, 101
Uncertainty reduction, 59–60,
    159–160
United Arab Emirates, 201
United Kingdom, 239
United Nations Commission
    on International Trade
    Law (UNICTRAL),
    216, 217, 219

United Nations Conference on Trade
and Development (UNCTAD):
on FDI flows, 4
on foreign direct investment, 30
on greenfield investments, 192
on international marketplace, 3
population/economy
of countries, 36–40
United States:
affective dichotomy and, 104
communication style of, 57
emotional culture of, 103
face in, 162
foreign direct investment
from, 30, 31
impact on cultures of Japan,
China, 55–56
individualistic culture of, 45
introductory method in, 68
NAFTA and, 188–189, 191
negotiation team in, 66–67
nonverbal behaviors in, 89–90
power distance in, 100
self-monitoring in, 139
Soviet Union and, 24
See also Americans
Universalism, 102–103
Ury, W.:
knowledge for negotiation, 50
knowledge of other party's
options, 60
on mediation, 220
negotiation approach, 64
negotiation as communication
process, 16
on problem solving, 155
separation of people from
problem, 59, 123
on verbal aggressiveness, 128
win-win negotiation strategy,
71–72
Users Councils, 217

Valencic, K. M.:
on communication characteristics, 121
on communication perspective,
119–120
on verbal aggressiveness, 129

Values:
cultural differences, 95–98
cultural values/international
business, 179, 181, 249
importance of, 84–85
Verbal aggressiveness, 127–132, 143
Verbal Aggressiveness Scale,
129, 143
Verbal agreement, 76–77
Verbal/nonverbal codes context, 58
Verweij, M. J., 72–73, 111
Violence, 129
Vlachou, E., 212
Volkema, R., 110

Wall, S., 43, 44
Walters, E. V., 155
Warsaw, Poland, 229–230
WATNA. *See* Worst alternative
to the negotiated agreement
Watson, A. K., 135
Webster, F. E., Jr., 8
Wengrowski, B. S.:
dialects in China, 56
on exchange of business
cards, 68
order of issues discussion, 70
West Asia, 37
Western cultures:
effectiveness in, 158
spatial relationship in, 92–93
Western perspective, 5–6
Westfield, E., 221
Wholly owned investments,
191–193
Wictor, I., 43
Wiemann, J. M., 155
Wigley, C. J., 128, 129, 143
Wilmot, W. W., 62, 73–74
Wilson, S. R.:
culture definition, 154
on effectiveness, 159
face-attacking need, 163
on strategic competency, 158
Win-lose approach, 64, 71
Win-win approach, 64–65
Win-win/cooperative/
integrative approach, 64

Wiseman, R. L., 129
Wolfe, R. N., 139
Women, 101–102
Workspace, 92–93
World Bank, 26–27
World Trade Organization (WTO), 195
Worst alternative to the negotiated
   agreement (WATNA):
   knowledge of, 60, 62
   in renegotiation, 211, 212
Wright, P., 110
Written agreements:
   advice for, 77
   cultural differences regarding, 94–95
   relationships and, 248–249

translators for, 88–89
   See also Agreement; Contract
WTO (World Trade Organization), 195

Yang, S., 139

Zaremba, A., 227–228, 242
Zarkada-Fraser, A., 110, 111
Zartman, I. W., 65
Zhao, J. J.:
   on agreements, 77
   on buyer/seller roles, 66
   on concessions, 75
   on relationship development, 68
   on win-lose approach, 64

About the Authors

Jill Rudd is currently an associate professor in the School of Communication at Cleveland State University. She has published in various journals, including *Mediation Quarterly, Human Communication Research, Communication Quarterly, Quarterly Journal of Speech, Communication Research Reports,* and *Women's Research in Communication.* Dr. Rudd's interest in interpersonal organizational communication and dispute resolution has been the key focus of her research. She has consulted for more than 100 organizations and businesses in negotiation, strategic planning, dispute resolution, and intercultural communication. Dr. Rudd was appointed by the governor of Ohio to serve on the Ohio Commission on Dispute Resolution and Conflict Management, and has also served on various community boards. Dr. Rudd's academic background and professional activities provide insight into the international negotiation process from both an individual and organizational perspective.

Diana Lawson holds a Ph.D. in marketing. Currently she serves as the Dean and Professor of Marketing at the G. R. Herberger College of Business at St. Cloud State University in Minnesota. Prior to her current position, Dr. Lawson held the Harvey Randall Wickes Chair in International Business at Saginaw Valley State University in Michigan. She also held various positions at the University of Maine Business School, including associate professor and associate dean. Dr. Lawson has published in a number of marketing and business journals, including *Journal of Business Research, International Business Review, Journal of Marketing Education, Journal of Nonprofit & Public Sector Marketing, Marketing Education Review, the Journal of Financial Services Marketing, International Journal of Management and Enterprise Development,* and *Journal of Euromarketing.* Dr. Lawson holds a visiting position at the University of Angers, France, and has taught in the Harvard Summer

Economics Program, in the Istanbul Chamber of Commerce in Turkey, and as a visiting scholar in Moldova. Through her international activities, Dr. Lawson has had the opportunity to experience firsthand intercultural similarities and differences and the changes within cultures over time as they relate to the international business environment.